AT THE END OF
THE STORM

AT THE END OF
THE STORM

STORIES FROM
LIVERPOOL'S HISTORIC TITLE WIN

OLIVER KAY · JAMES PEARCE · SIMON HUGHES

AND OTHER AWARD-WINNING WRITERS OF

The Athletic

POLARIS
PUBLISHING

BACKPAGE

First published in 2020 by

POLARIS PUBLISHING LTD
and
BACKPAGE PRESS

www.backpagepress.co.uk
www.polarispublishing.com

ISBN: 9781913538279
eBook ISBN: 9781913538286

British Library Cataloguing-in-Publication Data
A catalogue record for this book is available on request from the
British Library.

Designed and typeset by Polaris Publishing, Edinburgh

Printed and bound in Great Britain by Clays Ltd, Elcograf S.p.A.

CONTENTS

A

Introduction   vii

AUGUST

Liverpool chairman Tom Werner on glory in Madrid and Klopp's future   1

No big signings but electric Liverpool should continue to flourish under Klopp   11

How videos, NASA technology and 'carb power' helped Liverpool avoid "the biggest banana skin in history"   17

Fabinho's display against Arsenal shows how far Liverpool's 'lighthouse' has come   23

SEPTEMBER

Salah and Mane have already made up. There's friendly rivalry and occasional selfishness but a feud? No way   31

Tennis, teeth-whitening and making Liverpool tick – why Klopp and the Kop love eccentric Firmino   38

'Time wasting', nutrition and a pro surfer are giving Liverpool the edge in early days of the title race   44

Lederhosen, losing fat and beating Bayern – how Salzburg made Sadio Mane   48

OCTOBER

Despite the grumbles Salah is not struggling, he has simply evolved – the stats and his position prove it   57

NOVEMBER

How Man City and Liverpool compete for everything: from titles and £75m centre-backs to physios and youth stars   67

This was the day the shackles came off. To a man, Liverpool stepped up, puffed out their chests and delivered   77

The pride of Bambali. Watching Sadio score against City with the Mane family   82

'It's a penalty. That... is... a... penalty! How can you not give that?' Watching Liverpool v Man City with Kevin Keegan   94

Jurgen Klopp exclusive: When we start a team meeting the only thing I really know I am going to say is the first sentence   104

Virgil van Dijk: The man who transformed himself and his teams   118

DECEMBER

"It's all about surprising the opposition" – second string's win over Everton stems from Melwood atmosphere   149

"All you need is... Alisson Becker" – the video analysis behind save that proved Liverpool's keeper is back to his best   155

"Partying? No, I think a recovery rub will be my celebration." Relentless Liverpool are champions of the world — 160

Alexander-Arnold doesn't need midfield role to be centre of attention — he's the best right-back on the planet — 165

JANUARY

January has been Liverpool's nemesis before. Surely not this time? — 173

"Jurgen surprises me every day. His brain works differently to other people" — Exclusive interview with Klopp's No 2 Pep Lijnders — 178

Ninety minutes watching Virgil van Dijk, the world's best defender — 190

Liverpool also top the set-piece table — and it's all down to the unseen work of the 'team behind the team' — 196

The players' meeting that helped turn "lonely" Anfield into a genuine fortress — 200

FEBRUARY

The secrets of Fortress Anfield and "a pitch as finely tuned as the athletes who play on it" — 217

MARCH

How Liverpool react to defeat at Watford will define their season — 225

How Liverpool are helping their players and the community during pandemic — 229

APRIL

Inside Liverpool's U-turn: a "leak", a toxic backlash and real money worries — 237

Liverpool's Player of the Year: Mane, Salah, Henderson, Trent, Van Dijk...? — 243

JUNE

Controlled aggression, collective defence: Liverpool are league's cleanest team — 251

Resistance, pride and relief: What Liverpool's title will mean to a city — 256

This was a performance of champions — 268

Jurgen Klopp — the fist-pumping genius who turned dreams into reality — 273

Michael Edwards — the visionary behind Liverpool's remarkable rise — 302

Understanding Jurgen Klopp — "It's never about him" — 319

JULY

Liverpool have doubled their income in six years. Now they're chasing Man Utd — 327

Powering the champions: Apple juice laced with caffeine, sea salt and cherries — 339

Liverpool's title winners — by the coaches who discovered them — 344

Liverpool's season: Klopp's *Friends* quote, weight lifted, who's coming through? — 379

INTRODUCTION

When it comes to writing about sports, and particularly football, you always want as much time as possible.

An extra minute can be the difference between making a deadline and falling apart. A late goal can, if you haven't made adequate preparations, completely sink your entire piece.

For Liverpool fans who had waited 30 years for a league title, every extra minute of this season felt like agony. Stretched over months, the seeming inevitability of a first domestic title in three decades didn't temper the concern of wondering if this most unprecedented of seasons, a pandemic-disrupted campaign, might never be allowed to conclude.

Those fears had been narrowed by the Reds' final game before football was put on hold. A shock defeat to Atletico Madrid saw the holders of the Champions League eliminated. A week earlier, Chelsea had knocked them out of the FA Cup to leave Liverpool with a singular objective: the Premier League.

If the tagline for the season of Champions League glory a year earlier was 'this means more', the feeling was that, when it came to the Premier League title in 2020, 'this meant everything' to Liverpool.

Jurgen Klopp's men headed into football's pause with a virtually unassailable 25-point lead and needed just two wins after a three-month break to seal the league championship that had eluded them. Eventually, when Chelsea beat Manchester City in the final week of June, Liverpool won the Premier League title. It was the latest championship ever won, but better late than never.

At *The Athletic*, we took you through every step of Liverpool's record-breaking campaign.

From pre-season optimism and the use of spacesuit technology in recovering from their European Super Cup victory in August, we took Liverpool fans all over the world to provide the best coverage of their club.

Oliver Kay went to Bambali, in Senegal, to watch Sadio Mane play against Manchester City with the winger's family. He captured their pride as Mane scored. He witnessed the joy that a red blob on a tiny screen can generate from thousands of miles away.

In December, with Liverpool pulling away atop the league, James Pearce went to Qatar to see the Reds become champions of the world but this was a time for focus, not festivities.

"Partying?" asked Joe Gomez. "No, I think a recovery rub will be my celebration."

January saw six wins from seven as Liverpool pulled away domestically. February and March saw only a minor wobble until the pandemic hit and everything went on ice.

When it comes to writing about sports, and particularly football, you always want as much time as possible.

While this wait for football to resume was agony for Liverpool's supporters, for us at *The Athletic* it was an opportunity to re-focus and tell the most complete story possible of a historic title win.

And that is what we did.

As the final whistle blew on the game that sealed Liverpool's first-ever Premier League title, we unveiled a schedule encompassing a definitive long read every day for 10 days, taking in every aspect of the Reds' process, approach and success as well as in-depth podcasts breaking down the moments that mattered.

James Pearce and Simon Hughes went deep on Klopp, the fist-pumping genius who transformed the club. We spoke to Tom Werner, the club's chairman, we dissected the tactics, we asked how Liverpool could ensure this wasn't a one-off win. Daniel Taylor and Adam Crafton wrote in-depth about Michael Edwards, the club's secret weapon and Matt Slater did the same with the business decisions that funded a new, global red empire.

And we could do that because we had that precious time.

Our commitment to quality football writing and our business model means that we are uniquely positioned to afford our writers time and space to talk to the right people, to produce the best journalism and most wonderful writing possible.

The result was a season's worth of Liverpool coverage that we are immensely proud of.

The result is this book; a month-by-month journey through a momentous, unprecedented, remarkable season.

Ed Malyon
Managing Director (UK)
The Athletic

AUGUST

LIVERPOOL CHAIRMAN TOM WERNER ON GLORY IN MADRID AND KLOPP'S FUTURE

JAMES PEARCE

AUG 4, 2019

Tom Werner strides down the corridor towards me. "Welcome to Boston. Is it warm enough for you?"

It's 37 degrees outside and the capital of Massachusetts is experiencing its hottest day since 1991.

The handshake from the chairman of Liverpool Football Club is equally warm and the door is opened to his plush Fenway Park office on Jersey Street. It has recently had a makeover. Now taking pride of place in the centre of the wall is a large framed photograph from a cherished night in Madrid.

There is the captain Jordan Henderson, surrounded by his jubilant Liverpool team-mates, lifting the Champions League trophy towards the heavens on the podium. Ticker tape is raining down around them.

Images from the four World Series triumphs Boston Red Sox have enjoyed during Fenway Sports Group's (FSG) reign as owners are positioned around it. "It wasn't a problem making room for that picture. Something else had to leave," Werner smiles.

The 69-year-old American television producer and businessman shared the unbridled joy of Liverpool's sixth European crown with co-owners John W. Henry and Mike Gordon.

Their nine-year tenure at Anfield had been a tale of eye-catching progress – both on and off the field – but agonising near misses when it came to clinching silverware. The only trophy they had won in that time was the 2012 League Cup.

Three weeks before the Champions League final there was the heartache of missing out on the Premier League title to Manchester City by a solitary point but in the Estadio Metropolitano, Jurgen Klopp's side finally took the next step as a 2-0 victory over Tottenham delivered the biggest prize in club football.

"It was exhilarating," Werner says. "The whole experience leading up to the final was so remarkable. The match against Barcelona at Anfield (the semi-final second leg when Liverpool overturned a 3-0 deficit) was sensational and I've watched it again a few times since.

"As a person who loves sport, that was probably one of the most thrilling matches ever. Even then it was like, 'OK, well now you have to go and finish the job'. We were all in Kyiv for the final a year earlier and were sorely disappointed. We played quite well for the first 20, 25 minutes before Mo Salah was injured.

"As special as last season was for Liverpool, it was bittersweet towards the end. As successful as we were, we didn't finish the job in the Premier League. To have the opportunity to win the Champions League was so special. We came into this experience wanting to win trophies for the team and for our fans. It was really gratifying to witness that in Madrid. It was an extraordinary evening."

The post-match celebrations continued right through the night inside the club's private party in Madrid's luxurious Eurostars Hotel. Werner bowed out and headed for bed at 4am.

Mid-morning the owners flew back to Merseyside with the team to embark on a parade that attracted well over half a million people on to the streets of the city. It opened Werner's eyes to exactly what it meant to write a glorious new chapter in the club's proud European history.

"What it was like is pretty hard to articulate," Werner says. "A picture is worth a thousand words. On my iPhone I've got seven or eight videos from that parade. The relationship between our supporters and the players was so palpable, so special. If you hadn't been there, you'd have described it as remarkable. But it was something much greater than that."

How did it compare to winning the World Series?

"Well, we've now been fortunate enough to win the World Series four times after what was a long drought for the Red Sox," Werner says. "This Champions League win was very special. It's like your children and being asked to compare one against another; you can't."

Talking of droughts, it will be 30 years next May since Liverpool last won English football's top flight. The Premier League is the trophy that Kopites crave more than any other going into the 2019-20 campaign. The stage looks set for another intriguing battle with Manchester City.

"I think our fans are like our players, manager and us as owners, they want to win everything," Werner says. "Of course the league title is a big, big ambition but I think last season taught us the key is to focus on just winning the next game and being greedy to keep winning and see where that gets us.

"There's so much to compete for this season thanks to our success in Madrid. The Super Cup, the Club World Cup competition, domestic cups, the Champions League again and yes, the Premier League. We go into every one of them knowing we are good enough to be in the conversation to win them. I think that's pretty cool.

"The Liverpool team on that pitch over the past year was such a united team. Listen, we have to compliment Man City. They played flawless football in the Premier League for the final four months of last season. They didn't drop a point after January.

"I'm not taking anything away from our season, but City are a magnificent football team and it's going to be a big challenge for us again. I think last season was very good for the sport. It's important for the Premier League that the competition is there. We don't want a league like Serie A, where Juventus win it every year without any competition."

Gracing the Champions League felt a long way off when FSG (then known as New England Sports Ventures) completed their £300 million takeover of Liverpool back in October 2010. The club was in a mess. The debt-ridden and divisive reign of former American owners Tom Hicks and George Gillett had taken its toll.

Two days after winning a High Court battle to buy the club and signing the paperwork at the London offices of law firm Slaughter & May, the scale of the task facing FSG was underlined when Werner and Henry took their seats at Goodison Park for the Merseyside derby. Roy Hodgson's side slumped to a miserable 2-0 defeat, which left Liverpool 19th in the Premier League table – only goal difference kept them off the bottom. It was an unpleasant experience for the owners in more ways than one.

"There was a lot of chanting in the Everton stands that day," Werner recalls. "Everton won that match so it wasn't a particularly auspicious opening. After Everton scored one of their goals, one of their supporters spat at John and me. It was a somewhat rude welcome to English football. We've moved forward a lot since that moment. Gradually, the enormity of the task unfolded and revealed itself."

Within three months Hodgson had been sacked and one of the Kop's icons Kenny Dalglish returned for a second spell in charge to spearhead the resurgence. It's telling that the framed photo

4

of Werner and Henry with the 2012 League Cup at Wembley is tucked away on the shelf behind his chair in his Boston office.

FSG wanted more. They wanted Champions League football and Dalglish was replaced by Brendan Rodgers in a bid to make that happen. The Northern Irishman led Liverpool to the brink of Premier League title glory in 2014 before the wheels came off. It was the appointment of a world-class operator in Klopp in October 2015 that proved to be the real trigger. They have been on an upward curve from the moment he walked through the door.

"Our intention was obviously to progress each year. We've had some stumbles," Werner says. "There were some challenging moments. There's no question that it hasn't been a continually upward journey but our heart was always in the right place. Our credo was to under-promise and over-deliver."

One "stumble" arrived in February 2016 when some 10,000 angry fans walked out of Anfield during a game against Sunderland in protest at planned ticket price increases. Stung by the accusations of greed, FSG quickly shelved the changes and a price freeze has been in place ever since.

"We came into that whole discussion about raising ticket prices with the assumption that as long as we froze the vast majority of ticket prices that we could create a tier of seating that was new, not displacing anyone, and at a slightly higher price point," Werner says. "But we worked our way through that. That was one example of a good learning experience."

FSG found the perfect solution to the stadium issue they inherited by transforming Anfield with the impressive new £110 million Main Stand, which lifted the capacity to 54,000. "I'm especially proud of the accomplishment we made in figuring out the Main Stand challenge," Werner says. "There were some dark days early on. We not only had to come up with a scheme that made sense but Liverpool City Council had to convince home owners on Pulford Street to sell so we in turn could buy the land from the council.

"Without 100 per cent participation, we couldn't have moved forward. We had to slog through that. We were very focused on making sure that the result was as good as it's turned out. The whole point of it was to improve fan experience. I think we've done a good job on that. For the fourth year in a row, we were awarded an honour from the Premier League for providing the best fan experience in the league.

"Just as at Fenway Park, we believe we can somewhat affect the outcome by hopefully hiring a great coach and a great group of people around him. But we can certainly ensure that win or lose, when you come to Anfield that it's a special experience and I'm proud of what we've done."

With tickets so hard to come by, fans are keen for FSG to push on and redevelop the Anfield Road End. That would lift capacity past 60,000 but the owners are still considering their options.

"We continue to assess the feasibility of expanding Anfield Road and although the existing planning permission expires in September this year, if we decide to move forward with a different design, we would apply for a new planning permit," Werner says.

In total some £200 million has been invested in the club's infrastructure. A new £50 million training complex in Kirkby is taking shape and Klopp's squad will relocate there next summer when they leave their historic Melwood home.

"As we looked around the other training facilities in the Premier League, we didn't feel like we were near the top," Werner says. "With the input of the coaching staff, Jurgen, Michael Edwards (sporting director), Alex Inglethorpe (academy director) and Pep Lijnders (assistant manager), these people have all participated in helping to shape what we believe will be a first-class facility at Kirkby."

Financially, Liverpool are now a very different beast. Total annual revenues have leapt from £184 million in 2011 to £455 million for the year up to the end of May 2018. Champions League glory will inflate those figures still further. Hefty losses have been turned into healthy profits. *Forbes* magazine now values the club at £1.73 billion.

"We are exceptionally proud of the growth of the club commercially," Werner says. "We have narrowed the gap with Manchester United. We were talking about this theory of the virtuous circle – the stronger we are commercially, the stronger we can be on the pitch, the stronger we are on the pitch, the stronger we are commercially.

"We've had double-digit growth under the leadership of Billy Hogan (managing director and chief commercial officer). It's very important to us, as, among other things, that has enabled us to invest in our squad and invest in Kirkby."

There has also been a concerted effort to strengthen the club's bond with the local community. Werner is a trustee of the LFC Foundation, which was established as an independent charity back in 2010 to help those in need.

One in three children in Liverpool live below the poverty line. Life expectancy is lower than the national average and unemployment is higher.

The foundation focuses its work on helping children and families in areas of deprivation. Some 28,630 youngsters took part in the club's array of programmes in 2018-19 – an 86 per cent increase on the previous season. An annual legends match at Anfield raises about £1 million, which is used to help fund the foundation.

A collective sense of unity has propelled Liverpool forward. At the heart of it all is Klopp. His passion, drive, knowledge and tactical acumen inspires those around him. Securing his services has arguably been FSG's finest achievement.

"What comes through from Jurgen is what a kind, humble, intelligent, confident and good humoured leader he is," Werner says. "He's obviously the right person for Liverpool. We were convinced of that the first time John, Mike and I met him in New York.

"The match between the aspirations of our fan base, the history of the club and Jurgen, they match up in a way that is really perfect. I'm sure he could have taken a job at any other top club but I think this has been a great match.

"I think he would be a brilliant psychologist if he wasn't such a great manager. He brings out the best in players. The moment I'll remember more than any other from the final in Madrid is when the players embraced Jurgen and then threw him up in the air on the pitch. We can talk about what a remarkable coach he is but the love that you felt in that moment between Jurgen and his players was so great. There's so much respect for him and what he's done for them. There was great love in that moment."

Shrewd recruitment has been key to Liverpool's rise. They have bought wisely and sold even better. When you consider the quality of the star-studded squad they have now compared to the one Klopp inherited, it's remarkable that his net spend over four years is only about £105 million. The £142 million sale of Philippe Coutinho to Barcelona in January 2018 effectively paid for the world class duo of defender Virgil van Dijk and goalkeeper Alisson. The fees shelled out for Mohamed Salah (£43 million) and Sadio Mane (£30 million) now look like small change considering how their value has rocketed.

After the addition of £170 million worth of talent into Klopp's squad last summer, this transfer window has been decidedly quiet for Liverpool. There has been no big show of force from the European champions. At a time when the lure of Anfield is arguably greater than it has been at any point since the 1980s, Klopp has largely decided to stick with what he's got.

Quizzed about the lack of new arrivals, Werner says: "Jurgen has articulated the situation really well by pointing not only to the strength we already have but the strength we have to come back. Alex Oxlade-Chamberlain is back, Rhian Brewster is available properly for the first time I'd say, Naby Keita a year on, I could go on...

"It's also a very high-quality team and squad, which makes signing players who are better than we currently have more challenging. What I would say is that we always remain ambitious and we remain committed to keeping this amazing squad together and at a level where it can be competitive for all the big trophies."

Klopp has made Anfield a final destination for elite talent rather than a stepping stone, with Salah, Mane and Roberto Firmino all signing new long-term deals. But what about the manager's future? Klopp's contract runs until 2022. FSG would have happily rewarded him with a lucrative extension this summer but the manager has made it clear he's happy to wait.

"I'd rather not talk too much about private conversations that we've had but suffice to say that we all think he's just exceptional. Jurgen knows what we think of him," Werner says.

Liverpool remains a long-term project for FSG. The mission is to ensure that winning the Champions League marks the start of a golden era. "Our channel put out a video the day after we won the Champions League final, which showed the celebrations of our fans all around the world," he says. "You watch that and you realise that we are custodians of something that is so meaningful. It makes it all worthwhile. We know the relationship between our supporters and the club is extraordinary, it's unique.

"We certainly understand that there will be good days and bad days ahead. As owners, one has to have a bit of a thick skin to be involved in this. We're in it for the long haul. I'm excited about the path that we're on. We go into the season confident we'll be performing at a very high level again this year.

"There is going to be a target on our backs now against all the other teams that we play. We are back as one of the truly great clubs in the world and everyone will bring their best energy to try to beat Liverpool.

"But our players are still very hungry to be successful. By and large, they are quite young. I'm looking forward to seeing what we can achieve again this season."

There's still space on that wall for more iconic achievements. If Liverpool kick on as Werner expects, the hall of fame in his Boston office will require another rejig next May.

NO BIG SIGNINGS BUT ELECTRIC LIVERPOOL SHOULD CONTINUE TO FLOURISH UNDER KLOPP

JAMES PEARCE

AUG 4, 2019

The message from Jurgen Klopp has been clear. After a summer of wild celebrations for everyone connected with Liverpool Football Club, the time has come to look forward rather than back. The memories of June's Champions League final triumph over Tottenham will last a lifetime, but Klopp doesn't want that night in Madrid to go down in the history books as the pinnacle of his Anfield reign. Momentum has to be maintained.

"Let's be greedy" was Klopp's message to his players when they reassembled at Melwood for pre-season. And there's plenty to whet their appetite considering what's at stake over the next nine months.

Liverpool's status as European champions means Klopp must juggle the added demands of a Super Cup showdown with Chelsea in Istanbul on August 14 and December's FIFA Club World Cup in Qatar.

Emulating the dazzling achievements of 2018-19 won't be easy. Liverpool's 97 points in the Premier League was the highest tally in their 127-year history. They suffered only one league defeat all season, but it still wasn't enough to finish ahead of Manchester City.

The reality is that Klopp's men have the misfortune of competing against the most formidable winning machine English football has ever seen. City have collected 198 points over their back-to-back title campaigns.

Liverpool's latest pursuit of the Holy Grail has added significance as next May marks the 30th anniversary of their last top-flight crown. When the club previously fell agonisingly short in Premier League title races, in 2002, 2009 and 2014, on each occasion they regressed and soon slipped back into the chasing pack. It's hard to see history repeating itself. Not under this manager. Not with the array of talent at Klopp's disposal.

The same two-horse race looks a certainty. It's a rivalry which has been growing in intensity but the big question is: Have Liverpool really got enough in their armoury to depose Pep Guardiola's side?

There has been no booming statement of intent in the transfer market this summer. They certainly haven't sought to leapfrog City by getting the cheque book out. There have been just two signings. Firstly, young Dutch defender Sepp van den Berg, who has joined from PEC Zwolle for an initial fee of £1.3 million. Secondly, 16-year-old Fulham winger Harvey Elliott. Klopp insists that Liverpool's continued development as a team this season will come from within. He's adamant that he's got what he needs for the challenges ahead.

"We have solutions for all the situations," was the German's assessment.

Klopp's approach has divided opinion. Some regard it as a glaring missed opportunity at a time when Liverpool's pulling power is so strong after being crowned kings of Europe. Others have been quick to point out that the manager has earned their unwavering trust considering the transformation he has overseen at Anfield over the past four years.

His reign has already shown the value of waiting to land who he really wants rather than chasing after inferior options. Virgil van Dijk's £75 million move from Southampton was the perfect example. Klopp has never been one for stockpiling players and he likes operating with a tight-knit group where everyone feels they have a genuine chance of forcing their way in.

Ultimately, it comes down to depth and some concerns are understandable considering the schedule Liverpool are facing and the sheer calibre of City.

Klopp's dazzling front three are the envy of clubs worldwide. Mohamed Salah, Sadio Mane and Roberto Firmino will once again be tasked with tormenting defenders across the continent. They scored 91 goals between them in 2017-18 and a further 69 last term as Mane and Salah shared the Golden Boot with Arsenal's Pierre-Emerick Aubameyang.

All three are incredibly robust. Salah played 52 games for Liverpool last season with Mane (50) and Firmino (48) not far behind – but can they really be expected to hit the ground running and sustain it this time around? Their international commitments ensured it was deep into July before they got a breather after a gruelling 12 months and their pre-season has been brief.

Much will hinge on whether Klopp's back-up attacking options are able to deliver. Divock Origi achieved Kop icon status with his heroics in the second half of last season, culminating in him coming off the bench to slam home the goal that clinched the Champions League. However the Belgian striker, who recently penned a new long-term contract, still has plenty to prove as he looks to make the leap from impact sub to starter in order to ease the burden on Firmino.

Klopp will also need more from Xherdan Shaqiri, who has been hampered by injury in pre-season. The Switzerland forward made a big impact early on in his debut campaign following his arrival from Stoke City but then dropped out of favour. Shaqiri's quality on the ball isn't in doubt but his work off it is.

There is excitement inside Melwood around Rhian Brewster. This will be his breakthrough year. The 19-year-old frontman, who fired England to Under-17 World Cup glory two years ago, has returned to full fitness after 14 months out following ankle and knee operations. Brewster is quick, strong, works tirelessly for the cause and is a ruthless finisher. Klopp is convinced he's the real deal and has left the pathway clear for him.

It would be wrong to place too much responsibility on Brewster's young shoulders, but he has the personality as well as the ability to flourish. The former Chelsea youngster is effectively viewed as the replacement for Daniel Sturridge, who departed along with the left-back Alberto Moreno following the end of their contracts.

It is little wonder that Klopp didn't feel the need to bolster his midfield as that is an area of real strength. After a baptism of fire at Anfield during which he struggled to adjust to Liverpool's style and the speed of English football, Fabinho began to flourish and will undoubtedly start to get the wider adulation that he deserves. He is now the fulcrum of Klopp's midfield, a nailed-on starter.

The rest are battling it out for two spots. With Fabinho at ease in the holding role, the captain Jordan Henderson can be utilised further forward more regularly. The England midfielder's doubters have been silenced and Henderson now commands universal respect after leading the Reds to European glory. Mr Versatile, Gini Wijnaldum, is a model of consistency and the evergreen James Milner shows no signs of slowing down in the twilight of his career, while Naby Keita should kick on after a rollercoaster first season. There were flashes of brilliance from the Guinea international but he has yet to reproduce the form which lit up the Bundesliga during his time at RB Leipzig.

There are times when Liverpool's midfield lacks a creative spark. If Alex Oxlade-Chamberlain can stay fit then he will certainly provide it. The England international deserves some good fortune after battling back from a ruptured ACL. Adam Lallana is another midfielder looking to put fitness issues behind him after a torrid spell.

A year ago Klopp turned Liverpool into title contenders by tempering their attacking instincts and placing a greater emphasis on control and balance. He focused on marginal gains by dedicating more time on the training field to set-pieces and employed a specialist throw-in coach. They had the best defensive record in the top flight in 2018-19 and the foundations continue to look rock-solid.

Alisson Becker has been a revelation after joining from Roma last summer and was awarded the Golden Glove award for his 21 clean sheets in the Premier League. Liverpool haven't enjoyed such a commanding presence between the posts since Ray Clemence was in his prime.

In front of him is the Ballon d'Or contender Van Dijk. The Dutch centre-back is the best defender in world football, simply oozing calm and class. Joel Matip, Joe Gomez and Dejan Lovren will compete for the right to partner him, while on the flanks Liverpool continue to boast the most dazzling full-back combination in Europe in Trent Alexander-Arnold and Andy Robertson. They will provide a succession of ammunition for the frontline to fire.

For all those stellar names, Klopp remains Liverpool's biggest asset. His personality is infectious. He has galvanised the fanbase and the dressing room alike. Fortress Anfield has been rebuilt and there's a real sense of unity and spirit driving the club forward.

"Mentality monsters", was Klopp's colourful description of the guts and desire which ensured Liverpool surpassed all expectations last term. That will be needed in spades once again as they seek to add to their European crown.

With City so formidable and the margin for error in the Premier League so small, Klopp's inactivity in the transfer market does represent a gamble, but the feelgood factor on the back of Madrid remains strong. Now the current crop must justify their manager's big show of faith: that they can maintain the charge without a further sprinkling of star dust.

HOW VIDEOS, NASA TECHNOLOGY AND 'CARB POWER' HELPED LIVERPOOL AVOID "THE BIGGEST BANANA SKIN IN HISTORY"

JAMES PEARCE

AUG 18, 2019

As soon as the lap of honour was complete in Istanbul's Vodafone Park, Liverpool's backroom staff swung into action.

By that stage it was already the early hours of Thursday morning. There was little time to dwell on the glory of being crowned UEFA Super Cup winners after a penalty shootout victory over Chelsea.

There were ice baths to run, recovery shakes to be dished out and video analysis to be pored over. The next assignment was just around the corner and Jurgen Klopp knew that it was laced with danger.

Privately, the scheduling had angered the Liverpool manager. He couldn't understand why his side had been handed a Saturday afternoon showdown away to Southampton in the Premier League so soon after a 3,500-mile round trip to Turkey. But Klopp also knew that publicly complaining would achieve little other than giving his players a ready-made excuse to stumble on the south coast. Instead, a detailed plan had been drawn up to ensure that Liverpool did everything in their power to ensure that fatigue wasn't a determining factor against Saints, who had the luxury of a full week to prepare and were smarting from a heavy opening weekend defeat to Burnley.

The decision had been taken to stay at the luxurious Ritz-Carlton Hotel close to Besiktas' home in Istanbul post-match, rather than immediately fly home to Merseyside. It was just after 2am local time when the squad returned to their base, but all the clocks in the players' rooms had been put back two hours, in line with UK time.

Captain Jordan Henderson didn't return for a further hour-and-a-half as he was forced to wait in Vodafone Park, desperately trying to rehydrate after an exhausting night in order to provide a urine sample. Xherdan Shaqiri was also randomly selected for a drugs test but, having not featured over the course of the 120 minutes, had no such issues.

The following morning brought an early start for head physio Lee Nobes and long-serving masseur Paul Small as they got to work on weary limbs in the hotel. Among their five-strong team was physio Jose Luis Rodriguez Robledo. The Spaniard had enjoyed an eventful evening in Istanbul. Having gone into the stands to get his national flag for goalkeeper Adrian during the post-match celebrations, stewards mistook him for a pitch invader when he returned to the field. Twice, they tried to drag him away – much to the amusement of his fellow staff members.

After breakfast, those squad players who didn't get on in the Super Cup embarked on an intensive core session in the gym led by head of fitness and conditioning Andreas Kornmayer.

On their four-hour afternoon flight back to Liverpool the treatment continued for Klopp's walking wounded. Nobes, who joined the club from Manchester City last November, spent three of those hours working solidly on Adrian's ankle. It had swelled up considerably overnight after he had been wiped out by a supporter who had run on to the field after the penalty shootout. Without Nobes' expertise, the former West Ham keeper would have had no chance of playing at St Mary's. James Milner was also regarded as a major doubt with a heavily bruised leg after taking a kick against Chelsea and was tended to on the plane.

The 'Game Ready' icing machine was regularly filled and passed around the players. Developed by scientists and doctors using NASA space suit technology, it circulates cold water from an ice reservoir through a wrap which is applied to the injured area of the body. It provides compression as well as ice treatment.

Having landed back in Liverpool just before 4.30pm on Thursday, the players had cars at the airport and were able to head straight home to their families.

For Klopp and his staff, there was still work to be done. They got together to study the video analysis assistant boss Peter Krawietz and his team had pulled together on Southampton. They talked about dealing with Saints' threat from set-pieces, their direct style and how crucial it would be to win the second balls.

At 1pm on Friday the players reported back to Melwood, where the importance of rest and nutrition over the following 24 hours was drummed into them. Signs around the inner sanctum of the training ground read 'Carb Power'.

A light training session lasted less than an hour. Over-exerting the players would be counter-productive on what was essentially their second recovery day.

That work was preceded by the video analysis team meeting. The manager picked out examples of Southampton's strengths and weaknesses. "Massive," was how one staff member described the significance of that information to Saturday's outcome.

"It's so difficult trying to prepare when you only have one light session between games, so that's when the video becomes such a powerful tool. The manager was calm. He told everyone he wasn't interested in excuses."

At 6pm on Friday they flew to Southampton and headed to the Hilton at the Ageas Bowl. Nobes and Small were busy again. The players ate together, had treatment and then slept.

On Saturday morning Adrian passed a fitness test on his sore ankle, before the squad went for a leisurely stroll close to the home of Hampshire County Cricket Club.

Klopp had described the game to his players as "the biggest banana skin in history". "Everybody is waiting for it, probably all the headlines are written already," he said. "I would prefer the headline: 'The mentality giants were in town.'"

The manager had decided that fresh legs in midfield was vital. Henderson and Fabinho had played 120 minutes in the Super Cup so they would make way. Gini Wijnaldum and James Milner, who had each featured for an hour in Istanbul, would have Alex Oxlade-Chamberlain for company. Shifting Oxlade-Chamberlain from wide on the left to a central role created space for Roberto Firmino's return to the starting line-up.

It was a big show of faith in Oxlade-Chamberlain considering how he had struggled in the first half of the Super Cup. But he looked so much more comfortable in the middle and Klopp's gamble in handing him a first Premier League start since April 2018 paid off handsomely.

For most of the opening 45 minutes it was a scrappy, disjointed game. Possession was tossed away far too easily. As well as a predictable hangover of sorts from their midweek exploits, Liverpool were caught out by Saints' set-up. Instead of the 5-4-1 formation the visitors had planned for, it was 5-3-2. That gave Southampton more of a threat through the middle but also meant there was more space out wide for Klopp's men to exploit.

Liverpool's failure to make the most of that in the first half featured heavily in the half-time team talk at St Mary's. Sadio Mane's stunning finish had lifted the mood but the bar still needed to be raised. Full-backs Trent Alexander-Arnold and Andy Robertson were told in no uncertain terms that they needed to be operating further up the field.

Liverpool now switched play quickly from one flank to the other, stretching Southampton's compact formation, and began to dominate. Midfielders were quicker to get up in support of Mane, Firmino and Mohamed Salah. Rather than wilt physically, Liverpool grew stronger. They counter-pressed better as a unit. The rewards of the gruelling fitness drills during the pre-season training camp in Evian came to the fore.

So did Klopp's attention to detail and pursuit of marginal gains. Some were sceptical last season when it emerged that he had enlisted the services of throw-in coach Thomas Gronnemark. But the players have bought into it and the Dane's impact is clear. Both of Liverpool's goals at St Mary's came via that route. The second involved Mane robbing the ball off Jan Bednarek and feeding Firmino, who hammered home from the edge of the box. Nerves were jangling when Adrian's blunder enabled Danny Ings to pull one back, but Liverpool held on.

"It's a massive result for us," Robertson told *The Athletic*. "We got no favours playing Wednesday night in Turkey and being given a 3pm Saturday kick-off away. I think we could have been looked after a wee bit better but getting another three points on the board is all that matters. We knew we would have to dig deep, especially having had extra time in midweek.

"We stayed resilient and compact. Our mentality is so strong. When your preparation isn't ideal, it's all about finding a way to win and we did that."

An 11th straight league win – equalling the club's best run of the Premier League era – was all the sweeter as Manchester City were held by Tottenham later in the day. Liverpool still haven't dropped a point since March.

Despite the body blow of losing No 1 Alisson Becker to a torn calf, they emerged from an energy-sapping week with the Super Cup and six points out of six.

Their latest triumph owed much to the team behind the team. A truly collective effort.

In the away dressing room at St Mary's following Saturday's game, assistant boss Pep Lijnders declared that he had "good news and bad news".

"The bad news is that Adam (Lallana), Joe (Gomez) and Hendo (Jordan Henderson), you have to go back outside and run," he said. "The good news is that you've all got two days off."

Nobody can say they haven't earned a breather.

FABINHO'S DISPLAY AGAINST ARSENAL SHOWS HOW FAR LIVERPOOL'S 'LIGHTHOUSE' HAS COME

JAMES PEARCE

AUG 25, 2019

The contrast between then and now is stark.

The first time Fabinho locked horns with Arsenal in the Premier League it proved to be a chastening experience for the Liverpool midfielder. Last November's 1-1 draw at the Emirates opened his eyes to the pace and intensity of English football's top flight. It was only his second league start for the club following a £43 million summer move from Monaco and he had endured a difficult adaptation period. He had a habit of dropping too deep, wanting too many touches and being wasteful in possession. Arsenal swarmed all over him. "That was the night when I really understood the speed of the Premier League and the attention to detail that is required," Fabinho admitted.

Fast forward nine months and the Brazil international showcased his eye-catching development in Saturday's emphatic 3-1 victory over the Gunners at Anfield, which equalled a club record of 12 successive league wins. This time, Unai Emery's side couldn't lay a glove on him.

Mohamed Salah grabbed the headlines with his second-half double after Joel Matip's bullet header had ended Arsenal's stubborn resistance, but it was Fabinho who gave Liverpool the platform to dominate. He bossed proceedings in the holding midfield role which he has now made his own. Alert to the danger around him, he repeatedly won possession and put Jurgen Klopp's men back on the front foot with his intelligent use of the ball. The 25-year-old boasted a passing accuracy of 93 per cent and came out on top in 67 per cent of his duels. He also provided four key passes, including the classy assist for Salah's majestic second goal.

It was the perfect riposte to recent criticism from former Liverpool boss Graeme Souness, who suggested he had been wearing "lead boots" in the Super Cup triumph over Chelsea in Istanbul.

"Sensational," was a beaming Klopp's assessment of Fabinho's performance on Saturday. "There was one tackle from him that was just incredible – completely clean, winning the ball and passing it with his bum pretty much still on the floor!"

It wasn't a one-off. Fabinho has steadily grown in stature over the course of 2019 with his early struggles at Anfield now an increasingly distant memory.

Bought as a replacement for Emre Can, who left for Juventus as a free agent in 2018, he's proved himself to be a more dynamic and more imposing midfield enforcer than the Germany international, who always divided opinion at Anfield.

Liverpool's interest in Fabinho, who is represented by Jorge Mendes, dates back to the 2012-13 season, when the then teenager was on loan at Real Madrid Castilla, the La Liga giants' reserve team, from Portuguese outfit Rio Ave. He was a right-back at that time and the club's recruitment staff were monitoring his progress.

Born and raised in Campinas in Sao Paulo State, Fabinho was just 18 when he moved from his homeland to Europe after coming up through the youth ranks at Fluminense. There was one solitary appearance for Real Madrid's first team under Jose Mourinho before Monaco secured his services. Coach Leonardo Jardim transformed Fabinho into a defensive midfielder and he was instrumental in an exciting team which included Kylian Mbappe, Bernardo Silva and Benjamin Mendy. They won the Ligue 1 title in 2016-17 and reached the semi-finals of the Champions League.

The scouting reports over the course of the following season were glowing and the character references were also important in convincing Klopp that Fabinho would be the perfect fit, both on and off the field. It was felt that Fabinho's physical presence made him a better option than either Jorginho or Lucas Torreira, who had also come under consideration.

Liverpool sporting director Michael Edwards and head of recruitment Dave Fallows put in the hard yards to get the deal done. The announcement – 48 hours after the club's Champions League final defeat by Real Madrid in Kyiv – was a welcome pick-me-up for supporters.

Yet Klopp always knew that Fabinho would need time to get up to speed. It simply wasn't realistic to think he could hit the ground running considering the difference in styles between Monaco and Liverpool. Fabinho was used to having another holding midfielder alongside him. In France, he wasn't expected to cover anywhere near as much ground. There was work to be done both tactically and physically. He had to wait until late October for his Premier League debut.

The support of wife Rebeca and Brazilian team-mates Roberto Firmino and Alisson kept his spirits up during a frustrating spell. It had been a glowing recommendation from Firmino which had helped convince Fabinho to sign for Liverpool. "This manager demands a lot but he will improve you," Firmino told him.

Fabinho was given an extensive gym programme designed to strengthen his core in order to increase his power and fitness without affecting his mobility. Pep Lijnders was crucial in helping him to settle and make the necessary changes to his game. Fabinho was only just starting to learn English but Klopp's Dutch assistant is fluent in Portuguese following his spell at FC Porto.

"I was adapting to a new training method, a new league and a new country, which was completely different from the one I was used to," Fabinho recalled. "In the beginning I needed to be patient. I constantly looked to learn from my coaches and the players who had been playing here longer.

"Here, when you have the ball at your feet, you have less time to react. You always have one or two opponents on your back. In France, I was able to turn. Here, your reaction time has to be very quick."

The penny dropped and in the second half of last season, Fabinho was immense, never more than in a commanding display in the stunning Champions League semi-final fightback against Barcelona. With Fabinho operating on his own in front of the back four, Klopp is able to play his favoured 4-3-3 formation rather than 4-2-3-1. That has freed up Jordan Henderson to shift further forward. The Liverpool captain had been reinvented as a holding midfielder by Klopp, but he appreciates the qualities that Fabinho has brought to the fold. "I think if you look at Fab, it's quite natural to him. He's so good at what you need to do in that position," Henderson said.

Lijnders refers to Fabinho as "the lighthouse" in the "organised chaos" of Liverpool's brand of attacking football. As the storm rages around him with the brilliance of Sadio Mane, Firmino and Salah, Fabinho provides the control. "His timing, his vision, his calmness; it gives another dimension to our midfield," Lijnders said.

Fabinho is much more than a wrecking ball in the centre of the park. He set the tone on Saturday, surging forward with purpose before he was cynically chopped down by Granit Xhaka. His role in Liverpool's third goal was exquisite. When Trent Alexander-Arnold was under pressure close to the touchline, Fabinho dropped off to give him an outlet and promptly swept a first-time pass into the feet of Salah. Talk about vision. The Egyptian darted away from the hapless David Luiz and finished brilliantly.

Fabinho's reaction to Torreira ramming home a late consolation was also telling. He threw his arms up in disgust, his face contorted with rage. He wanted that clean sheet. The bar is set high.

It's no wonder that Fabinho has been recalled to the Brazil squad for next month's internationals against Peru and Colombia after being overlooked for the Copa America. He's now a vital cog in this Klopp machine. Liverpool haven't had a specialist holding midfielder operating at this level since Javier Mascherano a decade ago.

Interview requests from the waiting media were politely declined in the bowels of Anfield on Saturday evening. "I'm still learning English and my teacher isn't so good," joked Fabinho.

There's maybe some work to do off the pitch but on it, he's flourishing.

AUGUST RESULTS

Community Shield, August 4 2019
Liverpool 1 Man City 1 (City win 5-4 after pens)
Liverpool scorer: Matip 77

Premier League, August 9 2019
Liverpool 4 Norwich 1
Liverpool scorers: Hanley 7 OG, Salah 19, Van Dijk 28, Origi 42

UEFA Super Cup, August 14 2019
Liverpool 2 Chelsea 2 (Liverpool win 5-4 after pens)
Liverpool scorer: Mane 48, 95

Premier League, August 17 2019
Southampton 1 Liverpool 2
Liverpool scorers: Mane 45+1, Firmino 71

Premier League, August 24 2019
Liverpool 3 Arsenal 1
Liverpool scorers: Matip 41, Salah 49 pen, 58

Premier League, August 31 2019
Burnley 0 Liverpool 3
Liverpool scorers: Wood 33 OG, Mane 37, Firmino 80

SEPTEMBER

SALAH AND MANE HAVE ALREADY MADE UP. THERE'S FRIENDLY RIVALRY AND OCCASIONAL SELFISHNESS BUT A FEUD? NO WAY

JAMES PEARCE

SEP 1, 2019

Sadio Mane wasn't in the mood for talking when he left Turf Moor on Saturday evening. With his headphones in, the Liverpool attacker headed straight past the waiting media. Interview requests were turned down with a shake of the head. It was out of character for the amiable Senegal international – just like his outburst after being substituted in the closing stages of a record-breaking 3-0 win over Burnley.

As he made his way off the pitch after being granted a breather five minutes from time, Mane erupted. He was fuming over Mohamed Salah's failure to give him a pass, moments earlier. A slick counter-attack from Jurgen Klopp's side had seen Georginio Wijnaldum and Roberto Firmino link up down the right before the Brazilian picked out Salah inside him. The Egyptian had the opportunity to give Mane a tap-in but opted instead to turn back on to his right foot and go for goal himself. It was the wrong move. Erik Pieters was able to slide in and force the ball behind.

After being embraced by his manager on the touchline, Mane jabbed a finger in the direction of captain Jordan Henderson, who was sat on the bench after being forced off with a dead leg. Mane, who had received a rollicking off Henderson after a late error against Arsenal at Anfield a week earlier, clearly wanted to make a point to the skipper about Salah's decision-making. A training bib was thrown down in disgust as Mane continued to vent his frustration, before vice-captain James Milner wisely moved to take a seat next to Mane and helped to calm things down.

For the critics desperately trying to find a chink in Liverpool's armour after a club-record 13th successive top-flight win, it was manna from heaven. But social media talk about a feud between the two hottest properties in African football is ridiculous.

"It wasn't even an issue by the time the players got back to the dressing room," a source told *The Athletic*. "Sadio and Mo were chatting and everything was fine. It was just in the heat of the moment. It's all forgotten. It was a storm in a teacup."

Henderson, who revealed that Mane had been "laughing and joking" with his team-mates post-match, welcomed the show of passion. The skipper believes it was a sign of the high standards set by Klopp's European champions. "I quite like that now and again, I think we need it," Henderson said with a smile. "Sadio is fine, he's a great lad. That's just us pushing each other all the time. I think that's important. We all want to do better. We all want to improve. We're really close and I think we can deal with that."

The ESPN pundit Steve Nicol, a member of Liverpool's last title-winning side in 1990, nodded his head in agreement. "I think what you saw is the reason why Liverpool are so good and why Firmino, Salah and Mane are so good," Nicol said. "That desire and determination. Even at 3-0, they still weren't happy. They want goals and they want them all the time."

Salah certainly saw the funny side. He uploaded a video to his Instagram story on Saturday night of Firmino smirking at the camera as the Brazilian walked back down the tunnel between Salah and Mane at Turf Moor with the caption 'Wait for Roberto Firmino's face' with three laughing emojis.

It's not the first time that questions have been asked about the dynamic between Liverpool's two most potent weapons. Mane and Salah shared the Premier League Golden Boot with Arsenal's Pierre-Emerick Aubameyang last season and since the start of 2018-19 they have both scored 30 goals in all competitions for Klopp's side. There is a healthy rivalry. Klopp believes they bring out the best in each other and prides himself on the fact that they both put team success before individual glory.

Does Salah have a selfish streak? Of course. That self-belief and willingness to back himself is the reason why he boasts 74 goals in 110 appearances for the club and has broken a stack of records. There are times, like on Saturday, when he strives too hard and that same desire to score clouds his judgement. It's a fine line. If he had got the shot away before Pieters' last-ditch intervention and beaten Nick Pope then he would have been saluted for his individual brilliance, as he was at St Mary's in April, when he ran half the length of the pitch, ignored Firmino's lung-bursting run outside him and whipped an unstoppable left-foot shot into the bottom corner.

"Salah should have passed," Jamie Carragher, the Liverpool legend turned pundit, told Sky Sports on Saturday evening. "If he hasn't scored for 60 minutes then he looks as though he is absolutely desperate to score in the final 30 minutes and he starts shooting more."

A year ago the shoe was on the other foot, with Mane heavily criticised for failing to put one on a plate for Salah during a narrow victory over Tottenham at Wembley. Mane's Instagram post after that game received so many abusive messages from fuming Egyptian fans that he ended up deleting it. The Official Liverpool Supporters Club in Cairo subsequently issued an apology to Mane and branded the treatment of the player as "shameful".

Since Salah arrived at Anfield from Roma in the summer of 2017, Liverpool's first-choice frontline have scored a remarkable 169 goals in all competitions. Salah (74) leads the way followed by Mane (50) and Firmino (45).

During that time Opta stats for Premier League matches show that the most frequent combination in terms of passes between Klopp's attackers involves Salah finding Firmino (277). That's followed by Firmino to Salah (256), Firmino to Mane (222), Mane to Firmino (209), Mane to Salah (177) and Salah to Mane (172).

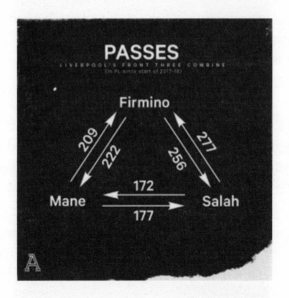

Given that Salah and Mane largely operate on opposite flanks, it's hardly surprising that Firmino links play more often.

Interestingly, in terms of creating chances for each other since the start of the 2017-18 season, Mane leads the way with 43 for Salah. Mane has provided Salah with seven assists. In return, Salah has created 25 chances for Mane and that has resulted in four assists. The Egyptian has created 34 chances for Firmino with five assists, while Firmino has created 33 chances for Salah with seven assists. Firmino has created 26 chances for Mane with five assists and Mane has created 17 for Firmino with two assists.

The fact that Mane's total passes to Salah is the second lowest of the six combinations but Mane to Salah is the highest for chances created shows that when they do combine it's in areas where they can really hurt teams. It was a pass from Mane which led to Salah slamming a first-half strike against the upright at Turf Moor. Mane is clearly a more productive source of opportunities for Salah than vice-versa, so maybe a sense of frustration at times is understandable.

Yet the stats make a mockery of the idea that Salah isn't a team man. Going back to the start of the 2017-18 season, he has contributed 20 assists in the Premier League and created 139 chances, with 968 successful passes in the final third. Over the same period Mane has chipped in with nine assists, 104 chances created and 848 successful passes in the final third. Firmino boasts 15 assists, 103 chances created and 878 successful passes in the final third. Salah has been the most dazzling creative force of the three – providing 1.92 chances per 90 minutes compared to 1.68 for Mane and 1.61 for Firmino.

One of the highlights of Liverpool's run to the Champions League final last term was Salah's exquisite assist with the outside of his left boot which was nodded home by Mane against Bayern Munich, silencing the Allianz Arena.

Off the pitch, the pair share a friendship and a mutual respect. Mane was Liverpool's Player of the Year when Salah arrived two years ago and found himself shifted from right wing to left in order to accommodate the new signing. However, that was never an issue for Mane. Humble and quiet around the training ground, he does not court the limelight or seek to be regarded as the main man. Mane went out of his way to help his fellow Muslim settle in two years ago and adjust to life on Merseyside. Since then Mane has done the same for Naby Keita, while Salah has developed a bond with Dejan Lovren.

"I am very close to Sadio," Salah said last season. "We're friends, we talk a lot to each other. We sit together in the dressing room in the same place just after matches. There's a real solidarity between us because we don't worry about who's going to score the most or first."

Speaking before June's Champions League final, Mane said: "Mo can score goals or Bobby or me, it doesn't matter. We do everything as a team." During a 'Bezzies' (best friends) feature on the club's TV channel last season, the only thing Salah and Mane couldn't agree on was who had the best fashion sense.

It's been a hectic and stressful period for them both: a gruelling season was followed by the Africa Cup of Nations which shortened their summer break. Both Mane and Salah will now benefit from some much-needed time off. Senegal and Egypt aren't in action during the current international break and Klopp has given all his players not on duty the coming week off. The squad will reconvene at Melwood next weekend to start preparations for the visit of Newcastle United.

"Everyone needs to calm down a little bit. Sadio is completely fine and everything is good. We still like each other," laughed Klopp at Turf Moor on Saturday. The Liverpool manager couldn't have been less concerned, either in front of the media or in the confines of the dressing room.

Mane will be embarrassed about losing his rag – hence his decision to stick those headphones in and keep walking past the waiting media. It's not his style. He knows he would have been better off saying his piece away from the cameras. But rather than unrest in the camp it was a sign of the winning mentality that Klopp has instilled in this incredibly gifted squad. There's a hunger driving Liverpool on in search of ending the club's painful 30-year wait for the title. Mane and Salah epitomise that.

TENNIS, TEETH-WHITENING AND MAKING LIVERPOOL TICK – WHY KLOPP AND THE KOP LOVE ECCENTRIC FIRMINO

JAMES PEARCE

SEP 15, 2019

It was just after 4.30pm on Saturday when a yellow Lamborghini slowly made its way down Anfield Road.

One eagle-eyed fan who had emerged from the throng of hundreds celebrating Liverpool's victory over Newcastle outside the popular haunt of Hotel Tia spotted who was sitting in the passenger seat.

"That's Bobby Firmino in there," he told his pal before darting across the road to deliver a message to the club's cherished No 9. "Bobby lad, there's something that the Kop wants you to know. We fucking love you."

Firmino, with his wife Larissa Pereira at the wheel, responded with a beaming white smile and a thumbs up before continuing the journey back home to Formby, 14 miles north of the stadium. The Brazil forward had the man of the match award in tow after delivering another masterclass at Anfield to cement Liverpool's place at the Premier League summit.

It was an afternoon that illustrated why Jurgen Klopp refers to Firmino as "the engine" of his team. He didn't score and was on the field for only 53 minutes but his impact was immense. Liverpool were misfiring at times before his introduction, but they purred when he was back leading the line.

"Bobby proved again that he's absolutely world-class," the left-back Andy Robertson told *The Athletic*.

"He set up two goals and probably could have had four assists. He changed the game when he came on. He's so important for us and makes us tick."

Klopp had wanted to give the 27-year-old a rest. After all, he had only returned to Merseyside with Fabinho late on Wednesday after starting games for Brazil against Peru and Colombia. Mindful of the lack of preparation time before Saturday's lunchtime kick-off, Liverpool had laid on a private plane to get the duo back from Los Angeles to John Lennon Airport as quickly as possible.

With Thursday a recovery day, Firmino only took part in a light session after the 5,000-mile journey, before training fully on Friday. He was desperate to start against Newcastle, but Klopp had to look at the bigger picture: Tuesday's Champions League group-opener away to Napoli is followed by a trip to Stamford Bridge next Sunday.

The decision was taken to rest him and bring Divock Origi into the side on the left, with Sadio Mane operating through the middle. However, just as in August's Super Cup clash with Chelsea, Klopp's plan for Firmino to put his feet up had to be swiftly reassessed.

In Istanbul, it was the paucity of Liverpool's first-half display that prompted his introduction straight after the break. Within three minutes that night, he created the equaliser for Mane and transformed the complexion of the contest.

On Saturday, the change was enforced by Origi limping off with an ankle problem eight minutes before the interval. Klopp could have turned to Xherdan Shaqiri but opted to unleash

Firmino instead. It enabled Mane, who had cancelled out Jetro Willems' opener with a classy finish into the top corner, to return to his favoured role on the left. Immediately, the balance of the side looked so much better.

Firmino needed only two minutes to showcase both the perspiration and the inspiration that he offers Liverpool. His tenacity robbed possession off Christian Atsu, before he picked out Mane's intelligent run with a perfectly-weighted pass. The Newcastle goalkeeper Martin Dubravka blundered and Mane tucked away his second of the afternoon. It was classic Firmino: dropping deep, hassling and harrying opponents and then hurting them with his creative spark. In the second half, he tormented Newcastle's overworked back line. There was magic in those garish pink boots.

Firmino is so elusive because he's always on the move. He's a master at finding pockets of space between the lines. Awe-inspiring tricks and flicks are combined with an unwavering work ethic. He created chances for rampaging full-backs Trent Alexander-Arnold and Robertson before the assist for Mohamed Salah, which had a capacity crowd off their seats.

When Salah rolled the ball into Firmino's feet, the Brazilian was 20 yards out with his back to goal. Five defenders patrolled the edge of the penalty box. What followed was exquisite, as he controlled with his right, rolled it on to his left and then executed a deft back-heel that flowed perfectly into the path of Salah, who scored before making a beeline for Firmino.

"That touch was so nice," Georginio Wijnaldum told *The Athletic*. "He's really important for us because he does a lot more than just playing as a striker. He defends well. He drops into the midfield at times and gives us an extra man in there. He does so many things extra that makes things easier for us. Bobby is quite shy off the field but on the field, he comes alive."

ROBERTO FIRMINO'S TOUCHES AGAINST NEWCASTLE

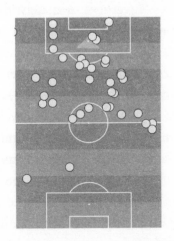

Liverpool's rise in recent years has been founded on outstanding recruitment and few transfers have proved shrewder than the £29 million deal they struck with Hoffenheim for Firmino in June 2015.

Brendan Rodgers had his doubts. He wanted Christian Benteke to be the focal point of his attack and it was a compromise that both the Belgian and Firmino were signed that summer. Sporting director Michael Edwards (who was director of technical performance at the time) was convinced that Firmino would be "a game-changer". The head of recruitment Dave Fallows and chief scout Barry Hunter agreed. That trio were key in putting in the groundwork to secure his signature.

Liverpool had kept close tabs on his progress in the Bundesliga since being alerted to his potential by Fernando Troiani, the club's head of South American scouting, when Firmino was on the books at Figueirense in his homeland as a teenager. Presented with an array of impressive data, glowing character references and Edwards' passionate belief in the player, Fenway Sports Group president Mike Gordon was so enthused that he vowed he was prepared to sanction "whatever it takes" to secure the signing.

"When I saw that Liverpool had signed him, I thought: 'How could Liverpool do this?'" Klopp said, shortly after his appointment at Anfield. "They were not in their 100 per cent best moment and other clubs would have spent more on him, so I thought immediately: 'What a good transfer for them.'"

Four years ago this week, Firmino found himself marooned out on the right wing by Rodgers during a miserable 3-1 defeat at Old Trafford. He was stuck on the periphery before being replaced by Jordon Ibe. Within a month, Klopp had taken over and Firmino started to blossom in a central role. He has never looked back. In 199 appearances for the club, he has scored 68 goals and contributed 52 assists.

Firmino, who socialises with fellow Brazilians Fabinho and Alisson, is happy and settled in Formby with his wife and young daughters Valentina and Bella. He lives in a house previously rented by Rodgers and is currently having tennis lessons.

He's eccentric. When he decided to have his teeth whitened he was offered shades four, three, two or one, in increasing degrees of brightness. Instead he told dentist Robbie Hughes he wanted "maximo, beyond one" and they created it especially for him. Over the summer, he had a new tattoo added to his back of him lifting the Champions League trophy in Madrid. It's been a year to cherish for him, as Copa America glory with Brazil followed soon after.

"Bobby is a connecting player, a finisher, a fighter, and our first defender," Klopp said, a reference to how he sets the tone with his pressing. He's also incredibly robust. In 2016-17 he featured in 35 of Liverpool's 38 Premier League games. He only missed one league game in 2017-18 and then sat out four last term.

Liverpool have won without him, most significantly when

they beat Barcelona 4-0 in the semi-final of the Champions League back in May, when Firmino was hampered by a groin problem. But he's arguably Klopp's most indispensable player because the manager simply doesn't have anyone else quite like him. Liverpool can't play the same way when he's not there.

After Saturday's game, he headed upstairs from the home dressing room to the Carlsberg Lounge to receive his man-of-the-match award. Inside, he was embraced by Ian Rush, the greatest goalscorer in Liverpool's history, who introduced him to an array of legends including David Fairclough, Terry McDermott and Roy Evans.

Fairclough, the former Liverpool striker, told *The Athletic*: "This is going back a long way, but Firmino actually reminds me of Alfredo Di Stefano, the Real Madrid great of the 1950s and 1960s. It's hard to put him in a box or describe him as a No 9 or a No 10 because he does so much for the team. He's excelled since Philippe Coutinho moved on."

Liverpool's love for their unique No 9 continues to grow.

'TIME WASTING', NUTRITION AND A PRO SURFER ARE GIVING LIVERPOOL THE EDGE IN EARLY DAYS OF THE TITLE RACE

JAMES PEARCE

SEP 22, 2019

The irony won't have been lost on those jubilant Liverpool fans in the Shed End. There was Stamford Bridge, collectively raging at the sight of Jurgen Klopp's Premier League leaders taking every possible opportunity to run the clock down as they protected their precious lead in the capital.

Andy Robertson was chastised by referee Michael Oliver for dallying over a throw-in and goalkeeper Adrian enraged the natives for doing likewise from a goal-kick. A fuming Frank Lampard approached the away dugout to voice his displeasure, only for Klopp to smile back at the Chelsea boss and respond with, "Oh, come on!"

Oliver's patience finally snapped when he booked Trent Alexander-Arnold for time wasting. Fabinho later cynically hauled down substitute Michy Batshuayi, the Brazilian midfielder taking a booking for the team after a mistake by Roberto Firmino, rather than running the risk of Chelsea bursting away and finding an equaliser on the counter-attack.

Of course, Chelsea are no stranger to the dark arts. Their former boss Jose Mourinho has a black belt and famously put them to good use on the day in April 2014 when the Londoners wrecked Liverpool's title dream at Anfield. The abiding memories of that afternoon involve Blues players untying their laces and going down with mystery bouts of cramp to stop the hosts building any momentum.

Liverpool haven't quite plumbed those depths, but what they are displaying in their pursuit of the title is a much-needed streetwise approach. They know when to slow the game down and when to try to take the sting out of proceedings.

"I don't think we were doing it deliberately," insisted Robertson to *The Athletic* when quizzed on Chelsea's allegations of time wasting. "Listen, you can't expect us to be quickly getting the ball back. We were 2-0 up, we weren't going to rush and jump in the stands to get it. Their fans got on the ref's back and then he was rushing us a bit."

Finishing top of the Premier League Fair Play Table for the past three seasons is admirable, but the reality is that there's only one top spot that Liverpool fans really care about. Currently, it belongs to their club and they will take some shifting after restoring their five-point lead at the summit.

It was a record-breaking afternoon, with Klopp's men becoming the first team to win their opening six matches of a top-flight season in two consecutive seasons. They also set a club record of seven successive away league wins and extended the club's best winning run in the league to 15 matches dating back to early March.

Good value for their 2-0 lead at the break, Liverpool rode their luck as Chelsea rallied in the second half. N'Golo Kante pulled one back and only a combination of gutsy last-ditch defending and shoddy finishing denied them a share of the spoils.

Fatigue undoubtedly played a part with the visitors looking leggy after their gruelling night in Naples in the Champions

League on Tuesday. But what ultimately proved the difference between success and failure was Klopp's attention to detail. Marginal gains is the watchword at Melwood as he tries to turn Liverpool from challengers into champions.

It was no coincidence that both of the visitors' goals came from set-pieces. Hours of hard graft on the training field paid a rich dividend. Mohamed Salah back-heeled a free-kick for Alexander-Arnold to unleash a thunderbolt into the top corner for his first goal since November. Then, full-backs Alexander-Arnold and Robertson combined from another free-kick, the latter whipping a beauty into the box for Firmino to nod home. It was the 23rd headed goal Liverpool have scored in the Premier League since the start of last season – seven more than any other side.

"We spend a lot of time on set-pieces," Robertson confirmed. "The assistant managers (Peter Krawietz and Pep Lijnders) take the sessions and we work hard on them because we all know how important they are in both penalty boxes. Luckily, two of them worked well for us."

Krawietz shows the squad video montages at Melwood ahead of each game, highlighting where he believes opponents are vulnerable. Chelsea's soft centre had been targeted.

"After the analysis we go out on the training pitch and try to replicate what he wants us to do," Robertson said. "It doesn't always work but we've scored some good goals from set-pieces already this season and long may that continue. We try to find weaknesses to exploit – that's part and parcel of the game.

"The first one was a piece of magic from Trent. The second one we'd been practising with the roll and the cross and thankfully Bobby was in the right place to put it away."

Last season, Liverpool failed to hold on to 1-0 leads against Arsenal, Leicester and West Ham and ended up drawing all three games 1-1. Having missed out to Manchester City by the narrowest of margins last term, Klopp is leaving no stone unturned. During their training camp in France back in July he asked German surfer Sebastian Steudtner to give his players a motivational speech about managing stress and dealing with panic. Klopp already boasts the world's only specialist throw-in coach in Thomas Gronnemark and he rates nutritionist Mona Nemmer, snapped up from Bayern Munich three years ago, as one of his most crucial additions.

"For us, it's not about gaining five per cent or 10 per cent here and there, because we are a very good team. It's about the small margins," Robertson said. "All those one per cents add up. The manager is very big on that. The throw-ins and the set-pieces improved a lot last season and we're looking to kick on again. We're getting the one per cents right at the minute and long may that continue. We'll keep looking for more."

This was a statement win for Liverpool.

Much had been made about the fact they had only taken nine points out of a possible 36 from their last dozen away league games against fellow top-six teams. Ultimately, it was ugly, but they dug deep to get the job done. The show of fight was epitomised by Robertson's lung-bursting run at the death to run down the clock.

For Klopp, it was a 92nd win in 150 league games in charge. No Liverpool boss has ever done better than that.

"Maybe there's a wee bit more maturity in the team now, on the back of going so close in the league and winning the Champions League last season. It's a case of using all that experience," Robertson added.

It is serving Klopp's increasingly streetwise Reds well.

LEDERHOSEN, LOSING FAT AND BEATING BAYERN – HOW SALZBURG MADE SADIO MANE

RAPHAEL HONIGSTEIN

SEP 30, 2019

Last month, Sadio Mane flew to Austria to take a peek at his past.

The Liverpool forward and one of his best friends, Red Bull Salzburg integration manager Mustapha 'Musti' Mesloub, stopped outside an unassuming house on Wehrgasse, a small U-shaped street that backs onto the Glanbach brook on the western outskirts of the city, and looked up to the one-bedroom flat that was Mane's abode for almost two years. They resisted the temptation to ring the doorbell and ask the present occupier to let them in, but then, they didn't have to. The memories from 2012-13 and 2013-14 are still very fresh.

"It was a rather cramped flat, with a beaten-up leather sofa in the lounge and not much else," another close friend recalls. "We spent a lot of time watching football on television there but Sadio could never sit still. He got some weights and other gym equipment from the club and was always doing core stability exercises. Sadio was obsessed with bettering himself, with getting rid of the last gram of fat on what was even then an unbelievably muscular body."

The Senegal international might have been living in modest environs then, but his ambition was already super-sized. Mane told his friend that his target was to win the Ballon d'Or. When his pal felt that he was perhaps aiming a little too high at this early stage in his career, Mane replied, "OK, then I want to be African Player of the Year first."

Getting the Sedhiou-born player to the hometown of Mozart had not been a straightforward endeavour. Salzburg's scouts had identified him as a possible target after his strong showings at the 2012 Olympics in London, but sporting director Ralf Rangnick first wanted to see the then 20-year-old in action for Metz, in France's third division.

"I went to their League Cup game against Tours," the 61-year-old told *The Athletic*. "Sadio played very well, which worked a little against us that day. I remember meeting with Metz's president after the game. He insisted that they would only sell him for €4 million. That was a huge fee for us, especially for a third-division player in France."

Rangnick phoned club owner Dieter Mateschitz and convinced him that Mane was worth the outlay.

The player arrived at a pivotal time for the club. They had just appointed Roger Schmidt, a trained engineer, to implement a high-energy pressing game and needed young professionals willing and able to play that kind of game.

"As much as Salzburg made Sadio as a player, he also had a huge hand in making Salzburg as a team," Schmidt says. "Thanks to him and other new arrivals, such as Kevin Kampl, we were able to change the style and really play the football we wanted to. From the first training session, it was immediately clear that he had all the raw ingredients to be a top player. He had to get to grips with some aspects of collective tactics but it took him no time at all to come up to speed. I've rarely seen a player willing to work as hard and selflessly for his team. For a coach, he was a dream."

However, according to Mesloub, who had been hired by Rangnick and was very close to Mane throughout his time at the Red Bull Arena, it took the player a bit more time to settle off the pitch.

"In Metz, there were plenty of Africans in the team and in the city but Salzburg was a very different story," the 59-year-old French-Algerian says. "One big problem was food. There was no African restaurant here at the time. We went to eat a lot of pasta, because that was the closest we could get to the rice-based cuisine of his home country."

People in the picturesque town at the foot of the Alps are friendly and good-natured, he adds, but they do take time before they open up to outsiders.

"Rangnick knew that a young player like him would be in danger of getting completely lost in such an environment, which is why I was employed to look after him pretty much 24-7," says Mesloub. "He spent a lot of time with me and my family and almost became an adopted son. He called me 'papa' once but I prefer that he calls me a 'big brother'. He already has a father."

Mane threw himself into learning German and soon spoke the language pretty well. He still does, incidentally, and with a clearly discernible Austrian accent.

"Little by little, he became more acquainted with the culture here," Mesloub says. "He even wore lederhosen to a friend's wedding. At first, he had been totally against wearing them but I talked him around. He got many compliments for the way he looked in them and was very pleased he had tried them in the end."

But there were some unhappier moments, too. Mesloub recalls Mane getting very upset when he smiled at a young child and the kid straight away started crying in fear. "The boy was maybe two or three years old and had probably never seen a black person before in his life. Salzburg is 99 per cent white. Sadio was deeply distraught by this incident."

A much worse case of prejudice was to follow in a league game against Sturm Graz. An opponent racially abused him during the first half and at the break, Mane came into the dressing room shouting "pourquoi?" (why?) over and over again, banging one of the lockers with his fist in angry disbelief. Schmidt told him not to let the provocations get to him. Some of his white team-mates took matters into their own hands. Three or four approached the Graz player and told him he'd better be quiet or face some physical retribution. That was the end of the matter.

In his second season, both he and the team really hit their stride. More and more scouts started sitting in the stands to check on the wide attacker, who scored 23 goals in all competitions. His most impressive performance came in a friendly, however. Mane scored and provided an assist in a 3-0 evisceration of Pep Guardiola's Bayern Munich at the Red Bull Arena in January 2014.

"He played a superb game against top defenders like David Alaba and Javi Martinez," says Mesloub. "Everywhere in the city, people went up to him and hugged him. Beating the European champions was a huge deal here. Salzburg had never taken on such a big team and won before. Everybody was happy about the win and Sadio was so happy about the love he was shown."

"Legendary," Rangnick calls the match. The former Hoffenheim boss was surprised Bayern never made a serious attempt to sign Mane. Liverpool, too, weren't convinced. "Michael Edwards said the player wasn't quite ready for the step up to the Premier League yet," he continued. "There was something about their scouting model not being able to properly evaluate the quality of an Austrian Bundesliga player, too, if I remember correctly."

A certain Jurgen Klopp, by contrast, was very much interested. The Borussia Dortmund manager met with Mane for a long chat. "I've never sat down with a coach and come out talking more than I did," he told a friend about the get-together, in which Klopp had tried to gauge the player's character. They immediately clicked on a personal level but the German and his club ultimately decided against pursuing a transfer, believing that they needed to strengthen elsewhere. "Kloppo once said not going for Sadio was one of his biggest mistakes," Rangnick says.

Salzburg's attempts to create an auction for the player in summer 2014 saw relations with the club suffer. Mane had his heart set on joining the Premier League, where West Ham United and Southampton were keen, but the Austrians were hoping to offload him to clubs with deeper pockets in more far-flung places. Their differences became irreconcilable when Mane arrived late for a meeting ahead of the second leg of a Champions League qualifier against Malmo in August, citing a headache. He was banished from the squad as Salzburg lost 3-0 in Sweden to miss out on the group stage once more. "Everyone has forgiven him now but, at the time, his team-mates were not happy," Rangnick says.

Mane was jeered by the RB crowd during a friendly with Southampton in 2015. It will be different in December, however, when Mane returns in Liverpool colours. "People are proud that one of the best in the world, a Champions League winner, made his breakthrough here," says Mesloub, whose family will be the player's guests of honour when Salzburg go to Anfield on Wednesday night.

The last time Mane came to check in on his friend and the city that put him on the path to super-stardom, they went to his favourite restaurant, Osteria Cavalli, a short stroll from the house where Mozart was born. Maybe one day, there'll be a plaque outside that house on Wehrgasse, too, commemorating a different type of maestro.

SEPTEMBER RESULTS

Premier League, September 14 2019
Liverpool 3 Norwich 1
Liverpool scorers: Mane 28, 40, Salah 72

Champions League, September 17 2019
Napoli 2 Liverpool 0

Premier League, September 22 2019
Chelsea 1 Liverpool 2
Liverpool scorers: Alexander-Arnold 14, Firmino 30

Carabao Cup, September 25 2019
MK Dons 0 Liverpool 2
Liverpool scorers: Milner 41, Hoever 69

Premier League, September 28 2009
Sheffield United 0 Liverpool 1
Liverpool scorer: Wijnaldum 70

OCTOBER

DESPITE THE GRUMBLES SALAH IS NOT STRUGGLING, HE HAS SIMPLY EVOLVED – THE STATS AND HIS POSITION PROVE IT

JAMES PEARCE

OCT 6, 2019

Mohamed Salah could hear the hat-trick of roars from a jubilant Anfield. The first coincided with referee Chris Kavanagh pointing to the spot deep into stoppage time; the second followed VAR confirming the award of the penalty and then, finally, came the eruption when James Milner held his nerve to slot home the winner against Leicester City.

Salah missed the wild celebrations that followed as Liverpool clinched a 17th successive Premier League victory in dramatic fashion – moving to within one of Manchester City's all-time top-flight record. The Egyptian forward was lying in the home dressing room having treatment on his swollen left ankle. News from outside helped to ease the pain. He had been forced off moments earlier after a challenge from Leicester City's substitute Hamza Choudhury, which Jurgen Klopp called "dangerous as hell".

Some 50 minutes after the final whistle, Salah emerged, stopping to embrace and chat with South Africa's Olympic 400-metre champion Wayde van Niekerk, a special guest of the club, who was waiting in the tunnel area to meet his heroes. Then, Salah continued on his way, limping through the mixed zone interview area, pulling along a suitcase on wheels that had a backpack perched on top of it.

The 27-year-old rarely stops to speak to the waiting media and wasn't keen to provide his thoughts on a bruising afternoon. When asked about his well-being, he simply smiled and offered: "I think I'm OK – we'll see. Thank you. Bye."

The initial assessment by medical staff indicated that Salah had avoided any significant damage to his ankle and Liverpool don't need to worry about any club-v-country issues during the international break.

Salah had already asked new Egypt coach Hossam El-Badry to excuse him from their upcoming friendly against Botswana in Cairo. "I agreed with him that it is in his best interests and those of the national team that he rests," El-Badry confirmed. Salah will have a well-earned week off before the Premier League leaders' focus turns to the trip to Old Trafford on October 20.

His form in the opening months of the campaign has been a source of much discussion among supporters. The general consensus is that while Sadio Mane and Roberto Firmino have both got off to a flyer, Salah is lacking his usual spark. He has certainly squandered some chances that you would have expected him to stick away and he has cut a frustrated figure at times.

But concerns need to be put in context. With six goals in all competitions by early October, Salah has found the net twice as many times as he had done at the same stage of last season. In the Premier League, Salah has chipped in with four goals and three assists so far. Mane has five goals and one assist, while Firmino has three goals and three assists. There isn't a weak link. There isn't anyone in that potent front line not pulling their weight.

In many ways, Salah is a victim of his own success. The standards he set during a record-breaking first season at Anfield were always going to prove impossible to replicate. Only Ian Rush has ever bettered his remarkable haul of 44 goals in all competitions in the 2017-18 season.

A year ago, he started slowly. He needed time to get back to his peak physically after the shoulder injury inflicted by Sergio Ramos in the Champions League final and found he could not do himself justice at the World Cup.

He got better and better as the campaign went on and ended up scoring 27 times. Talk of being a "one-season wonder" was emphatically put to bed. Having won the Golden Boot outright in 2017-18, he shared it with Mane and Pierre-Emerick Aubameyang in May.

This time around, he again missed out on having a proper pre-season due to his commitments at the Africa Cup of Nations. Bar the Carabao Cup tie with MK Dons, when Klopp fielded a shadow line-up, Salah has been ever-present.

His record of 77 goals in 116 games for the club is sensational but his importance to Klopp's team extends way beyond the frequency with which he finds the net.

There's no question that he's a much more complete player now than he was during his first year at Anfield, when the records kept tumbling. Back then, Salah had the element of surprise, darting in off the right to wreak havoc, bursting in behind defenders with his devastating turn of pace.

Since then, his role under Klopp has evolved. Salah's work off the ball has improved drastically. With Liverpool adopting a less gung-ho approach, Salah has had to embrace greater defensive duties.

He's much more than a conventional winger. Over the course of last season, Klopp regularly moved him into a central role. "Mo is young enough to involve a lot more things in his style of play. It's not just speed, it's not just finishing; it's between the lines, it's keeping the ball," Klopp said.

They worked extensively at Melwood on him dropping off into space and linking play. The end result was 13 assists in all competitions in 2018-19 – blowing out of the water the idea that Salah is a selfish, one-dimensional marksman.

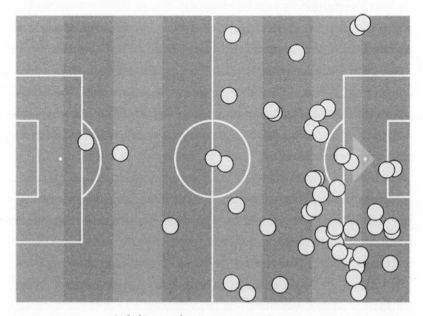

Salah's touch map against Leicester

Pep Lijnders, Liverpool's assistant coach, expanded on the decision to play Salah through the middle at times, rather than out on the right.

"Mo has the ability to create from the inside," the Dutchman said. "To have him in the last line as high as we can, with the speed he has, the goal threat he has, it makes it easier for us to create a freer role for Bobby. There's a hunger in this squad to become better and Mo is a good example of that. He's always searching for the next step."

Salah was given that central role for the visit of Brendan Rodgers' in-form Leicester side on Saturday. It was the first time Klopp has utilised him in that position from the start of a game this season.

It was effectively a 4-3-2-1 formation, with Mane and Firmino operating behind him as two No 10s. Klopp wanted Liverpool to have an element of surprise, in the belief that Leicester had spent the week preparing to have Mane and Salah flying at them down the flanks.

He showcased his strength early on, latching on to a throw-in and spinning away from Caglar Soyuncu in the box before forcing a low save from Kasper Schmeichel.

Salah provided the focal point for attack after attack as Liverpool took control. One minute he was dropping off into pockets of space to exchange passes with Milner, the next he was darting in behind the over-worked Ben Chilwell.

It was the day when the outstanding Mane reached 50 league goals for Liverpool in 100 games. No one in the club's history has ever got to that milestone quicker than Salah, who took just 69 matches, beating the likes of Fernando Torres (72), Luis Suarez (86) and Robbie Fowler (88).

Having struck a match-winning double against Salzburg in midweek, Salah was denied further reward by a fine reaction save from Schmeichel early in the second half.

Leicester's back line simply couldn't handle Salah's movement and trickery. Soyuncu was booked for cynically pulling him back and then fellow centre-back Jonny Evans was carded for a bout of wrestling.

But for a last-ditch tackle from Evans, Salah would have laid on one of the goals of the season after combining with Mane to expertly carve the visitors apart. He also put Andy Robertson through on goal.

Shortly before his afternoon was prematurely ended by Choudhury's lunge, there were groans from the stands when Salah twice misplaced passes that could have released Mane. That will cloud the final judgement for some, but Salah left battered and bruised having done exactly what Klopp asked of him. In total, he had 50 touches, completed 21 of his 28 passes (75 per cent), made three key passes and had five shots, of which two forced saves.

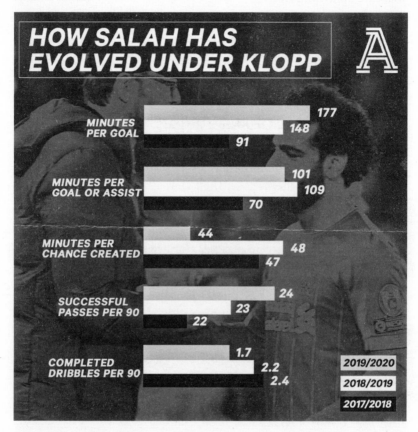

HOW SALAH HAS EVOLVED UNDER KLOPP

	2019/2020	2018/2019	2017/2018
MINUTES PER GOAL	177	148	91
MINUTES PER GOAL OR ASSIST	101	109	70
MINUTES PER CHANCE CREATED	44	48	47
SUCCESSFUL PASSES PER 90	24	23	22
COMPLETED DRIBBLES PER 90	1.7	2.2	2.4

Salah created a chance for Liverpool every 48 minutes in the Premier League last season. That figure so far this term stands at 44 minutes. There was either a goal or an assist from him every 109 minutes in the top flight in 2018-19 and it's every 101 minutes so far in 2019-20. He's also completing more successful passes per 90 minutes.

"Of course I want the Golden Boot but for me, the team trophies come first, especially the Premier League," Salah said on the eve of the new season. "It's not just my job to score. It's about assists, playing with the midfield and defending, too."

Salah has embraced that. He's putting in the hard yards. He's helped launch Liverpool's title charge without being at his absolute sparkling best.

The break will do him good. The fact there's so much more to come from him spells bad news for the rest of the Premier League.

OCTOBER RESULTS

Champions League, October 2 2019
Liverpool 4 Red Bull Salzburg 3
Liverpool scorers: Mane 9, Robertson 25, Salah 36, 69

Premier League, October 5 2019
Liverpool 2 Leicester 1
Liverpool scorers: Mane 40, Milner 90+5 pen

Premier League, October 20 2019
Manchester United 1 Liverpool 1
Liverpool scorer: Lallana 85

Champions League, October 23 2019
Genk 1 Liverpool 4
Liverpool scorers: Oxlade-Chamberlain 2, 57, Mane 77, Salah 87

Premier League, October 27 2019
Liverpool 2 Spurs 1
Liverpool scorers: Henderson 52, Salah 75 pen

Carabao Cup, October 30 2019
Liverpool 5 Arsenal 5 (Liverpool win 5-4 after pens)
Liverpool scorers: Mustafi 6 OG, Milner 43 pen, Oxlade-Chamberlain 58, Origi 62, 90+4

NOVEMBER

HOW MAN CITY AND LIVERPOOL COMPETE FOR EVERYTHING: FROM TITLES AND £75M CENTRE-BACKS TO PHYSIOS AND YOUTH STARS

SAM LEE and JAMES PEARCE

NOV 7, 2019

"No but they can't be serious, come on." That was the verdict of Manchester City chairman Khaldoon Al Mubarak when told how much Southampton wanted for Virgil van Dijk this time two years ago. With the asking price set at £75 million City decided – as they often do – that they did not see the fee as sensible, and walked away. Given they turned their attentions to Aymeric Laporte, who has barely put a foot wrong since signing from Athletic Bilbao for £57 million and whose absence has been so keenly felt this season, there are very few, if any, regrets about that decision.

Perhaps the only tinge would be that, had City's senior figures decided that £75 million was a fair price to pay for Van Dijk, then the defender would not have had the transformative effect on Liverpool, who have been a thorn in the club's side for the past 18 months, and who could take the title from them this season. Yet had City signed Van Dijk, then Liverpool might have moved for Laporte and the difference would not have been so significant. It is but one example of the constant off-field battle that the two clubs are locked into.

The Fenway Sports Group president Mike Gordon and Liverpool sporting director Michael Edwards had no concerns about the fee for Van Dijk. They were convinced that he would transform a porous backline that had lacked a true leader since Jamie Carragher's retirement in 2013. Jurgen Klopp shared that belief in the Dutchman's quality but sought reassurances from the Anfield hierarchy that the club wouldn't be overstretching themselves by sanctioning a record-breaking deal for a defender.

Liverpool viewed the capture of Van Dijk as a significant triumph. The previous summer the former Celtic defender had made it clear that after weighing up his options he favoured Merseyside over City and Chelsea when all three were vying for his services.

Klopp had sold Van Dijk his vision for a trophy-laden future and the player had been won over. The passion of Liverpool's fans also influenced his decision. Van Dijk attended the 2017 Champions League final in Cardiff as a fan and was besieged by supporters urging him to head for Anfield.

When Liverpool were accused of tapping up Van Dijk and issued a public apology to Southampton, both parties agreed to sit tight until the January window. Gordon repaired relations with the Southampton chairman Ralph Krueger to get the deal done.

Liverpool believe the real reason City didn't meet the asking price for Van Dijk is because they had been given no encouragement that he wanted to go there.

If City had got Van Dijk then it's highly likely that Laporte would be a Liverpool player. The club's recruitment staff had tracked in excess of 30 centre-backs from across Europe over an 18-month period. A list of four "A-grade" targets was drawn up. Van Dijk was the priority with Laporte, who had a £57 million release clause, viewed as the perfect alternative. Napoli's

Kalidou Koulibaly and Bayern Munich's Jerome Boateng were also considered.

The *All or Nothing* documentary that charted City's 2017-18 season showed the ins and outs of Laporte's arrival, with chief operating officer Omar Berrada and club lawyers sent to Madrid to pay the Frenchman's buy-out clause. It offered an interesting glimpse into the world of top-level transfers, but did omit one very common element; a last-ditch moving of the goalposts.

Already aboard the club-chartered private jet, Laporte's lawyer suddenly asked for more money, leading to hurried conversations between Berrada and his colleagues back in Manchester. City have ended transfer moves over similar hiccups, but found a compromise to land them their "absolute priority" target.

It is inevitable that England's two top clubs, who both play a high-intensity, attacking brand of football, and have both seemingly set an upper limit on their spending on any one player, will often have scouts at matches across the world, keeping their eyes on exactly the same player.

High-profile transfer deals, though, are only one area in which the Premier League's leading clubs are going head to head.

———————————— **A** ————————————

It recently came to light that Liverpool paid City £1 million in a legal settlement back in 2013 after allegedly hacking into one of the club's scouting platforms, using the log-in of a City employee. The payment was made without the club, or the individuals named (Edwards, Dave Fallows and Julian Ward), accepting any liability or wrongdoing. Both clubs have since remained tight-lipped about the allegations. It was an unprecedented breach of security and one that the FA is still investigating, but it helps tell the story of the off-field battle that top clubs across Europe, and not least these two, are engaged in.

Whatever information or data Liverpool gleaned it appears to have had little impact on their transfer dealings between June 2012 and February 2013, which has come under scrutiny considering their recruits included Fabio Borini, Joe Allen, Iago Aspas, Simon Mignolet and Mamadou Sakho.

Edwards secured the services of both Fallows and Barry Hunter from City in 2012 when Liverpool overhauled their recruitment staff after the departures of the director of football Damien Comolli and the manager Kenny Dalglish. The club later hired another three City scouts in Ward, Andy Sayer and Kevin Hunt.

Klopp credits Fallows, the head of recruitment, and the chief scout Hunter as playing key roles in Liverpool's resurgence through their contribution to the club's dealings in the transfer market. They were pivotal in pushing the claims of Roberto Firmino, Mohamed Salah and Fabinho.

Ward, who was a South American scout for City, is also highly respected at Liverpool. In 2015, he was promoted from European scouting manager for Spain and Portugal to the role of loan pathways and football partnerships manager.

The world of top-level scouting and transfers is often contradictory. For one thing, there is a global scouting WhatsApp group that contains the most senior figures of football's biggest clubs, as well as scouts and coaches in youth academies. It is one big chat, and on any given weekend it will be buzzing about whichever big matches are taking place – City's 5-0 victory over Liverpool in 2017-18 among them, for example. And by the time a transfer market rolls around, many top clubs know more or less what their rivals are looking for, either in terms of positions or more specific names. However, much of the process before that is shrouded in secrecy, locked away on encrypted laptops and discussed in hushed tones, even in top-level meetings; City's 'Senior Leadership Team', which includes the chief executive Ferran Soriano, director of football Txiki Begiristain and Berrada, as well as their assistants, lawyers and communications and HR staff, regularly meet to discuss important issues, but the names of specific transfer targets are withheld. Only the inner circle, including Soriano, Begiristain and Berrada, as well as chairman al-Mubarak, are party to the players under consideration.

Coaching is similar. Guardiola's staff came up with new passing combinations designed to work especially well in the Champions League last season, which were stored on password-protected laptops. When FA staff have been at the City training ground for whatever reason, tactics boards and notes have been covered or hidden.

A year ago City's whole security system was upgraded and made more robust in light of the Football Leaks hacks, with staff of all levels also required to change their email passwords every month.

City use a range of different online scouting tools to inform their transfer plans. Wyscout, InStat and Scout7 are among them, each serving similar but different purposes. Any player in the world can be searched and each of his moves are broken down into different areas, such as defensive positioning, crossing or link-up play, but Scout7, which was the program Liverpool's staff used to access City's data, is best used for exporting information to apps and creating detailed reports on players.

Although transfer meetings between the most senior staff utilise a lot of video, decisions are not based solely on technology. City boast a vast network of scouts who watch players in person and compile detailed reports on their personalities, with a view to ensuring any new player will fit into the dressing room and adapt to a new environment. City's recent success in recruitment has played a key part in their success, but they have been creating those reports for years. They helped inform moves for David Silva and Sergio Aguero, among others.

SportsCode is a common programme used to analyse matches by clubs across the country, and it also helps inform transfer planning. Guardiola watches City games back before passing on timestamps to his analysts and charging them with relaying their findings back to the players. The data collected helps build a profile of the type of player for any given position, and potential signings can then be scouted on that basis.

City's senior figures also use their contacts around the world to inform on potential targets. Ronald Koeman, Pep Guardiola's former Barcelona team-mate, was consulted on the pursuit of Ajax's Frenkie de Jong, for example. De Jong was identified as a 'Category A' target, as opposed to B or C. With most of the world's biggest and richest clubs vying for the same players, City try to catch their rivals off guard by acting early, and after deciding what they are willing to pay for a player between al-Mubarak, Soriano and Begiristain, they work to tie up signings long before the window opens. Manchester United are known to open talks with several players for the same position all at the same time, before closing in on one at the end of the process. City, by contrast, identify their top target for one position and get to work as early as possible on signing him and him alone. This has led to them securing a large majority of their top targets during the Guardiola era, including Ilkay Gundogan, Bernardo Silva, Ederson, Benjamin Mendy, Kyle Walker, Riyad Mahrez and Rodri, give or take a bit of haggling later down the line. But it has also led to near misses on several priority targets, and due to the months of groundwork they put into transfers, they have been unable to find alternative options at relatively short notice, which has angered Guardiola on several occasions.

De Jong is one such example. Around this time 12 months ago Barcelona officials were resigned to losing out on the promising Dutchman. Begiristain had held several meetings with Ajax and the player's agent, and personal terms had been agreed. After missing out on Jorginho that summer, Guardiola and his staff had made it clear De Jong was the one they wanted.

Barcelona, however, decided to pull out all the stops last December, dispatching their own delegation to Amsterdam with the aim of signing the youngster no matter what. In the end they paid him upwards of €200,000 per week, as well as €5 million to the agent. City lost a top-tier target, but only after a competitor had moved beyond their valuation of the player.

It was a similar situation when they decided not to match the £85 million that United were willing to pay Leicester for Harry Maguire, who had already agreed terms with City but was equally happy to move to Old Trafford, where he saw himself as a guaranteed starter and potential captain.

Guardiola and his assistant Mikel Arteta's anger was sparked again in the wake of Laporte's injury in August. The two coaches wondered how their current options at centre-back would leave them able to win at Anfield. Yes, that is the barometer.

The battle for young talent is no less competitive, and it is a race that also includes United and Everton. Even top sporting brands have their own scouts who are charged with beating their business rivals to the country's most coveted prospects. Pairs of boots are often sent to players in a bid to woo them.

As far as City and Liverpool are concerned, there is a huge financial gap in academy expenditure. Liverpool's is run on an annual budget of around £10 million. They estimate that City's costs are more than double that.

Under academy director Alex Inglethorpe, Liverpool took the decision to limit most first-year professionals to a basic salary of around £40,000 per year. Contracts are heavily incentivised with bonuses linked to appearances and promotion to the first-team squad. That structure aims to ensure teenagers retain their hunger and Inglethorpe is convinced it is effective. "I've never worked with a player who has fulfilled his potential and been overpaid when he was young," he says.

Liverpool, who operate with smaller youth squads than City,

picked up Rafael Camacho from their rivals after he was released in 2016 and sold him to Sporting Lisbon in a £7 million deal last month. City were also fuming when they lost highly-rated attacking midfielder James Balagizi to Liverpool's youth ranks at the age of 11. The passage of time has only strengthened the belief that it could prove to be a significant capture. Now 16, Balagizi is one of the top talents in Liverpool Under-18s and in the England Under-17s squad having developed into an impressive centre-forward.

Liverpool also signed Bobby Duncan from City's youth ranks in 2018, after the England youth international had been locked in a protracted contract dispute with the Manchester club. Liverpool paid £200,000 in compensation for him and made a hefty profit when he demanded a move and was sold to Fiorentina for £1.8 million in September. Duncan didn't have the patience to wait for his opportunity, but Klopp has already handed out six debuts this season – that is a big help to academy staff making their sales pitch to in-demand young footballers.

Liverpool have channelled resources into getting recruitment right at pre-academy level. They believe if they can educate parents of seven-year-olds and eight-year-olds about why Liverpool is the best place for their kids to develop then they will stay put and resist the lure of the Etihad Campus.

"This area is even more competitive for recruitment than London," Inglethorpe says. "Here, you have four very big clubs within an hour-and-a-half's drive. You have to try to get it right at an early stage but you also have to be careful that you don't stop looking after that."

Academy games between the clubs carry an extra edge which made Liverpool's FA Youth Cup final triumph over City on penalties at the Etihad Campus back in April all the sweeter for them.

Both City and Liverpool have been found guilty of breaching youth player recruitment rules by the FA in recent years. Within scouting and coaching circles, such infringements are viewed as boundary testing and a common occurrence.

It is a competitive business and all the north-west clubs are in constant battles to sign the best young talents, and like Beswick leaving City for United, and Fallows, Ward and Hunter moving to Liverpool, several youth coaches and scouts have also left Melwood for Manchester.

Rodolfo Borrell, now part of Guardiola's senior coaching set-up, left Liverpool's academy for City in 2013. The Spaniard is credited with developing several Reds youngsters, including Raheem Sterling.

Around that time Stephen Torpey and Darren Hughes, two Liverpudlians, also made the move to City, the former becoming head of coaching and the latter the Under-11s coach. City have also taken a kit man from Liverpool in recent years, yet despite the competition for the best young players, there is an acceptance that, at this level, these are normal people changing jobs for the same reasons anybody else would.

That is best summed up by Guardiola after physio Lee Nobes left City after 11 years to join Liverpool last season. "He's a brilliant guy, but there's always going to be interesting jobs elsewhere and everyone's free to make that choice," he says in the book *Pep's City*. "He'd been at City for a long time and wanted to try something new." It was Nobes that Guardiola rang after June's Champions League final, concluding his congratulatory message by asking to speak to Klopp. That was a show of respect but there's also been hostility and animosity in this very modern rivalry.

City were outraged by the damage done to their team coach outside Anfield prior to the 2018 Champions League quarter-final. Liverpool officials were stunned by the footage of City players singing a derogatory version of *Allez Allez Allez* on their plane home after pipping Liverpool to the Premier League title back in May. City's subsequent statement, which included no apology, only served to pour petrol on the flames. Guardiola mentioning Liverpool's "diving" and Klopp responding by referencing City's "tactical fouls" cranked things up again.

These are two elite clubs competing for everything, on and off the field.

THIS WAS THE DAY THE SHACKLES CAME OFF. TO A MAN, LIVERPOOL STEPPED UP, PUFFED OUT THEIR CHESTS AND DELIVERED

JAMES PEARCE

NOV 10, 2019

"I'm not a clown," a beaming Jurgen Klopp told the over-eager cameraman who was urging him to deliver a flurry of his trademark fist pumps in front of the jubilant Kop. Instead the Liverpool boss applauded his adoring public, raised a clenched fist and repeatedly patted the liver bird on his chest, before jogging over to the touchline to embrace Andy Robertson.

The noise was deafening as Anfield paid homage to the genius who is making their dreams come true. The stirring rendition of *You'll Never Walk Alone* shortly before the final whistle was laced with pride.

This was a statement victory. The magnitude of the outcome was writ large on the faces of players and managers alike. As Pep Guardiola held his head in his hands, Manchester City's stars remonstrated with the officials. Forget talk about VAR and any burning sense of injustice. That wasn't the story here. This was the day when Liverpool deservedly took a giant step closer to the promised land.

Their lead at the top of the table is eight points and they are nine clear of Guardiola's side. Only Manchester United in 1993-94 have ever had a bigger advantage at this stage of a Premier League campaign. "Nothing is decided today, not even close to it," Klopp wrote in his programme notes and the message was the same post-match.

He's right but this juggernaut he has created is going to take some stopping. No team has ever made a better start to a top-flight season. Liverpool have lost just one of their past 51 league matches. Their consistency has been remarkable.

All season talk has centred on how Liverpool have been winning without performing anywhere near their best – functional and effective rather than eye-catching and dominant. But this was the day when the shackles came off. To a man, Liverpool stepped up, puffed out their chests and delivered. They succeeded in making the most expensively assembled squad in the history of football look distinctly average. City's defensive frailties were exposed.

Klopp had demanded a show of bravery and that "even the hot dog seller needs to be in top shape". That clarion call was answered. Nobody let him down. Not even the guy frying the onions.

Here were the fruits of his labour. This was the perfect illustration of what he has created over the past four years through his tactical acumen, shrewd recruitment and the sheer force of his personality. Klopp has fashioned a team in his own image. It's jam-packed with quality but they are bound by a relentless work ethic. There are no big egos or cliques, they play for each other and that spirit and unity was there in abundance as City were brushed aside.

"They are ripping teams to shreds," said Roy Keane in the Sky Sports studio. "The way they are playing is fantastic. There's no shame in losing to this Liverpool team, they're amazing."

The intensity of Liverpool's dazzling early burst was key. City looked shell-shocked, scarcely able to believe that they were 2-0 down inside 13 minutes. From the first goal to the second,

Liverpool had just four touches in the final third. But they certainly made them count.

Ilkay Gundogan's weak clearance was punished by the outstanding Fabinho, who hammered home the opener from 25 yards. The second goal was a thing of beauty. Trent Alexander-Arnold switched play intelligently out to the left and Robertson's delivery from out wide was majestic. Mohamed Salah didn't even have to break his stride as he nodded past the hapless Claudio Bravo. City had been ripped to shreds.

Liverpool's xG was 1.1 which underlines just how clinical they were. City's was 1.29. Alexander-Arnold had 89 touches, 23 more than any other Liverpool player. He was at his marauding best. His battle with Raheem Sterling was pivotal and the 21-year-old full-back emerged triumphant. It was another chastening Anfield return for Sterling, whose every touch was jeered.

City had their moments, with Angelino striking the post, but defensively Liverpool generally stood firm. Alisson was alert to thwart Sergio Aguero and the Brazil No 1 oozed class and composure. In front of him, Dejan Lovren more than justified his selection after getting the nod ahead of Joe Gomez to partner Virgil van Dijk. City targeted Lovren, but he wasn't the weak link they thought he would be. The former Southampton defender put his body on the line and did brilliantly to turn Sterling's effort over the bar in the second half.

Klopp had gone for solidity and control rather than adventure with his midfield selection and it worked a treat. There isn't a better holding midfielder in Europe than Fabinho, who is growing in stature with every passing week. The quiet Brazilian wasn't even trusted to start against City in either fixture last season. How far he's come since.

In front of him, Jordan Henderson defied the virus that had sidelined him from training earlier in the week to put in a real captain's shift for an hour. Georginio Wijnaldum was equally as dynamic as he ran himself into the ground and produced his best display of the season.

Henderson helped put the game beyond doubt when he darted down the right and curled in the pinpoint cross which Sadio Mane headed inside Bravo's near post. For Mane, it was the perfect riposte to Guardiola's pre-match talk about him diving. Sunday was his 100th Premier League start for Liverpool. He has scored 18 goals in his last 17 starts at Anfield.

Liverpool's front three of Salah, Mane and Roberto Firmino never allowed City's depleted backline to settle. Mane made four tackles – no player on either side made more. At 3-0, Liverpool showcased their maturity and streetwise nature as they slowed the game down. 'Poetry in motion,' echoed around Anfield.

Last season's two battles with City were decided by fine margins. This one wasn't. Liverpool could have done even more damage with their blistering counter-attacks.

Late on, fatigue kicked in and Liverpool dropped deep. Considering the energy which had been expended to get into a position of such control, it was hardly surprising. Bernardo Silva pulled one back and City could have had greater reward, but the outcome was never in doubt. It was the ninth time Klopp has beaten Guardiola in 18 meetings – no manager has inflicted more losses on the Spaniard. Guardiola described Anfield as "the most difficult stadium in the world right now".

"Nine points is a lot, they lost just one game last season," he conceded.

Liverpool have won 13 successive home league games – the club's best run since 1985. Having gone 29 league games unbeaten, they are closing in on the club record of 31 set in 1988. This is a special team producing incredible feats. They are one slick, unified, powerful force. The European champions crave English football's biggest prize and ending that painful 30-year wait for a 19th league crown.

Last season a healthy lead in the New Year was frittered away. But the scalp of City will rightly fuel the belief that this time they simply won't be denied.

THE PRIDE OF BAMBALI. WATCHING SADIO SCORE AGAINST CITY WITH THE MANE FAMILY

OLIVER KAY

NOV 11, 2019

The biggest game of the Premier League season so far is just an hour away and, in Bambali, a village in a remote part of Senegal some 3,000 miles from Anfield, one of Sadio Mane's cousins claps his hands and declares it is time to eat.

We venture outside, into the sweltering mid-afternoon heat, and are directed towards a shady spot in the yard of the huge mansion that Mane has had built for his extended family. "Around 40 of us live here," one of his uncles, Ibrahim Toure, says. "Brothers, sisters, uncles, aunts, cousins, nephews, nieces, grandparents, grandchildren; all the family together. It's a normal thing in Senegal."

Another cousin struggles over with a huge vat, plonks it down on the floor and removes the lid, releasing a beautiful smell across the yard. This, he announces, is *thiou tiir*, a local stew made of fish, sun-dried tomatoes, onions and rice. He passes me a spoon, while others are invited to tuck in with their hands. It tastes just as good as it smells and there is just enough to feed a family of 40 plus one hungry guest.

It is simple moments like this, in the bosom of his family, that Mane has missed since initially defying his mother's wishes by leaving Bambali as a 15-year-old to pursue his dream. More on that remarkable act of single-minded defiance later, as well as his extraordinary generosity.

There will be no time for Mane to drift off into wistfulness on this particular afternoon, though. On Merseyside, his focus is firmly on the task in hand. It will be his 100th Premier League start for Liverpool and, with Manchester City the opposition, the match feels integral to the title race. Bambali, where time seems to stand still, waits in a rare state of anxiety.

———————————— **A** ————————————

Did *The Athletic* really know what it would entail when they came up with the idea of dispatching me to Senegal to watch the Liverpool-City encounter from Mane's village?

A phrase like "off the beaten track" doesn't really suffice when it comes to describing Bambali, on the banks of the Casamance River. From the capital Dakar, in the north-west, it is seven hours by road, including border crossings into and out of The Gambia. The nearest airport is in Ziguinchor, a two-and-a-half-hour drive away.

From Ziguinchor, there are two potential routes. On Sunday morning, my driver, Salif, a former footballer, follows the scenic route on dusty, potholed roads through the forests before taking the ferry from Ndieba to Marsassou, where we watch the pelicans fly overhead, and proceeding through more forest land. Every few miles, we are slowed down by loose cattle, goats or donkeys.

On our first visit, the previous day, he prefers the quicker route, setting off in a north-eastward direction on the Trans-Gambia Highway – better, faster, and safer roads – before dropping down towards the south. The towns we pass through blur into one: stalls on the roadsides selling fruit or charcoal, or clothes or electrical goods, or plant pots or long strips of metal, all of it procured in the hope of turning a small profit. There is little obvious demand.

In the town of Sedhiou, birthplace of former Newcastle United forward Papiss Cisse, that imbalance between supply and demand appears even more stark, yet there is none of the aggressive hawking you might expect in a place where landing a sale or two might be the difference between feeding your family and not. Every face wears a smile. Sales are hoped for, rather than anticipated.

The same smiles are visible in the villages but there is no such commercial scene. Men and women, young and old, sit in the shade outside their homes while their children amuse themselves, playing with battered-looking footballs, chasing the chickens or using the local well as a climbing frame. Some of the houses are made of stone, but these are outnumbered by the shacks made of corrugated iron and – by far the most numerous – shacks made of mud or sticks, many of them with dishes drying on a thatched roof.

Whichever route you take the terrain changes in the final half-hour of the journey towards Bambali. It becomes much more agricultural, with banana and maize plantations in the fields as asphalt gives way to red sand. The only other traffic is the occasional farmer's cart, pulled by donkeys.

Eventually, the signs say we have reached Bambali. There are signs announcing the village has been the recipient of American aid. The first business we reach is a shack offering photocopying and scanning services. The second, in the shack next door, is a hairdresser. A little further on is a local DJ. Several of the shacks are decorated with the same poster, lauding Sadio Mane as *l'enfant de Bambali, le fier de toute une nation* (child of Bambali, pride of a whole nation).

We ask some local children where Mane's house is and, a little quizzically, they point us down the road. There it is, a huge house on the left-hand side. Five of the children playing outside are wearing Liverpool No 10 shirts. It is safe to say we have come to the right place.

Hanging from an upstairs window at the Mane mansion is a banner lauding *Nianthio*. "In the southern Senegalese dialect, it's a name that means lion and warrior," one of Mane's many cousins explains later. "When we say Sadio Mane, we say, *Nianthio*. He is a lion. He is a warrior. Like a lion, like a warrior, he will succeed, no matter what is put in his way."

———————————— **A** ————————————

Mane's uncle Ibrahim, his mother's older brother, is showing me around what he calls "the compound".

There are at least 30 children playing in the yard – Mane's nephews and nieces, but also many of their friends from the village. Some of them are playing football. Others chase the chickens, while the smallest girl cuddles a toy cat. There are numerous Liverpool shirts around, all of them bearing Mane's name. Barcelona are represented. So too are City, but the boy with the Sergio Aguero shirt seems oblivious to what it symbolises. "*Liverpool de Sadio Mane. Sadio Mane de Bambali*," the boys shout in unison.

There are cows in the field, a few goats here and there, but Ibrahim is keen to point out a rather ugly-looking shack with a corrugated-iron roof, just next to the main property. "Sadio has come from a poor, poor family," Ibrahim says. "His father died when he was young and the family had no money. He grew up in a house just like this one, with his mother and his sisters and the wider family."

Can we see the house? Is it still standing? "No, it was just next to this one, right where we're standing," Ibrahim says. "This house [the mansion] was built on the site where he grew up. It's symbolic, really."

AT THE END OF THE STORM

Ibrahim gestures towards the fields where a young Mane was sent to work on the family's farm. "Every day after school, he had to go to the fields to work," he says. "Every evening, he had to learn from the Koran, learn how to pray. His uncle was the local imam here. We expected him to work on the farm, to cultivate the land."

Mane did not want to be a farmer, though. He had been kicking a ball around the dust-swept lanes of Bambali for as long as he could remember – and he was faster, more skilful, better than anyone else in the village. When his teams played against those from other villages, his talent stood out. "He was better than everyone," his friend Bacary Diatta says, "even those who were older than him. But I remember him saying, 'Every day, I have to go out into the field. But I'm not going to be a farmer. I'm going to be an international footballer'."

As for what happened next, when he was 15, Mane has offered two rather different versions of events in interviews. One story is that he talked things over with his mother and uncle in a civil manner, which led to them agreeing to send him to Dakar to join a football academy. The alternative, much more dramatic, media-friendly narrative is that he upped and left without telling a soul, such was his desperation to follow his dream, and took a bus on the seven-hour journey to the capital.

So which is it? "He fled Bambali," Ibrahim says, laughing. "He fled in secret, without informing anyone. Walked a long, long way, and then took the bus to Dakar.

"His mother was very worried and the family were not at all happy. We knew he was in Dakar. After two months, we went to Dakar and brought him home. His mother felt and I felt it was difficult to become a footballer. How could someone from Bambali become a footballer?

"Six or seven months after that, this time, Sadio sat down and said to us, 'I want to be a footballer. I believe I can become a star. I want to show you I can do it'."

At that point, Mane's family believed they could no longer stand in his way. They would at least allow him the opportunity to give it a shot. He went – and he has never really looked back.

──────────── **A** ────────────

Ibrahima Diarra, who has coached top-flight Senegalese clubs such as Casa Sport, is trying to explain just how difficult it is for a player like Mane, in a small village as remote as Bambali, to reach the big time.

"There are so many talented young players all over Senegal, all over Africa," he says. "Every single one of them dreams of going to Europe and becoming a professional.

"In a place like Bambali, there is very little organised football. Even in Ziguinchor, we don't have the resources. We might have 50 boys but only two or three coaches. Balls are expensive. There is a synthetic pitch at the stadium, but most of the pitches are sand. We have licensed football schools, but we don't have a *centre de formation*.

"The only big academies exist in Dakar, like Generation Foot, where Sadio and Papiss Cisse went, Diambars, where Idrissa Gana Gueye went, and Sacre Coeur. Generation Foot has a partnership with Metz. Sacre Coeur has a partnership with Lyon. But many, many players join these academies – not just from Dakar but all over Senegal, from The Gambia, from Guinea-Bissau, etc. Only two or three each year go to those clubs in France. Most of the players who go to the academies come back again."

Mane was one of the chosen few, offered the chance to join Metz. This time, with his family's blessing, he took the chance.

For any African teenager, moving to a city in northern France would be a huge culture shock. It was certainly the case for Mane. His friends in Bambali understand that he would sometimes stay at the training ground all afternoon or even well into the evening – not just out of a desire to improve but because he liked the staff there and he was not sure what he would do with his time otherwise.

He at least felt safe at Metz, where there were numerous other African players and where his landlady looked after him and took care of his laundry. He signed a new five-year contract after they were relegated to the third tier. He was horrified when the club's president informed him they had accepted an offer from Red Bull Salzburg. "Metz was my new home and I didn't want to leave," he told Canal+. "The president told me, 'Look, they offered €4 million, so I have no choice'. That day, I cried like a kid."

Those two years in Salzburg were the making of Mane. It has been non-stop since then: two seasons as a free-scoring winger for RB Salzburg, who won the Austrian Bundesliga in his second campaign there; an £11.8 million transfer to the Premier League to join Southampton, where he excelled for two seasons; and a £35 million move to Liverpool, where he has played in two Champions League finals, scoring in the first, winning the second. He narrowly missed out on Africa Cup of Nations glory this summer, with Senegal beaten by Algeria in the final, but, at Anfield, all eyes are now on the Premier League title bid.

"Liverpool will win," his uncle Ibrahim says. "And Sadio will score. You will see."

———————————— **A** ————————————

The Mane house in Bambali is awaiting refurbishment, so the grown-ups sit on plastic chairs while the children sit on the floor in front of the TV. There are cheers and shouts when Mane's face appears on screen during the pre-match warm-up, but there is a call for quiet as we listen to Robert Pires and Olivier Dacourt discussing his recent impact, including the debate over whether he has been guilty of what Pires, who knows a thing about such matters, calls *plonger* (diving). The jury in Bambali, it is safe to say, rejects Pep Guardiola's view on the matter.

There is a rhythmic clap from the boys at the front as the two teams emerge from the tunnel but there is tense silence as the game kicks off. Then, seconds after a penalty appeal at the other end of the pitch, Mane streaks away down the left-hand side and crosses the ball into the penalty area. Eventually, the ball reaches Fabinho, who lets fly – 1-0 to Liverpool and the place goes wild. Nobody here even stops to consider the possibility of a VAR check. Even the boy in the Aguero shirt is jumping for joy.

Seven minutes later, Mohamed Salah makes it 2-0 and Liverpool are firmly in control. More and more and more children – including more girls now – file into the living room, where there is a celebration. An exception is one Mane elder at the front, who, even with his team firmly in the ascendancy, remains as agitated as Jurgen Klopp and Guardiola combined.

The first half whizzes by, with a steady procession of soft drinks and cups of tea along the way. One of the boys looks bored, building a tower from drinks cans, but everyone else is captivated. It has been one of Mane's quieter games – only six successful passes, one dribble and no shots before half-time – but he is working his flank in the way that Klopp so admires, grafting for his team. "Not playing for himself. Putting the team first," one of his cousins says.

——————————— **A** ———————————

A five-minute walk from the Mane house is the Lycee Moderne Bambali, a school. Until recently, it consisted of two old single-storey teaching blocks. Now, there are three two-storey blocks, equipped with bigger classrooms and modern teaching facilities.

It was built last year at a cost of 152 million Central African Francs (around £200,000), which came entirely from Mane. "He built this," Diatta says. "Not with his hands, but with his feet. He wanted to build something for the people of Bambali."

Diatta takes me around the corner to a building site, where a new hospital is under construction. "All from Sadio," he says. "It will serve not just Bambali but the other villages nearby."

Mane's generosity is legendary in these parts. It was widely reported that when his team reached the Champions League final against Real Madrid last year, he sent a huge parcel of Liverpool shirts – 350 of them, his uncle Ibrahim estimates – for the children of Bambali to wear while cheering him on.

Less well-known is that Mane sends every family in Bambali and the nearby villages a gift at Ramadan every year. "It's something like XAF 50,000 (around £65) for every person," Ibrahim says. "Sadio is such a generous man. He's also very sentimental, maybe even too sentimental. That is his nature. He just wants to help people."

It tallies nicely with a video which emerged on social media one Saturday last year, when, rather than paint the town red after scoring for Liverpool during the afternoon, he was to be found helping a friend clean the toilets at Al Rahma mosque in the Toxteth area of Liverpool. "Sadio requested that no video was sent out," Abu Usamah Al-Tahabi, the local imam, told the BBC on that occasion. "He wanted to remain discreet. He wasn't doing it for publicity. He's not a person looking for fanfare. There's no arrogance."

In an interview last month with TeleDakar, Mane said: "Why would I want to have 10 Ferraris, 20 watches with diamonds and two aeroplanes? What would these objects do for me and for the world?

"I've been hungry. I had to work in the fields. I played football barefoot. But today, with what I earn through football, I can help my people. I don't need to display luxury cars, luxury homes, trips or, even less, aeroplanes. I prefer that my people receive a little of what life has given me."

———————————————— **A** ————————————————

For a moment, belief is suspended. Everyone in the room sees that Jordan Henderson has crossed the ball from the right-hand side towards the far post, where Mane's run has taken him away from the defender. Everyone sees him meet the ball with a firm header. Everyone sees Claudio Bravo, the City goalkeeper, scrambling desperately, but it takes a second or two for the Mane household to be certain that their hero has scored.

An explosion of ecstasy follows. There are yells and shrieks and the boys at the front are doing whatever their bodies are telling them to do. One of them skids across the floor. Another leaps through the air, on to his backside, and then uses his arms to flip himself upwards again. One female relative looks overjoyed, as if she has just heard the most wonderful news. Liverpool appear to be home and dry and their Sadio, the child of Bambali, the pride of a whole nation, their blessed *Nianthio*, is the hero.

More and more people file in after that, attracted from outside by the noise, wanting to share Mane's moment with his family. I start counting but lose track, certain that there are well over 100 people there. There is an air of celebration and, if there is tension at Anfield after Bernardo Silva's late goal, which forces Mane and his team-mates to work even harder in the final moments, there is nothing of the sort in Bambali, where the outcome has not been in doubt since Fabinho's early goal. "I told you Sadio would score," Ibrahim says at the final whistle as everyone headed outside to celebrate.

Their fervour on Liverpool's behalf is genuine but, truly, their allegiance is to Mane. The more you look at it, through their eyes, the more extraordinary it must be to see Sadio up on the big screen, not only representing Senegal but playing for one of the most famous clubs in world football, winning the Champions League, being crowned African Player of the Year, coming fifth in the running for the FIFA Best Men's Player award, putting himself in contention to win the Ballon d'Or.

Consider the Liverpool supporters' pride at seeing a local lad, Trent Alexander-Arnold, playing a starring role – or the City fans' pride on their glimpses of Phil Foden, or even Harry Kane at Tottenham or Jack Grealish at Aston Villa – and then consider how it must feel not just for the people of Senegal but for the people of Bambali to see "one of our own" scaling such heights on the biggest stages in world football.

To get to Anfield from here has taken five huge steps: from Bambali to Dakar to Metz to Salzburg to Southampton to Liverpool. Arguably the sixth step, from an eye-catching Premier League forward to a reliably brilliant one, thriving in the Champions League, has been the most difficult of all, yet nothing seems to get in Mane's way. "Incredible," Diatta says. "Nobody thought it would happen, even if we all dreamed it."

He came back to Bambali in July to get over the disappointment of defeat in the Africa Cup of Nations final. As the word of his homecoming spread, children walked from other villages, further up the Casamance, to see if they could catch a glimpse of him. It was easier than they imagined. He was happy to walk among them in a pair of shorts and flip-flops, spreading joy, taking the opportunity to visit the school and, above all, relaxing with his friends and family, particularly his sisters and his mother.

I ask Ibrahim whether the woman who sat behind me, looking so emotional, was Mane's mother. "No," he says. "Sadio's mother is outside."

He takes me to her. She has spent the entire afternoon sitting outside in a state of high anxiety. She doesn't feel able to watch Sadio play. It is too nerve-wracking. "Too much emotion," her brother Ibrahim says. She smiles at that suggestion. She will watch the match in a more relaxed state later on, now that she knows the outcome for her son is positive.

She does not wish to be interviewed, preferring for Ibrahim to speak on the family's behalf. "She is incredibly proud of Sadio," he says. "Every one of us in Bambali is. Not just for what he does as a footballer but for everything that he does as a person. He does it for all the family, for the people of Bambali, for all of Senegal."

The child of Bambali, the pride of a whole nation, Sadio Mane, their esteemed *Nianthio*, continues to inspire. "He told us he had to pursue his dream," Ibrahim says. "And that dream has become a reality."

"IT'S A PENALTY. THAT... IS... A... PENALTY! HOW CAN YOU NOT GIVE THAT?" WATCHING LIVERPOOL V MAN CITY WITH KEVIN KEEGAN

DANIEL TAYLOR

NOV 11, 2019

It is quite some feeling to get your hands on an old Ballon d'Or trophy, even if it does appear to have a rattle on the rare occasions when Kevin Keegan, its owner for the past 40 years, can be persuaded to go through his football possessions. It is certainly lighter than you might expect, more akin to the kind of trophy you might get in a pool competition at your local pub rather than the hulk of silver that Lionel Messi and Cristiano Ronaldo have shared for the past decade. Look closely and you can see the line of glue where the plaque has been stuck on the wooden base. The metal started to discolour a long time ago and, if you are wondering why there is a rattle, it sounds like there is a bolt floating around inside the base. Keegan likes to tell the story about the time he had it valued. It still tickles him that the guy in the shop told him, in all seriousness, that it was worth a tenner.

It is approaching kick-off time: Liverpool v Manchester City, and a man with so much history at both clubs – a European Cup winner and category-A superstar for Liverpool, as well as being the longest-serving City manager since the 1970s – has invited *The Athletic* to join him for the biggest match of the season so far.

Keegan has the remote control beside him on the settee. *You'll Never Walk Alone* is reverberating round Anfield. He turns up the volume to get his fix of nostalgia and, in these *Gogglebox* moments, we talk about whether Liverpool opening up a nine-point gap on Manchester City would mean the title race is all but over.

Keegan thinks it would be. "When was the last time the title was decided in November?" he asks. But then he pauses and there is a knowing smile. That might sound a bit strange, he has realised, coming from a man whose Newcastle United side infamously once blew a 12-point lead at the top of the table.

His trophies are safely stored away with the England caps, the souvenir shirts, and some of his more unorthodox memorabilia, including an old pair of Pirelli 'KK' slippers, a model ship from Hamburg, and the bust that was given to him by some university students in Newcastle and then subsequently redecorated to make the hair the right colour (Terry McDermott, he explains, did not think it was realistic enough and sprinkled talcum powder where there was once that famous perm).

The teams have just been announced and Keegan, only half-joking, is wondering whether it might be one of those 4-3 occasions for which he will be always remembered (including one game at Anfield when nobody seems to remember it was actually Kenny Dalglish, not Keegan, in charge of Newcastle). The two managers are in the dugouts and it feels like a good moment to remember there was once a time that Keegan was one of a young Jurgen Klopp's major football influences.

Klopp – or *Klopple*, meaning Little Klopp, as he was known to friends back then – was approaching his 11th birthday when Keegan, having won the European Cup as a leaving present for Liverpool, arrived in the Bundesliga.

Keegan was on a mission to show that English footballers could thrive abroad and Klopp, like so many boys of that age in Germany, became obsessed with the story of *Machtig Maus* (Mighty Mouse) winning the Ballon d'Or twice. First in 1978, Keegan's introductory season at Hamburg. Then, again, the following season, as Hamburg clinched their first league championship since 1960.

Klopp was in the junior ranks of SV Glatten, growing up as a fan of Stuttgart, the runners-up to Hamburg in 1979. His hero was the West Germany international Karl-Heinz Forster, but he will happily reminisce about the years when Keegan entered his life. He has also sent a message, 40 years on, that Keegan is always welcome to visit at Melwood, Liverpool's training ground. Klopp would love to meet. And it doesn't take long with Keegan to realise that the admiration goes both ways.

"He just *gets* it. He understands what Liverpool is, and what their fans want. His teams always want to attack. Three up front, attacking full-backs. It's lovely to watch. You come away from every game thinking, wow, that was entertaining. And isn't that what football is all about?"

———————— **A** ————————

Right from the start, the game has fallen in favour of the home team. "Let me tell you something, straight away, from Liverpool's point of view," Keegan says, barely a minute in. "They must have won the toss. Just look at the way they are kicking."

As the television cameras look at the pitch, Liverpool are heading from right to left, attacking the smallest of the four stands. Just as they wanted it.

"That was always the thing at Liverpool," Keegan explains. "If you win the toss, make sure you are attacking the Kop in the second half. And if your opponents won the toss they would always say: 'Make sure we don't let them go the way they want.' It's a massive thing, for both teams.

"I had six years as a player at Liverpool and I know what it is like to be playing towards the Kop. It feels like you are running down a hill. There is no hill but, boy, it can feel that way sometimes."

Except it turns out that City, in those early exchanges, are intent on making it clear they are no ordinary opponent. The ball is in the penalty area. There are a couple of ricochets and, out of the congestion, Sergio Aguero is chasing after the referee. Kevin De Bruyne and Raheem Sterling are not far behind. Sometimes, in football, you know when players are trying it on and when they genuinely feel there is an injustice. Aguero's eyes are blazing.

Keegan is thinking the same ("he's so sure!"). His instinct is telling him it must have been a handball and a penalty. But the referee is running away, following the play, and in a few seconds the ball is launched off Fabinho's boot. It is flying past Claudio Bravo, City's stand-in goalkeeper, and now there are more players in blue running over to Michael Oliver and imploring him to speak to whoever is on the other end of that earpiece.

It is a heck of a strike and later, in one of the game's few quiet moments, Keegan can see a likeness with some of the goals that McDermott, one of his great old friends, used to score on the same ground. "Gary Neville (the Sky co-commentator) has been critical of the goalkeeper. OK, it's not gone right in the corner, so I know what he is saying. But I tell you what, he doesn't half hit it," he says. "I don't think you can really blame Bravo there."

But he is confused, like the rest of us, about how the goal has been allowed, why VAR has missed the ball striking Trent Alexander-Arnold's right arm in the other penalty area, and why it took so little time to reach a decision when, the previous day, the game between Tottenham and Sheffield United needed three and a half minutes to go through all the relevant checks after John Lundstram's toe strayed offside.

Keegan is leaning forward, making his own commentary, and in these moments he is just like you or me: utterly confused about whether it is going to be given as a goal at one end or a penalty at the other.

"This will be laughable... this will be major... it's killed the celebration... what a shame... the ref's right there... this is a game-changer," he says.

Sky shows the replay and now we have a better understanding of why Aguero was so aggrieved.

"It's a penalty. That... is... a... penalty! How can you not give that?"

Not, however, in the eyes of VAR. Keegan is laughing. But it is the kind of laughter that says: what the hell is going on here? It takes a while for everything to sink in and, even then, there are still so many questions about VAR, its inconsistencies and the potential consequences for City when it could have been them, not Liverpool, with a 1-0 lead.

More than that, there is something bordering on sadness, and it is tinged with a certain amount of weariness, too. Keegan knows that, whatever happens next, the game has been scarred by controversy. "We're going to have to get used to it because this is the way football is now," he says.

That doesn't necessarily mean he likes it, though. And it is a strange feeling to be sitting with one of the football greats, a former England captain and two-time European footballer of the year, as he adds it to the list of VAR controversies that have disfigured the sport.

Pep Guardiola looks on the point of spontaneous combustion. The crowd's goal celebrations have been interrupted for a video review that nobody inside the ground can see and, in those moments, Keegan is reminded that it wasn't such a bad thing to belong to an era when everything seemed so much more straightforward.

A

It's half-time. Keegan has gone to fetch a pear from the fruit bowl and, when he comes back, he is recalling his time as City manager. He has heard it being said that City have not won at Anfield for 16 years and it has set him off thinking. "That must have been me," he says, without sounding entirely sure. And the beauty of the internet is that it is only a click away to find the footage online.

May 3, 2003.

Once again, it's red versus blue at Anfield. Milan Baros has given Liverpool the lead, early in the second half, but Anfield was not quite as impregnable back then as it is now. Nicolas Anelka has equalised from the penalty spot. And then, with the game entering its third minute of stoppage time, there is one last attack from City's players. Anelka is running on to a pass from Shaun Wright-Phillips. The striker is pulling back his left boot, directly in front of the Kop, and the voice of the television commentator, Jon Champion, has gone to a different pitch.

"Rejected by Gerard Houllier, this is Nicolas Anelka's response… and it may well cost Liverpool a place in the Champions League!"

Liverpool 1, Manchester City 2

Anelka is running to the corner flag to celebrate and Keegan, watching back the footage and knowing how divisive the Frenchman could be in the dressing room, is not completely surprised that Robbie Fowler, another of City's ex-Liverpool players, has decided against joining the victory scrum.

It was a defeat for Liverpool, in the penultimate match of the 2002-03 season, that meant they ultimately had to make do with UEFA Cup qualification.

"It was always a place where I thought my teams had a chance," Keegan says. "And I will tell you why I think we did OK: we took them on. Even when we were beaten, we always made sure it was a tough game for them. Other teams might sit back and, over the years, Liverpool came to expect that approach.

"I always thought that if you had a go at them it could take them by surprise and can knock them out of their rhythm. That was always my approach. You've got to have the courage to do it but, more than anything, you've got to have the players."

Keegan was City's manager for nearly four years. There is only Tony Book, from 1974 to 1979, who stayed in the position for longer over the past five decades and, as always with Keegan, he wanted it to be fun. His team were promoted to the Premier League with 99 points and 108 goals and, to put that into context, it was three points and 16 more goals than the Newcastle side he took up, who became known as 'The Entertainers'.

Keegan enjoyed his time at City so much that he and his family put down roots in the north-west. The photographs of his grandchildren in one downstairs room show two of them wearing City's colours. He remains very fond of the club, even if it is also true that City's priorities have vastly changed since Abu Dhabi's royal family took control, as opposed to the joint owners of JD Sports.

Here, though, Keegan has recognised a vulnerability in City's defence even before the game has started. "You see that back four?" he asks, when the teams flash up. "That's their weakness."

Ederson's absence has meant Guardiola having to place his trust in Bravo. Aymeric Laporte has not played since early in the season and Keegan, an admirer of the centre-half, thinks that might be crucial. "They have put Fernandinho back there. But I don't care how good you are as a defensive midfield player, you are still a midfielder, not a defender. Playing at the back... it's a step into the unknown. When to push up, when to drop off, when to hold your line – these are all things that are drilled into you, as a defender, when you are 15 or 16 years old."

Liverpool have a much more assured back four and when the conversation turns to Alexander-Arnold and Andy Robertson it is a reminder that Keegan – the manager who played Wright-Phillips at right-back for City – always did like an attacking full-back, even in an era when that was not particularly fashionable.

Klopp, he says, has two of the best in the business. "They are so vital to this team. They just have so much desire and energy to keep bombing on. They're just going to get better, too. Robertson, in particular, hugely impresses me. His energy, the amount of ground he covers, the number of goals he creates… what a buy he has been, how much was he from Hull City?"

There isn't time to answer. Alexander-Arnold has played one of his long, diagonal passes, right to left, to switch the play and pick out the movement of Liverpool's left-back. Robertson is surging down the wing. And Keegan has paused.

"This guy… "

That's all that needs to be said. Robertson, bang on cue, has arced the ball into the space that Mohamed Salah is attacking. Bravo has been beaten again and Robertson, with an impeccable sense of timing, has made Keegan's point.

————————— A —————————

What does a manager do when his team find themselves 3-0 down in a game of this magnitude? Sadio Mane has continued City's ordeal with a 51st-minute header. Guardiola is slumped in his seat and, in the commentary box, Neville has said that the players in blue look like they "want the game to end". Yet Keegan disagrees. "I don't think they do want the game to end," he says. "If they can just get one goal… "

City are one of the few sides in the world – and Guardiola one of the few managers – who might think they can still save themselves. Bernardo Silva, one of the City players Keegan likes the most, slams one in. Sterling is shimmering with menace.

De Bruyne has slipped a few times and not always had his usual precision with his passes. But the Belgian's influence is growing and, even when things are not going well, he always wants the ball.

Keegan is surprised, though, when Guardiola decides to take off Aguero. It is a straight swap for Gabriel Jesus and, not too long before, Aguero has tried to run behind the Liverpool defence only to be flagged for offside. He has gone too early and Keegan wonders whether it was over-eagerness or whether, a few years ago, Aguero might have held back for a split-second. "Is he getting to the age when he hasn't quite got that pace?" he asks.

One certainty: Anfield is Aguero's bogey ground. He has gone 782 minutes without scoring a goal on this ground. It's a remarkable statistic for a player with his goals record and, by the end, he looks frustrated in the extreme.

Keegan, nonetheless, would have kept him on and removed Ilkay Gundogan instead. "You need a goal. Aguero's your top scorer. He's scored big goals over the years. Is he really quick? No. Is he really tricky? No. But he can still get the job done. He can score a goal when you have never really seen him. He's a great player and a great goalscorer. I would have put Jesus on beside him. What have you got to lose? I would be more positive. But that's me."

As it is, the clock is ticking down and it is becoming clear there is not going to be a feat of escapology. Keegan has enjoyed what he has seen. It has been a breathless match and, though he knows from personal experience how a great champion never gives up (Newcastle were 12 points clear of Manchester United in January 1996), he cannot see Klopp's men blowing it from this position. Liverpool, he is convinced, have struck a decisive blow.

"I'm pleased for Liverpool. It's been 30 years since they won the league and that's too long," he says. "We've seen two great teams. Nobody comes near them. I've got a feeling that Liverpool win the league and City will win the European Cup. And I think both teams would settle for that."

Then it's that song again. We are in stoppage time. City have the ball and they are still coming back for more, still pushing forward. But the score is 3-1 and the crowd know they can finally relax. *You'll Never Walk Alone* is getting another airing.

Keegan told me once, collaborating on his autobiography, that there were times during matches when Liverpool's anthem would move him to tears. He has turned up the volume again. "If you can imagine my first game at Anfield, there were 23,000 stood on that Kop. Nowadays they can't fit in anything like the same number," he says. "Yet it's still unique. And it goes on, doesn't it? You think it is going to stop, but the crowd just keep singing, over and again.

"Where else do you get that? You don't have to be a Liverpool fan to enjoy that. It's true: it used to make my eyes water when I was a player. Even now, it can still make me emotional. It always gets me. Always gets me. The day it doesn't get me, I will be dead."

JURGEN KLOPP EXCLUSIVE: WHEN WE START A TEAM MEETING THE ONLY THING I REALLY KNOW I AM GOING TO SAY IS THE FIRST SENTENCE

JAMES PEARCE

NOV 21, 2019

Jurgen Klopp throws open the door to his Melwood office.

"Oh, if I'd known it was you, I wouldn't have bothered having a shower," he jokes, his booming laugh echoing down the corridor. "How's the new job?"

The Liverpool boss is armed with a large bowl of fruit and yoghurt from the canteen. It's mid-morning and he's back at his desk after a week's break in Cape Town with his wife Ulla. Wearing a red New Balance hoodie, black tracksuit bottoms and white trainers, he looks refreshed and ready for what lies ahead as he takes a seat on one of the three cream sofas.

Klopp radiates positivity. In the space of four years he has transformed the club from one that had lost its way into the champions of Europe and the runaway Premier League leaders. No-one has had a bigger impact on Liverpool Football Club since Bill Shankly's appointment 60 years ago.

Shrewd recruitment and the manager's tactical acumen have been key, but what's most striking about Klopp is his man-management. Spending time in his company provides a fascinating insight into how he's able to drain every last drop of both talent and effort from those he works with and the close bond that is fuelling their pursuit of more silverware.

"Mentality monsters" was how he described his Liverpool team towards the back end of last season and that resilience has been crucial in maintaining momentum as they look to add domestic glory to the club's sixth European crown.

"How important is the mental side in football? It's all, if you like," Klopp says. "You can have the best technical ability but if you aren't ready to show it then you can't make the best of it. It's no different in football than it is in normal life. The first step to achieve whatever you achieve is to think you can do it. You want to do it, you want to achieve it then you have to find a way to go there.

"It's constantly like question and answer, question and answer. Right, not right, trial and error. That's how we do it and in football it's no different. If you are a naturally confident person you take challenges like this. If you are naturally an insecure person then you are pretty much constantly afraid of failing."

Liverpool, who have suffered just one defeat in their past 51 Premier League matches, keep on finding a way to win. A cherished victory over champions Manchester City prior to the international break put them eight points clear at the summit. Only Manchester United in 1993-94 have ever had a bigger lead after 12 games of a Premier League season.

Klopp's men have collected 10 points from losing positions already this season – more than any other team. On the last seven occasions when they have conceded the opening goal, they have won six and drawn one. Fitness is one factor, but Klopp knows it goes much deeper than that.

"Of course it's all about that," he says, tapping the side of his head. "But you can't just order it and then assume the boys will deliver it. If it was that easy then you could just tell them in the moment when you are 1-0 down with 10 minutes to play, 'you still have to believe'.

"You have to create something and what we have created all together started long ago. I already feel uncomfortable talking about it because I don't take it for granted, not for one second. It's not that I'm thinking five minutes before we go 1-0 down, 'no problem, you can score'. It's happened more often than not that we've come back which is good, very good, but [we are] not allowed to take it for granted. It's just that because it's happened so often, psychologically it's clear. If you do something good then it's absolutely likely that the next time you do it, it will work out again. If you fail at something, then you need to convince yourself 'I can do it'. You have to at least see the chance that it can work out. That's what the boys have worked for over the past four years. Everything is different now."

Klopp's impact on Liverpool's mindset extends way beyond the dressing room. A fanbase has been energised and fortress Anfield has been rebuilt. Liverpool are unbeaten in 46 home league games dating back to April 2017 – the second-longest run in the club's history.

It's a far cry from four years ago, when Klopp felt "pretty alone" at the sight of fans leaving early when his side trailed 2-1 to Crystal Palace in the closing stages.

"Just after I came in we spoke about why people leave the stadium early. I never understood it in my life, but I can imagine all the issues with traffic," he says. "I did it myself when I went to watch games as a manager. I'd leave the stadium 15 minutes from the end and run to the car park so I could get out. But as a supporter? I didn't understand that. We had to work a lot on that.

"We have this story here that we've been writing for four years. Some of the players have been here for the full four years, others for less. They all realise that we can do what we do in a specific way because we get so much power from outside – from the club, from the crowd, from the history.

"We spoke about history when I came in and that it could be a burden. Now it feels more like a trampoline. You can jump and jump again. That all changed. How we changed it? I have no idea. We just worked since the first day on it because it was always clear that you need to create a mood where it's easier to perform than when I arrived."

Klopp's squad is littered with examples of players who had to battle in the face of adversity and overcome difficulties to reach the highest level.

"Yeah for sure that helps," he continued. "It means you learn to fight pretty early in your life. You want something that a lot of people would say is not possible. You have to stay stubborn and say 'no, it is possible, I want to try it, I want to do it'.

"There are some players who everyone saw at the first moment and thought 'oh, that's so special'. But the biggest player in the world nowadays, probably Lionel Messi, when he was a kid he was pretty little so no-one thought he could get the physicality to be ready for professional football. Obviously, he made his way.

"That's the story – it shows to everyone that it is possible. But without luck in decisive moments, you still have no chance. The right people need to see you in the right moments, in the right games to think 'yes, I see something in him'. We are not completely alone responsible for our careers. We always need to get picked by people."

——————————— **A** ———————————

There's a shelf in Klopp's office where a copy of James Milner's new book *Ask A Footballer* sits alongside pots of chewing gum and a couple of Liverpool FC branded caps. There's also a DVD of the BBC drama *Care* written by Liverpool-born Jimmy McGovern. On the opposite wall there's a nod to past glories: a collection of black-and-white framed photos of Anfield icons Shankly and Bob Paisley. His desk, which looks out over Melwood's training pitches, is at the far end.

With so much focus on the emotion and passion that Klopp brings to the job, the attention to detail of the man crowned FIFA Coach of the Year for 2019 is often overlooked. He prides himself on the marginal gains that have been made through the appointment of personnel such as head of nutrition Mona Nemmer and throw-in coach Thomas Gronnemark. Klopp surrounds himself with specialists in their particular fields and *The Athletic* can exclusively reveal that Liverpool brought on board another one last summer.

Sports psychologist Lee Richardson has been working with the club's players since July and has his own office at Melwood, where he's based for three days each week. The former Watford, Blackburn Rovers and Aberdeen midfielder was recruited from Hull City by Liverpool's medical rehabilitation and performance manager Phil Jacobsen.

Richardson had a brief stint in management with Chesterfield a decade ago, before changing careers. He has previously been part of Sam Allardyce's staff as psychologist for West Ham and then Crystal Palace. During Brendan Rodgers' reign, Liverpool secured the services of sports psychiatrist Steve Peters, who was credited with helping cyclists Sir Chris Hoy and Victoria Pendleton achieve Olympic success. However, that partnership ended shortly after Klopp's arrival in 2015. In recent years Liverpool utilised the services of performance psychologist Yvie Ryan. A popular and respected figure around the club, she now works on a part-time basis with the academy teams in Kirkby.

"He works very specifically with the boys and I have no idea what they are talking about," said Klopp. "I am not interested. It's just a nice add on.

"It's difficult to find the right people with how I see it in that part of the business. Now we feel pretty good with him on board and that's cool."

Whereas Peters needed to feel that he was central to everything at Liverpool, Richardson is content with a more ad hoc role. Going to see him is optional for the players and he isn't involved on match days. It's a better fit for Klopp's style of management. In reality, when it comes to personnel delivering on the field, Klopp himself is Liverpool's psychologist.

"I don't know what the boys think but yes, I'm responsible for that," he says. "When it comes to performing, physical investment, stuff like this, how much they want to do instead of how much they have to do – that's my job, that's how I understand it. If that's psychology, I have no idea, I've never thought about it like that. Of course, I must be influential in their thinking process.

"It takes time to create an atmosphere where players listen to you like that or where players tell you about some issues. My job is to watch them constantly and to find out what they do and why they do it. If I can understand why they do it then I can be influential. If I don't know why they do things then I have no clue.

"That's why I say when we win the players are responsible, when we lose I am responsible. That's how I see it. If we lose then it means my message didn't come across. It's my job to make sure they understand it. For me to ensure they understand it, I need to know as much as I can about them.

"I already have the issue with my language. If I have another issue with understanding the boys then we have got a problem. Knowing more about the players is the biggest help I can get."

For someone who isn't a native speaker, Klopp has a remarkable knack of finding the right words at the right times. After Liverpool overhauled a 3-0 first-leg deficit in stunning fashion to beat Barcelona in the semi-finals of the Champions League back in May, a number of his players referenced the inspirational speech he had delivered in the team meeting at the city's Hope Street Hotel before the coach left for Anfield. "The world outside is saying it is not possible," he told them. "And let's be honest, it's probably impossible. But because it's you? Because it's you, we have a chance."

Captain Jordan Henderson recalled: "The players could see that the manager believed, which helped us believe in what he said. The manager has ingrained that belief into us: no matter what happens you keep fighting right to the end."

Asked about working with Klopp, striker Roberto Firmino said: "Jurgen motivates us in a different way every day."

Where does it come from? A smile creeps across Klopp's face. "Sorry, I would write a book about the things I do if I knew why I did them," he says. "But I could never write a book because I have no clue about how these things work. I just react in situations. My job, my life is 24/7 thinking about what happens here.

"The training sessions are one-and-a-half hours or two hours a day. There are still 22 hours left! There are so many things that influence the boys.

"The meetings are based on our past if you want – what happened after the last game, what happened yesterday, things like this. What can we use? I always react.

"I don't usually remember what I say. If the boys didn't say things in the press afterwards then I wouldn't even know I'd said it. I remember Divock Origi after the Dortmund game (in the quarter-final of the Europa League in 2016 when Liverpool fought back from 3-1 down to win 4-3). He said: 'The boss told us at half-time that if we turned the game around it would be a story we'd all be able to tell our grandchildren about so it would be really worth giving it a try.'

"But if it was that easy I'd tell them things like that constantly! We always want stories to tell the grandkids! When we start a team meeting the only thing I really know that I am going to say is the first sentence."

Really? So the rest is just off the cuff?

"All that happens through the week, it stays in my mind, I don't write anything down," he explains. "I just think about what's worth telling the boys. Shit session, very good session, whatever, little things. I know how it sounds and it should not sound like this – like I know always to say the right words. But I do trust myself 100 per cent to find the right words.

"I only know the first sentence. I am not nervous because I don't know yet the second sentence. I always realise after a meeting that I sweat here [he points to his brow]. That's when I feel the intensity of the meeting. I don't realise that it's intense until the drops come down my face and I think 'it's not that warm'. I am obviously pretty much 'in it'.

"If the meeting before a game was the only moment when we speak about football then it would take two-and-a-half hours. But it's only 10 to 15 minutes max. Most of the things are already said.

"It's about repeating the things we've said during the week. Then I think it always makes sense to give the boys a little hint about why it's so worth it, why it's so valuable to do it more intensely than others.

"We all have to come in a mood where we can reach the highest. You cannot get up in the morning at 8am having got pissed the night before and try to climb the Rocky Mountains or Mount Everest. It's just not possible. We have to come in a mood where we say 'now this step, now that step'. That's what we try to create constantly."

Sports psychology formed part of the diploma in sports science that Klopp completed at Goethe University, Frankfurt, during his playing career with Mainz in the mid-1990s. It was a topic that legendary German manager Wolfgang Frank was passionate about. Frank, who had two spells as Mainz boss, was a huge influence on Klopp's move into coaching but he didn't always follow his orders.

"Yeah, Wolfgang was constantly reading books," Klopp says. "He actually told us players that we had to spend at least 10 per cent of our wages on books about psychology. I never bought one!

"To be honest, we had players that even if the books they bought had been the other way around, they wouldn't have known any different. They didn't even understand the titles! They just got them because the boss told us to do it.

"I only read what I needed to read to prepare for my final diploma exam. I remember going to see the professor in sports psychology. I opened the door and he said from his desk 'if you want to talk about motivation get out of my office!'

"Everyone wanted to make the exam about motivation. I had 'mo…' on my lips actually, but I said: 'oh no, I actually want to talk about something else.' I didn't read many books about psychology to be honest. If there were more books about common sense then I would probably read them.

"If you ask me 'do you have a strength?' I'd say it's not my right foot, not my left foot, I'm not really smart but common sense? Yes. I can really judge things in the right way – as long as I'm not emotionally involved, like during a game.

"Before and after a game, I'm completely in the middle. If you tell me about a problem, I'll be able to tell you if it's really serious or not and how you can deal with it. That's one of my strengths. It was always like this. That's my thing – common sense more than psychology. Make the big things big and leave the small things small."

Win or lose, Klopp says little to his players in the dressing room immediately after games. He prefers to wait until the dust has settled. The real debriefs take place at Melwood the following morning.

"There's no need straight after," he explains. "We have two, maybe three minutes max. What I say straight after a game is very spontaneous and brief – very good or very bad is easy. Mediocre isn't too interesting, so we can talk about that the next day. Straight after a game you are emotionally involved but it's also that you are too busy. Players are off doing media or drugs tests. When you want to say the right things, you should think about it and I have no time to think about it at that time.

"I don't need to read newspapers to know if we were good or bad. I know that before I read anything. I tell them that the only opinion that really counts is my opinion. The day after is when I tell the boys how it was and why it was."

It's a measure of what Klopp has created that he rarely has to contend with any dissenting voices. Even those on the fringes, with limited game-time, feel like they are part of something special at Liverpool. A desire to protect and enhance that unity and spirit is one of the reasons why the 52-year-old prefers to operate with a relatively small senior squad.

"There's a lot of responsibility on the boys themselves. A person who doesn't want to feel needed, I cannot help," Klopp says. "If you play in the first XI and it's 'yeah!' or if you don't play and it's 'oh, you can all fuck off' then you cannot exist in this kind of environment, it's not possible. Yes, I get that it feels different if you haven't played, but you must always be ready for the moment when you come on.

"How do I keep them motivated? I treat them all the same, 100 per cent. You score four goals or no goals, for me you are the same person. When we talk about football it's easier for me to speak with the guy who scored four goals, but on a personal level they're all the same for me. I like them all a lot – that's why they are all here. It's not that anyone has forced me to get around with these guys. They are all wonderful. Different, but wonderful. I like being around them. Hopefully, they know that and they feel that."

Over the course of this interview, there are knocks on the door from head physio Lee Nobes and head of fitness and conditioning Andreas Kornmayer. You can guarantee that they wanted to discuss the various states of fitness that the club's international contingent have returned to Melwood in.

This is Klopp's life. He's always dealing with problems and challenges. His door is always open for staff and players alike. Does he ever find it draining?

"No, this for me is absolutely energy-giving, not energy-taking, 100 per cent," he says. "Life is all about these things. I like being alone. I have no problem with being alone sometimes, but actually I love having people around, speaking to them, listening to them. I really think that listening to people is the best teacher in life in general. The best thing is to listen to smart people. Not all people are smart, but it's still interesting. I really constantly try to understand the people I have to deal with.

"It's not at all draining. It's actually pretty much the best part of my job to be around these guys and to have the opportunity to help them and get the best out of them. That's the plan of a career – to make the best career you can make. Only some of us will know that it was the best career we could get. All the others will be a little bit in doubt in terms of 'if only I'd done more here or there'. Coming close to your personal perfect career – that's my target for the boys."

Can Klopp ever truly switch off?

"I would say yes, Ulla would probably say no," he laughs. "But I'm much better. On holiday in the summer, if it's say four weeks, then I'd say the first week is difficult and the last week is difficult. But in between, yes I can completely switch off."

But what about being able to savour a victory? It was telling that when Klopp faced the media straight after Liverpool's win over title rivals Manchester City he was bemoaning the lack of preparation time he would have for this weekend's trip to Crystal Palace. Even after such a statement triumph, he was immediately looking to the next hurdle that needed to be cleared rather than living in the moment.

"Yes because I hate the internationals! From a personal point of view, I just hate it," he says. "Sadio Mane played in Swaziland (for Senegal). You know nothing about games like this. He went off straight after half-time and you are thinking 'oh'. These are the situations that kill me, to be honest. It's just not knowing about what is exactly happening, trying to find out what we can do, what we have to do. As soon as Sadio got a phone we could get in contact, but he's the player, he's not the guy who organises everything else around it. Dealing with things like this is not cool. That's why the last game before an international break is always difficult for me. The final whistle goes and then I'm thinking 'now they leave'. That's the biggest problem in my working life.

"You know the best game of the season so far for me to enjoy? It was Arsenal in the Carabao Cup (when a youthful Liverpool line up fought back from 4-2 down to win 5-4 on penalties after a thrilling 5-5 draw).

"When we were 3-1 down I was thinking 'come on, don't give them a knock, don't lose 4-1 or 5-1 as that wouldn't be nice'. Then we started scoring again. That was my game to enjoy. I don't have that a lot. The boys made it a special night and I loved it. The atmosphere was brilliant and buzzing. We've had a lot of good moments at Anfield."

———————————— **A** ————————————

Liverpool will need plenty more good moments if they are going to end the club's painful 30-year wait for English football's top-flight crown. Winning the title isn't so much a target as an obsession on Merseyside. Supporters crave it so much that the emotion can become overwhelming. Last season Liverpool agonisingly missed out to City by a solitary point – a club record 97-point haul was in vain – before rallying to lift the Champions League in Madrid. This time around Klopp's men find themselves in a position of strength domestically and the manager knows that holding their nerve will go a long way to deciding the outcome.

"The difference is not too big to last season," he insists. "I know people will get nervous. Everybody thinks we need to win all the games otherwise they will catch us. But in those moments when people imagine that, they think the other teams won't drop any more points themselves. Last season City didn't lose any more games when we were both fighting for the title. But that doesn't mean it will be like this again.

"Last season was very helpful for the future of all of us. We were completely concentrated on a specific game. We knew we had to win it. The Champions League final: going there with my personal history in finals, not too cool, and the history of the team with losing the final the year before, not too cool. But if you use history in the right way then it can always help.

"We're all human beings and it's natural to have doubts. I was actually afraid of the three or four hours alone in the hotel room before the final because I'd have no interaction with anyone. Usually, I'd just sit there on the chair or on the bed and prepare. But on the day of the final I went in my room and I slept for two hours. I surprised myself. I woke up and I was still in a good mood. I have no clue why that happened. It's not that I forced myself to be in a good mood. I was just really looking forward to the game.

"It comes down to the faith and the trust I have in these boys. Not that we will make it, because you can't guarantee that, but that we will make the best out of it. I was really positive before the game. It was so nice."

His players repaid that faith in abundance on the biggest of stages and they have continued in similar fashion since. With the Super Cup already added to the Champions League and next month's Club World Cup on the horizon, the stage is set for a golden era. This is Liverpool's time.

"The experiences we've had certainly help," Klopp adds. "Last season showed us again that we have to keep going until the last match day. If you look throughout my career, you will see that I've pretty much always gone until the last match day. It's unbelievable. When we became German champions with Dortmund it was the third to last match day, but there was a cup final still to come at the end of the season. It's always until the bitter end. Ulla doesn't like that too much, but that's part of my career. I should get used to it. We always try to squeeze out everything that we possibly can."

Time is up. Klopp has staff to liaise with and an afternoon training session to oversee. The relentless pursuit of perfection goes on.

VIRGIL VAN DIJK: THE MAN WHO TRANSFORMED HIMSELF AND HIS TEAMS

SIMON HUGHES, KIERAN DEVLIN,

CARL ANKA and JAMES PEARCE

NOV 29, 2019

Groningen – 'All the scouts made a mistake with him'

Pieter Huistra lives in Tashkent now, the capital of Uzbekistan. His football career has taken him all over the world. There have been spells as a coach in Slovakia, Indonesia and Japan. As a player, he was at Rangers when the club dominated Scottish football under Graeme Souness, then Walter Smith. In Glasgow, Huistra lasted five years – his longest spell at any club during 17 seasons as a professional.

"I am a wanderer," he says, knowing it is way past midnight in Central Asia when he takes *The Athletic*'s call. If there is one place he calls home in a football sense, though, it is Groningen in northern Holland – the club he has represented on four separate occasions. He began playing for Groningen in 1984 before returning as a player 12 years later. As a coach, he started out with the club's under-19s before moving on to Vitesse Arnhem and Ajax, where he combined roles as assistant manager and second-team head coach. That was when he agreed to go back to

Groningen again at the start of 2010. For the next two seasons, he was their manager.

"It was February and the first conversation was about players," he recalls. "I was interested to know which targets they had in mind. The standard of the player reflected the ambition of the club. One of the players they were hopeful about was Virgil van Dijk. Their plan was to start him in the second team. Groningen was far away from Breda (where Van Dijk is from) and they wanted to break him in slowly. For Virgil, it was a new city and a new club. He'd never lived by himself before. Groningen is a bit different to other parts of Holland."

Groningen rarely win league titles, but they know about developing young footballers. Arjen Robben and Luis Suarez are two of those. Years before, there was Ronald Koeman. Huistra believes the city's geography and the source of its economy impacts on its football team. Supporters tend to be grounded and therefore, they want to see graft before anything else.

"Groningen is a very down-to-earth club," he says. "You are expected to behave normally, not to act like a big star. I think this is because of Groningen's location. It is far away in the north and surrounded by farmland. The nearest club is a fair distance away. It feels like its own place. There is an intensity in the passion for Groningen that doesn't exist everywhere. The winters are very cold and the agriculture leads the way of life. People have to work hard to get by. They want to see this identity in their football team. There is a big difference between Van Dijk's hometown of Breda and Groningen. In the south, it is a little bit more easy-going. In the north, they are very committed towards work and they don't accept any less."

In the Dutch Eredivisie, Ajax, Feyenoord and PSV Eindhoven are expected to compete for the league each season. Groningen are towards the bottom of the second-tier clubs that might have a chance of pushing them if the breaks go their way. AZ Alkmaar and Utrecht also fall into that category. "This also carries an expectation," Huistra says. "Maybe you are not expected to beat the big three all of the time, but at least sometimes. When you play those clubs, you are expected to put on a performance, at home at the very least. Then, you must beat the other teams. This means there is pressure. Virgil came from Willem II. Down there, near Breda, it's not quite the same."

Huistra was still at Ajax when he started driving towards Breda to see what he was working with the following season. Van Dijk had not broken into a Willem II team struggling for survival in the Eredivisie. Not only was their manager, Alfons Groenendijk, reluctant to place his faith in youth in such circumstances, Van Dijk was so far away from his consideration that Groenendijk supposedly did not even know the young defender's name. Instead, he leaned on experience. One such player was Ibrahim Kargbo. A decade later, around the time Van Dijk was on the way towards becoming a Champions League winner, Kargbo's football career was finishing at Dulwich Hamlet in England's National League South. That end was confirmed when he was banned for match-fixing international games with Sierra Leone.

Huistra looked at Van Dijk and saw both talent and room for improvement. He was very tall, but not at his full physical capacity. There had been growth problems as a teenager. At 16, his younger brother by two years was taller than him but suddenly, across one summer and autumn, he grew by five inches. This led to issues with his groin and knee, sometimes his back. He needed to be bigger to become a footballer, but that process simultaneously hindered his sporting development. For several months, while others were asked to train with the first team, he was instead trying to bulk up muscles with which to support his rapidly-changing frame.

In Breda, as a child, Van Dijk had divided his Sundays between church gatherings in the morning and football in the afternoon, playing on five-a-side courts financed by the Johan Cruyff Foundation. Each city in Holland had at least one. Games were unorganised. The team that won stayed on and the team that lost faced a wait. While this helped his technical ability, it also increased his endurance.

His mother came from the former Dutch colony of Surinam, in South America, and his father was Dutch. His grandfather had been the first of the Van Dijk clan to play football, though he was a better referee. Van Dijk's junior team WDS'19 had a partnership with professional side NAC Breda but they missed out on him altogether. Nobody from the club was willing to explain to *The Athletic* why he instead joined Willem II, a club based half-an-hour away in Tilburg. His break came because of Frank Brugel, whose son Jordy played as a goalkeeper behind Van Dijk at WDS'19. Brugel had been a pro at Willem II. It was something about the way Van Dijk took care of the ball that made him take notice.

When Van Dijk was aged 10, Jan van Loon noticed how few strikers could outpace the young centre-back. Willem's academy director also recognised how sometimes he'd switch off. Coaches who worked regularly with him could not decide whether he was too slow to spot danger or whether he simply tended to find football easy and this would lead to lapses in concentration. At 18, both Willem II and Van Dijk had a decision to make. Van Loon wanted to keep him but not every coach was convinced they should, with some technical directors happy to cut him loose. Some thought he'd make it as a centre-back, others as a right-back. Van Dijk felt let down not just by the lack of confidence shown in him, but the lack of guidance he was receiving.

Hans Nijland, Groningen's sporting director, believed he had become rusty at Willem, having had the same relationships with the same coaches, who were giving him the same instructions for such a long time. He needed new voices as well as a fresh environment to bring about a new focus.

Initially, there was also a feeling amongst the coaching staff at Groningen that Van Dijk was too laid-back. He was intelligent and talented, but did he have the drive to push himself all the way to the top? He'd occasionally give opponents too much space and though he was able to recover, he was told he might not be able to at senior level, where the top strikers think and act more quickly. He had a tendency to forget to push up and play a high defensive line as per the coach's request. Van Dijk was told he needed to sharpen up.

By his own admission, he had not eaten healthily as a teenager, finishing nights out with friends with a McDonald's burger near to Breda's Grote Markt. At least, he reasoned, he was spending his own money, having taken a job as a dishwasher at a restaurant to supplement his modest income. He enjoyed riding his bike to training sessions in Groningen, but his progress was interrupted by serious illness: he lost a stone following a stomach infection from an appendix operation which kept him in hospital for 13 nights. He had been in his first full season in Groningen's first team and he was preparing for the derby with Heerenveen when he began to feel sick.

The 2011-12 season ended in high drama. His first start was against Den Haag in the second leg of a domestic play-off to reach the Europa League. Groningen had lost the first leg away 5-1. "Everyone was down," Huistra remembered. "Instead of driving back to Groningen straight away, I took the players to a restaurant at a hotel and gave my team talk for the next game. I wanted to give them the feeling that there was a possibility to come back from such a bad moment even though understandably, nobody believed in us. I wanted the players to use their anger and aggression and show everybody that this was a one-off, that this was not Groningen."

Huistra decided on some tactical and personnel tweaks. Van Dijk was introduced to the team as a striker. The return leg in Groningen did not start well, with Den Haag taking a 1-0 lead. At half-time, the aggregate score was Groningen 2, Den Haag 6.

"But we kept believing. In the second half, we scored four goals, taking the tie to extra-time, where we also had some good chances. Virgil scored two of our goals. It was an incredible comeback. Many people had bought tickets from the first game but decided not to come to the ground because they thought the tie was dead. It was virtually empty at the beginning. Gradually, the stadium started filling up. They heard the score on the radio. By extra-time it was almost full."

Groningen lost on penalties, an agonising end to a remarkable comeback. Huistra, though, had learned he could rely on Van Dijk to deliver when the pressure was on. Coaches and scouts from other clubs came to watch him, but only occasionally. That changed only after Huistra left following a disappointing 2011-12 campaign, when Groningen finished just six points above the relegation zone. Soon, Huistra was fielding calls about Van Dijk. "But all the coaches and all the scouts made a mistake with him," he says. "They confused the ease at which he played with him being too easy-going. On the rare occasion he made a mistake, it was because – they thought – of a loss of concentration. For me, he was never like that. He was focused and always desperate to win. When you are young, you sometimes make the wrong choices. For example, he might pick the wrong pass and it gets intercepted. This was translated by people watching him, who didn't really know his game, as lapses in concentration. I don't think it was like that. He was young, he had time to develop and sometimes he was playing against a more experienced opponent. He suffered because he made most things look so, so easy."

The summer Van Dijk moved from Groningen to Celtic, Mike van der Hoorn left Utrecht for Ajax. Huistra told Ajax that they were making a mistake by not going for Van Dijk instead of Van der Hoorn, who now plays for Swansea City in the Championship.

"And Ajax were not the only club interested in him," Huistra says. "Their scouts always came to me with questions. 'He does not do this, he does not do that…' They all had at least two reasons to prefer someone else. These scouts, they repeated each other. This is what happens. They always speak to each other and they are so afraid that they miss something."

"I think Virgil's case is similar to Jaap Stam's," Huistra concludes. "He started at small clubs, going from small club, to small club to small club. When you start at a small club in Holland, there's a sort of bias. They (the bigger clubs) say, 'Ah, he cannot be good enough for us – there must be a player from our own academy that is better than him'. He spent the rest of his career playing for the best clubs in Europe. I think with Virgil, it was the same. Groningen was a bigger club than Willem II but maybe Groningen needed to overachieve for Virgil to convince everyone."

Simon Hughes

Celtic – 'The biggest talent I've ever managed'

Van Dijk arrived at Celtic in the post-season of 2012-13. It was an aberration of a campaign – the first without Rangers in the Scottish Premiership and the high of reaching the Champions League last 16 was tempered by a woeful loss to St Mirren in the Scottish League Cup semi-final. Celtic would beat the Barcelona of Lionel Messi, Andres Iniesta and Xavi and then, four days later, draw at home to St Johnstone.

With the homesick Kelvin Wilson returning south to Nottingham Forest, Celtic manager Neil Lennon knew before the season's end that another first-choice, quick centre-back with a good range of passing was the club's priority, and tasked chief scout John Park accordingly. Park brought Lennon footage of players via Wyscout, and Van Dijk stood out as being surreally good, a player so seemingly complete that it was assumed something invisible to video scouting platforms must have been missed.

Yet Lennon watched Van Dijk play for Groningen against Ajax, and he really *did* seem that good. Van Dijk joined for £2.8 million in June 2013, with Celtic batting away more monied interest from Russian side Kuban Krasnodar.

His first season at Celtic was really quite strange. After a difficult bedding-in period – including a 2-2 draw against Inverness on his full debut, and losing the first leg of a Champions League play-off 2-0 away to Shakhter Karagandy – something clicked, almost overnight, and he became the best player in the country. He was almost unbeatable in the air, won tackles that looked foregone conclusions, and pre-empted attacks as soon as the opposition instigated them.

In February 2014, Van Dijk, striding and immovable in front of his future Southampton team-mate Fraser Forster, was crucial to Celtic breaking the league record for consecutive clean sheets with 13 in a row, and the league record for time without conceding, at 1,256 minutes.

Van Dijk was also a goalscorer, grabbing 15 across his two years at Celtic. He was lethal from set-pieces, with two headers in one game against Ross County; he dribbled from inside his own half against St Johnstone to toe-poke in an absurd goal; and he developed into one of Celtic's primary free-kick takers, with rockets against Hibernian and Dundee.

After winning the Scottish Premiership, being named in the PFA Team of the Year for 2013-14 and being nominated for the PFA Players' Player of the Year, Van Dijk was touted for a call-up to the Holland squad for the 2014 World Cup. But coach Louis van Gaal looked elsewhere, including Terence Kongolo and

Bruno Martins Indi, who would both go on to be relegated from the Premier League with Huddersfield and Stoke respectively. Van Gaal told the newspaper *Volkskrant* that Van Dijk "didn't defend forward", as in he didn't defend proactively and utilise space well enough to be a Holland international.

Dutch scouts had also suggested to Van Gaal that Van Dijk had a tendency for complacency, lapses in concentration that led to him losing his man or not tracking back quickly enough.

Norwegian coach Ronny Deila took charge of Celtic for 2014-15 after Lennon's departure at the end of the previous season and met with Van Dijk. Conversation quickly turned to his omission from the World Cup squad.

"We were talking about that at the beginning because he was disappointed that he wasn't picked," Deila tells *The Athletic*. "He was asking me how he could improve. I asked him, 'Why do you feel you weren't picked for the World Cup?' and he replied that he didn't know, and that he felt it was unfair and that he was good enough. I told him he wasn't there because he obviously wasn't thought of as good enough, so the only way to become a big pick for the national team was to improve, to get better at what you can do because that's what you can control."

Deila also highlighted to Van Dijk the criticisms of complacency and how they were holding him back: "Sometimes, he felt it was too easy in Scotland, but you have to perform. To be the best, you have to show the attitude that you take everybody seriously and be focused 24 hours a day."

If Van Dijk's first season at Celtic instituted in him a psychological zealousness for winning, at a club where every dropped point represents a crisis, the second was more about physical development, about adopting the vigorous fitness regime of an elite professional athlete. Deila immediately instituted a stricter diet policy at the club: "When I came in, I thought he was too heavy. He was a fantastic player, and very physical, but to reach the next level he had to become fitter."

There were few Celtic players that clicked with the nutrition regime more than Van Dijk, and his weight-loss – and improved agility as a result – was remarkable, as Deila explains to *The Athletic*: "If you're carrying around too much weight, it makes you move slower, think slower, and makes you do everything slower.

"He lost 9kg. Van Dijk weighed 104kg when I arrived, and when he left for Southampton a year later, he was 95kg and looked like a real athlete – 9kg impacts your ability to quickly move around the pitch."

It wasn't just the benefits of better nutrition and fitness that prefigured Van Dijk's time at Liverpool, a club so fixated on marginal gains that they employ a throw-in coach, but the style of football which he played under Deila: a rough draft of Jurgen Klopp's gegenpressing, with a fluid 4-2-3-1 dependent on ball-playing centre-backs. This style also introduced Van Dijk to Van Gaal's treasured concept of defending forward, with the Dutchman encouraged to press liberally and trust his positional instincts more.

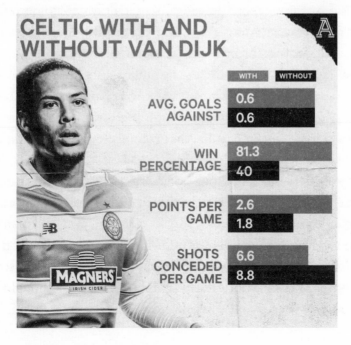

CELTIC WITH AND WITHOUT VAN DIJK

	WITH	WITHOUT
AVG. GOALS AGAINST	0.6	0.6
WIN PERCENTAGE	81.3	40
POINTS PER GAME	2.6	1.8
SHOTS CONCEDED PER GAME	6.6	8.8

Under Deila, Van Dijk was even more confident in carrying the ball from the back and in breaking opposition lines with his passing.

"He started training differently," Deila continues. "He became more motivated and focused on every detail of his training and tactical awareness, and started to realise he had to give 100 per cent in everything he did to reach the next level. He had to match the work with the talent.

"He started to take care of himself outside the pitch, to get fit, and at the same time, to focus more on training, to work on his tactical side of the game too."

Van Dijk was also a charismatic figure inside the dressing room. "He was really relaxed outside the pitch," Deila says. "But on it he was a winner. You could see in his eyes that something changed when he went onto the pitch but off it, he was relaxed, social, and thoughtful. He was close friends with Stefan Johansen and those two had a really good effect on each other.

"There was a good dressing-room culture that year, a lot of young players coming up, and those players looked up to him. But he was the star, the best player by far, and everyone appreciated that."

That season, he struck up an incredible partnership with the-then Manchester City loanee Jason Denayer, now captain of Lyon. Both were similar players, technically gifted and capable in possession, yet also resolute 18-yard-box stoppers. They were complete defenders, in other words, even from an early age (Van Dijk the elder at 23, Denayer only 19) and Celtic only conceded 17 league goals all season.

So was Van Dijk a good tutor for his fellow defender? "I think Jason was actually teaching Virgil how to defend!" says Deila. "Denayer was fantastic. He was unbelievable at the basics of defending. The two of them were quite close in training. Van

Dijk was much more of a leader, so calm on the ball and could control the game, but those two together were incredible."

They also scored 15 goals between them in 2014-15 and Van Dijk even turned provider for the Belgian teenager against Dundee United in March 2015.

There were highs during the campaign, not least John Guidetti's last-minute equaliser in a 3-3 classic against Inter Milan at Celtic Park but, arguably, the season's most exciting evolution was the development of this centre-back partnership destined for bigger and better things. Their fleeting brilliance together has become almost mythical over time, given neither of them were present in green and white for 2015-16, a harsh reality check that contributed towards the regression of Deila's Celtic.

Just as it was at Groningen and would be at Southampton, two years was enough for Van Dijk at Celtic, but he's only remembered fondly by Deila. "I think he was fantastic after Christmas that season. He was the biggest talent I've ever managed. So quick, calm, strong, good in the air, good on the ball. He was a bit sloppy at times and needed to focus his mentality on and off the pitch, but he improved that a lot in the last six months. We knew he was never going to stay in Scotland."

Kieran Devlin

Southampton – 'The wounds are still raw'

Talk to enough Southampton fans and they will make it clear Van Dijk was one of the best defenders in the world *before* he left for Liverpool. Talk to the same Southampton fans for long enough and they will make it clear they don't particularly want to talk about his time at their club.

The Dutchman spent three years on the south coast, sharpening his reading of the game and ironing out the occasional overconfident lapses in concentration that raised eyebrows when he was at Celtic.

He was one of the greatest players to wear Southampton colours, loved by the fans. He was their man. Then, very suddenly, he wasn't. And, after a few loveless months, he left.

The 2015-16 season was Southampton's modern zenith as they finished sixth, their highest top-flight position since they were First Division runners-up in 1983-84. While the main story of that campaign will always be Leicester City winning the 5,000-1 title and Tottenham Hotspur finishing third in a two-horse race, a closer peek at the table will show Southampton finished only three points off the Champions League places.

It was Southampton at their apex: multi-faceted, multi-talented and boasting a few faces that would shape the Premier League, and indeed European football for the second half of the decade.

Jose Fonte and Van Dijk partnered each other in central defence; Sadio Mane provided the X factor from the wing; Dusan Tadic – Van Dijk's old Groningen team-mate – toyed with possession in midfield and Ronald Koeman surveyed from the dugout. And come season's end, a then 24-year-old Van Dijk won player of the season awards from both the fans and his team-mates. Watching the Dutchman collecting both awards, you see a young man slowly realising his burgeoning abilities.

"I think the first day I came here I felt very welcome, straightaway," Van Dijk said upon receiving the players' player of the season gong. "I knew a lot of people around the club, a lot of players who I play with already and who I have played against. All the lads in the group. It's been amazing and you know the team is perfect."

He is not quite the cool operator we now know today, but there are glimpses of an emerging leader. His interviewer Ed

Chamberlin asks him about signing a six-year deal after his debut campaign for Southampton. He stresses every word: Six. Year. Deal – as a smile appears on Van Dijk's face and the audience cheers. It would be a contract extension that is now viewed with derision.

As he receives his second award, fans chant his name and Van Dijk stands there with a nervous smile. Then he turns to Fonte, who is sat in the crowd.

"He's a great guy," says Van Dijk. "A lot of qualities. Great captain. Good role model for everyone at the club and… yeah, he's a good player, that's the most important thing." Cue laughter from the audience and the Portuguese defender.

Nearly four years later, Van Dijk still makes Fonte smile. "When he arrived I could see… everyone could see immediately that physically he was a force of nature," Fonte tells *The Athletic*.

"We all can see his pace, his power, his strength. It was very easy to see that he is just a different class, a different kind of defender. He won every duel, he won every header; he was good on the ball as well, so we could immediately see the potential and the quality. When we started playing together, we developed a good partnership and you can see that today, he's the best defender in the world. But I could see it back then, that he could achieve that.

"He wasn't as polished as he is today, but after two months, three months, he was a different player than when he arrived. We started to talk about our partnership, what we should be doing and how we should be playing, and very quickly we got a good understanding between the two of us."

Fonte and Van Dijk formed the bedrock of Southampton's 2015-16 season, making 37 and 34 league appearances respectively. Southampton went unbeaten for almost two months at the start of 2016, keeping six clean sheets on the spin and not conceding for 667 minutes.

"We were the two guys that spoke the most during the games: to our full-backs, the midfield, to everyone," says Fonte. He was one of the leaders that was very good at communicating – especially on the left side of defence with (Ryan) Bertrand at the time. It's no surprise that we had such a good defensive record back then."

For Fonte, communication between a back line and midfield pivots is vital to proper defending. A relay of information to one player to adjust their on-field position by five yards can save the entire defence from having to retreat 35 yards when a ball goes over the top.

The one key adjustment Fonte recalls his new partner requiring was to temper the marauding runs he had developed in Scotland. "It was more about trying to keep him calm," says Fonte. "He used to dribble a lot throughout the defence, he used to try to go forward a lot. It was more about trying to keep it simple, stay at the back so we don't concede goals. Once he started doing that, I think he took a big, big step up."

Van Dijk's first season was a triumph. He became a Southampton fan favourite and, after signing that six-year contract, looked set to become the lynchpin of the side as they attempted to establish themselves as a Europa League-competing team for the rest of the decade.

While the Koeman factor helped to convince Van Dijk to choose Southampton from a number of suitors, Claude Puel claims to have also played a part in his development in the 2016-17 season, after succeeding the Dutch manager following his departure to Everton in the summer of 2016.

"When I came in at Southampton, he was, of course, a good player but he was in his comfort [zone]. He liked to defend deep on the pitch without covering his full-back and was taking some risks to dribble," said the French manager in January 2019, as the then-Leicester manager.

"At the beginning, it was a little difficult to discuss with him and to change and evaluate. I think, step by step, he took the intensity and feeling to defend with sometimes 50 metres behind him. Or to defend one-against-one without risk. I think it was important to make good cover and to move from the box and not just to remain in place."

Van Dijk was indeed impressive during the time he played in the 16-17 season, a commanding performance in a 2-1 home victory over Inter Milan in the Europa League that November being a particular bright spot.

However, on January 22, 2017, everything changed. Southampton were 2-0 up and cruising in a Sunday match against Leicester. Van Dijk had been named captain following Fonte's move to West Ham five days earlier. Early in the second half, he cleared a low cross aimed at Jamie Vardy, but collapsed in a heap after the striker connected with his ankle. He would be out for the rest of the season.

Southampton fans rue that collision. Firstly, because it meant the Dutchman missed the League Cup final against Manchester United a few weeks later. If they had Van Dijk to defend against United's match-winner Zlatan Ibrahimovic, maybe things would have turned out differently. Secondly, they know that, at some point during Van Dijk's recovery, the Dutchman had his head turned by Liverpool.

Every now and again, a football player and their fanbase will enter into an unspoken agreement: The Plus One Season. Football fans are wise to market forces and the power structures of European football. They understand that, save for a few European superclubs, any talented player can and will eventually be sold on. The Plus One Season is a sort of secret agreement between the two parties. A player is quite clear in their intention to leave, but stays for one more season, to leave the club in a strong position. Eden Hazard was exemplary during his last campaign for Chelsea, helping the club secure Champions League football and winning the Europa League. Luis Suarez scored 31 league goals in 2013-14, and almost led Liverpool to an elusive Premier League title before departing for Barcelona. Cristiano Ronaldo had a 26-goal title-winning Plus One Season at Manchester United in 2008-09. Thierry Henry's at Arsenal in 2006-07 was unfortunately marred by injury. Paul Pogba could be serving his at Manchester United as you read this.

Many Southampton fans believe Van Dijk didn't fulfil his Plus One Season on the south coast. The Dutchman stayed put in the summer of 2017 as Liverpool publicly apologised for their approach and temporarily cooled their interest, and so it was hoped Southampton could get one more season out of Van Dijk, where they could stabilise under another new manager, Mauricio Pellegrino. Unfortunately, Van Dijk made only 12 appearances in 2017-18, and was criticised among the support for a perceived dip in the level and intensity of his performance. There was a cloud over the club, but chairman Ralph Krueger believed in his vision and insisted they could climb back up the table. Unfortunately, that long-term plan has now gone awry.

This is part of the reason that makes questions about Van Dijk difficult to ask around Southampton. Speak to those at St Mary's and the Staplewood training ground about his influence and you get a sense fans and those associated with the club would rather not talk about a glorious season-and-a-half that quickly turned sour. To some fans, not only had Liverpool turned the head of their best player and robbed them of a final season that would have allowed them to rebuild, they then dominated the narrative: the story became one where Van Dijk only became a world-beater *after* making the journey up the M6. Worse still, in many ways, his departure meant the end of Southampton as a leading force in the second tier of the Premier League.

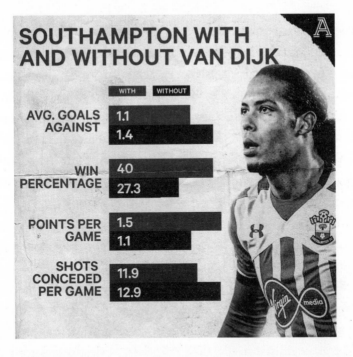

SOUTHAMPTON WITH AND WITHOUT VAN DIJK

	WITH	WITHOUT
AVG. GOALS AGAINST	1.1	1.4
WIN PERCENTAGE	40	27.3
POINTS PER GAME	1.5	1.1
SHOTS CONCEDED PER GAME	11.9	12.9

As John Bailey from the Saints FC Podcast put it: "Virgil van Dijk is a story of what might have been for Saints. We were on the cusp of greatness and we were bullied by the big boys and now sit with our more familiar peer group in the relegation zone. That's why no-one wants to talk. The wounds are still raw. He's moved on to bigger things and we have not. Talking about him is taking the big step and going to counselling because you have a skeleton in your closet that you haven't dealt with yet. It still hurts."

Carl Anka

Liverpool – 'A massive fee but there's no superstar status'

Van Dijk isn't perfect. Just ask anyone present in the picturesque setting of Evian's Hotel Royal, overlooking Lake Geneva, in late July 2018.

It was the Liverpool defender's first pre-season with the club and keeping with tradition, he had to deliver his initiation song along with Jurgen Klopp's other new arrivals during the karaoke night on their summer training camp. Van Dijk stepped up and delivered a 'unique' version of the R&B hit *So Into You* by Canadian singer Tamia in front of team-mates and staff.

"There was a lot of laughter from the boys and then some sympathetic applause," revealed one staff member to *The Athletic*. "It was definitely a case of 'don't give up the day job'."

Van Dijk's thunder was stolen that night by goalkeeper Alisson's rendition of *Don't Look Back In Anger* by Oasis, which sparked a rapturous ovation.

Fellow Liverpool centre-back Dejan Lovren found another chink in the Dutchman's armour when it came to shooting hoops after training at Melwood.

"Virgil is calm on the field but he's not calm when I beat him in basketball. I am the champion," smiled the Croatia international.

Yet when it comes to doing what Liverpool actually bought him for, Van Dijk simply has no peers. He hasn't just lived up to sky-high expectations since his £75 million move to Anfield from Southampton in January 2018 – he's surpassed them. After Klopp made Van Dijk the most expensive defender in world football, the manager declared: "The first thing all Liverpool supporters should do is forget the price." At the time, it seemed like wishful thinking, but within a matter of weeks, the centre-back's astonishing impact had well and truly silenced any debate over his transfer fee.

It helped that both Liverpool and Van Dijk were absolutely convinced from the off that they were the perfect fit for each other. Van Dijk had made his decision in June 2017. He had told those close to him that his heart was set on Anfield – despite the fact he was also being pursued by both Manchester City and Chelsea.

Klopp's charm offensive had paid off. He had left Van Dijk in no doubt about his admiration for his defensive qualities and his burning desire to work with him, describing him as "a game-changer" in helping Liverpool make the leap from contenders to trophy winners.

Captain Jordan Henderson also played his part. They share an agent in Neil Fewings and Henderson gave Van Dijk the lowdown on working with Klopp, the dynamic of the dressing room, and why he felt Merseyside would be the best place for his development.

The passion of the club's fans was another factor. Van Dijk attended the 2017 Champions League final in Cardiff between Juventus and Real Madrid and during his time in the Welsh capital, he was besieged by Liverpool supporters urging him to head for Anfield.

However, Liverpool's joy initially proved to be short-lived. Reports that Klopp had met Van Dijk in Blackpool to sell him his vision for the future and that he had been offered a contract worth £180,000 per week infuriated Southampton. At that time, Liverpool had yet to officially open negotiations over the fee. Southampton complained to the Premier League and accused Liverpool of making an illegal approach. After a series of emergency meetings, Fenway Sports Group president Mike Gordon felt the club had no option but to climb down and issue an embarrassing public apology. A club statement included the line: "We have ended any interest in the player."

The reality was very different. Despite the clamour from a section of the fanbase to move on and pursue a Plan B, Klopp had no intention of lowering his sights. Liverpool had tracked in excess of 30 centre-backs from across Europe over an 18-month period and Van Dijk came out on top on all the metrics. Aymeric Laporte, Kalidou Koulibaly and Jerome Boateng also made the shortlist but Van Dijk was viewed in a class of his own.

FSG's stance was that Liverpool could only be seen to be back in the market for Van Dijk if Southampton were actively considering bids for his services. That wasn't the case towards the end of the summer window in 2017 as the south coast outfit dug their heels in – despite Van Dijk issuing a transfer request. Klopp, sporting director Michael Edwards and Gordon all decided to sit tight until the January window, when they felt that tensions would ease and completing a deal would be much more straightforward. They were safe in the knowledge that Van Dijk's desire to head for Anfield was unwavering.

Gordon worked behind the scenes over the months that followed, helping to repair relations with Southampton's chairman, Krueger. With Van Dijk still unsettled and Southampton in a relegation scrap, the St Mary's hierarchy relented and a price of £75 million was set in late December. Edwards and Gordon had no concerns about meeting it. They were convinced that he would transform a porous back line that had lacked a true leader since Jamie Carragher's retirement in 2013. Klopp shared their belief in the Dutchman's ability but sought reassurances from the Anfield hierarchy that the club wouldn't be overstretching themselves by sanctioning the deal. Liverpool's transfer record was duly shattered.

After undergoing a medical with club doctor Andy Massey in Bournemouth, Van Dijk headed north and watched Liverpool's 2-1 win over Leicester City at Anfield on December 30, 2017, from the directors' box. There was a warm greeting from Kop icon Kenny Dalglish, who gave him his mobile number and told him: "Call me anytime."

Van Dijk was officially registered as a Liverpool player on January 2, 2018. Three days later, there was the small matter of an FA Cup third-round tie with Everton at Anfield. Van Dijk wasn't due to start that night. After such a whirlwind few days, Klopp had planned to put him on the bench. However, the manager changed his mind on the morning of the all-Merseyside clash after deciding that Lovren and Ragnar Klavan both needed a breather after a demanding festive period. "Are you ready?" Klopp asked Van Dijk. The response was instant: "Of course."

Van Dijk was thrown in at the deep end and he oozed class on his debut alongside Joel Matip. Six minutes from time, with the tie deadlocked at 1-1, Alex Oxlade-Chamberlain swung a corner into the penalty box and Van Dijk soared in front of the Kop to nod the winner past Jordan Pickford.

"A fairytale in a world with not a lot of fairytales anymore," beamed Klopp in his post-match press conference.

Off to a flyer on the pitch, what helped Van Dijk off it was the fact that the squad flew straight to Dubai after the game on a bonding trip sanctioned by the manager.

Van Dijk confirms: "Dubai was the perfect kind of trip for me so soon after joining. I'd never experienced coming to a club mid-season before, but we had a good laugh and it clicked immediately."

Liverpool's new No 4 kicked on. Commanding in the air, strong in the tackle, ice-cool with the ball at his feet and with an excellent range of passing, he added composure, organisation and leadership to Klopp's back line. He provided the perfect injection of both silk and steel.

What impact did he have on the team's style?

"We can play a higher line with Virgil," says assistant boss Pep Lijnders. "We can play more aggressive with him because of how he deals with space and longer balls into our back line. The centre-backs lead. They organise protection and the base for good pressing is the positioning of the last line – they are responsible for this."

What was an area of glaring weakness for the club soon became one of huge strength. Van Dijk's presence improved those around him, including Lovren. Their partnership helped

Liverpool excel as they swept Manchester City and Roma aside to reach the Champions League final.

"Virgil brought stability and leadership to the defence and that was desperately needed," says goalkeeper Simon Mignolet, who moved on to Club Brugge last summer. "I don't remember him losing a challenge in the air. He dealt with so many balls into the box before they became dangerous. He really helped to settle the team and ensured that we didn't get flustered."

A top-four Premier League finish was wrapped up with a final-day rout of Brighton, before the agony of Kyiv, when Loris Karius' meltdown gifted the trophy to Real Madrid.

Van Dijk went to the next level after the arrival of Alisson from Roma for £65 million in the summer of 2018. Suddenly, he had a world-class performer operating behind him with a similar swagger and his level of consistency was remarkable. In the first half of the campaign, his partnership with Joe Gomez was rock-solid. Liverpool conceded just seven goals in their opening 19 league matches.

Gomez describes Van Dijk, who is six years older than him, as "like my big brother". "He's been unbelievable," he says. "He came for a massive fee but there's no superstar status to him. He's grateful for what he has. He's come from humble beginnings and he's had to work for everything he's got. I'm lucky to have someone like him around to learn from."

Van Dijk's mental toughness is underlined by the fact he hasn't missed a Premier League game for Liverpool since January 2018. He should have done.

In September 2018, he was forced off against his former club Southampton after taking a painful blow to the ribs – four days after damaging them in the Champions League win over Paris Saint-Germain. Van Dijk was a major doubt for the subsequent trip to Chelsea, having sat out training at Melwood all week, but he dosed up on painkillers and declared himself fit for duty.

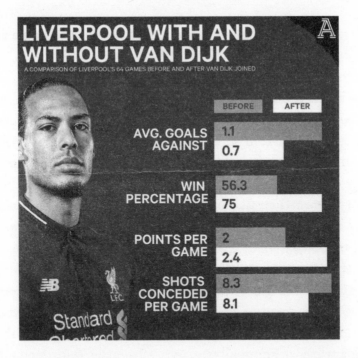

LIVERPOOL WITH AND WITHOUT VAN DIJK

A COMPARISON OF LIVERPOOL'S 64 GAMES BEFORE AND AFTER VAN DIJK JOINED

	BEFORE	AFTER
AVG. GOALS AGAINST	1.1	0.7
WIN PERCENTAGE	56.3	75
POINTS PER GAME	2	2.4
SHOTS CONCEDED PER GAME	8.3	8.1

Klopp described the injury as "bruising" but Holland boss Ronald Koeman later revealed that Van Dijk had been playing with two cracked ribs. "You never really play completely pain-free," Van Dijk says. "You are always going to have something – you are never going to be 100 per cent totally fit throughout the season. It was about managing it and giving everything for the team and for the fans."

With Henderson and vice-captain James Milner both sidelined by injury the following month, Klopp needed a new skipper for the visit of Red Star Belgrade. He held a vote among the squad and unsurprisingly, Van Dijk won it by a landslide, with Wijnaldum in second place. Many outside the club expected Van Dijk to take the armband from Henderson on a permanent basis but that theory overlooked two things. Firstly, how highly Klopp rates the role played by Henderson in keeping a happy, unified dressing room and secondly, the fact Van Dijk doesn't need the captaincy to have a big influence on those around him.

He's not shy to dish out a bollocking on the field when he feels one is required. Both of Liverpool's rampaging full-backs have been on the receiving end at times.

"Virgil is vocal but he's also a lovely person off the pitch," says left-back Andy Robertson. "What he brings on and off the pitch is special. It makes it so much easier when you have someone running at you and you know Virgil is alongside you. He is very rarely out of position and is the best centre-back in the world."

Right-back Trent Alexander-Arnold adds: "He has dominated every attacker I've seen him come up against. It's so rare to see someone operating at that kind of level every single week and it motivates us all as players. You know within yourself that the attacker has got no chance against him. You can see that attackers are scared to go on his side. It means that strikers tend to pull out on to my side more than the left! It just goes to show what a presence he's got."

There was one notable occasion in 2018-19 when Van Dijk endured the wrath of Klopp. It was half-time in the Allianz Arena with Liverpool's Champions League last-16 tie with Bayern Munich in the balance at 1-1 on aggregate. Van Dijk had produced arguably the pass of the season to create the opening goal as he pinged the ball 50 yards into the feet of Mane, who turned and finished brilliantly. However, Klopp was fuming about the manner of Bayern's equaliser shortly before the break. Serge Gnabry had got in behind Robertson and the boss felt that Van Dijk could have done more to cut out the cross which was turned into his own net by Matip. "Normally, I'm there to protect him, but I didn't," Van Dijk says. "The manager came in and shouted at me. He always tells you the truth. That's something I really appreciate."

It was a rare blip. For the most part, Klopp has simply watched in admiration. Some strikers have tried to out-pace him, others have tried to bully him, but both approaches have failed.

Van Dijk helped Liverpool boast the best defensive record in the Premier League in 2018-19 – keeping 21 clean sheets from 38 games and conceding just 22 goals. On the European stage, he locked horns with the finest attackers in world football: Kylian Mbappe, Neymar, Robert Lewandowski, Luis Suarez and Lionel Messi all struggled to get much change out of him.

"Great players make the job look easy and Virgil is one of them," says legendary Liverpool keeper Ray Clemence. "He's always in control and he's such a quick thinker. He sorts out in his brain how to put attacking players in disadvantageous positions.

"I think about Tottenham at home in March when they had the two-v-one breakaway and (Moussa) Sissoko was through. Van Dijk had it sussed out. He knew that Sissoko wanted to make the pass to Son (Heung-min) rather than take the shot on himself. He knew that Son would probably score if he got the ball, so he blocked that path, Sissoko had to shoot and he skied it."

Van Dijk thwarted the same opposition again with a man-of-the-match display in the Champions League final in Madrid. When Son threatened to restore parity in the second half, he cruised effortlessly across the turf to take the ball from him and restore calm.

That afternoon, Van Dijk had lay on his bed in the Eurostars Hotel watching videos on social media from the fanpark in the Spanish capital's Plaza Mayor where 50,000 travelling Liverpool fans joined Liverpool musician Jamie Webster to sing the centre-back's song, which goes to the tune of the Dubliners' classic *Dirty Old Town*. Usually, he has a pre-match nap but he couldn't sleep. The adrenaline was pumping.

When Divock Origi rammed home the late goal that sealed Liverpool's sixth European Cup, Van Dijk dropped to the turf with his hands covering his face. He was exhausted and overwhelmed by emotion. Long after the stadium had emptied, he was still out on the field, his medal around his neck as he rolled around in the confetti with his wife Rike and their two young daughters. By then, he was already the PFA Player of the Year – the first defender to be given the trophy since John Terry in 2005.

More accolades soon followed. He saw off competition from Cristiano Ronaldo and Messi to be crowned UEFA Men's Player of the Year. He finished second to Messi in the battle for the Best FIFA award. When Van Dijk lifted the UEFA prize, Klopp told his team-mates that he did so on behalf of them all. Van Dijk nodded his head in agreement. "At Liverpool, we're all part of one unit," he said.

When he's showered with plaudits, Van Dijk is always quick to turn the conversation to others. He was full of praise for the contribution of Matip in the early months of this season as Liverpool flew out of the blocks in pursuit of a first top-flight title in 30 years. With Matip hampered by a knee injury, momentum has been maintained with Lovren enjoying a revival alongside the Holland skipper.

Van Dijk is also so widely loved because of the contribution he's made off the field. He gives back to the community which welcomed him with open arms. Chris Geldard put out an appeal on Twitter for birthday messages from Liverpool stars for his son Oliver, who was in hospital for spinal traction treatment. Van Dijk went a step further by sending him a signed kit and boots. There are many similar tales.

Van Dijk read about the work of the Owen McVeigh Foundation, which was set up by Mark and Joanne McVeigh in memory of their son, who passed away at the age of 11 in 2015 following a short battle with leukaemia. The foundation was established to enrich the lives of children suffering from cancer and to provide help for their families. Van Dijk got in contact with them to say he and Rike wanted to get involved. They planned and paid for a Christmas party for 120 kids, who received presents from Father Christmas and a trip to the pantomime. "Virgil didn't want any media there. He just wanted to help put smiles on faces," says Mark McVeigh. Van Dijk has also given the foundation use of his hospitality box at Anfield.

He's a talismanic figure – both on and off the field. He's Klopp's colossus.

NOVEMBER RESULTS

Premier League, November 2 2019
Aston Villa 1 Liverpool 2
Liverpool scorers: Robertson 87, Mane 90+4

Champions League, November 5 2019
Liverpool 2 KRC Genk 0
Liverpool scorers: Wijnaldum 14, Oxlade-Chamberlain 53

Premier League, November 10 2019
Liverpool 3 Man City 1
Liverpool scorers: Fabinho 6, Salah 13, Mane 51

Premier League, November 23 2019
Crystal Palace 1 Liverpool 2
Liverpool scorers: Mane 49, Firmino 85

Champions League, November 27 2019
Liverpool 1 Napoli 1
Liverpool scorer: Lovren 65

Premier League, November 30 2019
Liverpool 2 Brighton 1
Liverpool scorer: Van Dijk 18, 24

DECEMBER

"IT'S ALL ABOUT SURPRISING THE OPPOSITION" – SECOND STRING'S WIN OVER EVERTON STEMS FROM MELWOOD ATMOSPHERE

JAMES PEARCE

DEC 5, 2019

Not bad for a B team.

Jurgen Klopp gambled and hit the jackpot on another record-breaking night at Anfield. This will be remembered as the demolition derby after title-chasing Liverpool stunned their struggling neighbours.

What a way to register the longest unbeaten top-flight run in the club's 127-year history. It now stands at 32 matches dating back to January after Liverpool stuck five past Everton for the first time since 1982.

For Klopp, there was the honour of accumulating 100 league wins faster than any of his illustrious predecessors at Anfield. He has reached that milestone in 159 matches – eight fewer games than Kenny Dalglish, who previously held that accolade.

Liverpool's stranglehold on English football's most-played derby now stands at 20 meetings. Everton's pursuit of an elusive victory across Stanley Park will enter a third decade. The gap between the clubs is now a chasm – 29 points after just 15 matches. Yet this triumph for the Premier League leaders was worth so much more than simply re-establishing their eight-point lead at the summit and heaping more misery on Everton. It was a night which set the perfect tone for a potentially season-defining December – the first of nine matches across four different competitions in the space of 25 days.

Klopp put his faith in the depth of the squad he has assembled at Anfield and his trust in those who have been on the fringes to deliver was handsomely repaid. Liverpool were without six of their starting line-up from June's Champions League final triumph over Tottenham in Madrid. With Alisson banned and Joel Matip and Fabinho both injured, Klopp opted to rest Jordan Henderson, Mohamed Salah and Roberto Firmino.

If it had backfired, Klopp would have stood accused of being reckless and jeopardising the club's pursuit of glory with his tinkering. Instead, he looked like a genius after Divock Origi and Xherdan Shaqiri emerged from the shadows to help the sensational Sadio Mane light up Anfield.

A year after grabbing a dramatic 96th-minute derby winner, Origi extended his impressive record against Everton with a classy double. Shaqiri, who hadn't started for Liverpool since the Champions League semi-final second-leg miracle against Barcelona in May, was equally influential.

"We have to use the squad, especially at this time of year," left-back Andy Robertson told *The Athletic*. "We've got such a good squad that we all believe that whoever comes in will do a great job for us. The boys who came into the team were magnificent. They really stepped up to the plate. It pushes everyone on when players come into the team and perform like that.

"It was a big performance. I'm sure there will be more rotation over the coming games – there has to be with the number of games we've got. [The performance] showed how deep the squad really is."

Klopp sprung a surprise by making five changes and switching to 4-2-3-1. Adam Lallana performed admirably after being handed only his second Premier League start since March. Evergreen stand-in skipper James Milner led by example with his combative edge. However, it was the manager's decision to shake up Liverpool's established front three which truly injected some much-needed dynamism and energy to their attack. Salah and Firmino, who both dropped to the bench, have been some way short of their blistering best so far this season and the stats prove it. Having scored a Premier League goal every 91 minutes in 2017-18, that figure for Salah climbed to 148 last season and 169 so far in 2019-20. He produced a goal or assist every 70 minutes in 2017-18 but that was 109 minutes in 2018-19 and 113 so far this campaign. It was 47 minutes per chance created in 2017-18, edging up to 48 minutes in 2018-19 and 56 in 2019-20.

As for Firmino, he scored a league goal every 185 minutes in 2017-18 but that figure climbed to 218 minutes in 2018-19 and 296 minutes so far this season. He provided either a goal or an assist every 126 minutes in 2017-18, every 145 minutes in 2018-19 and every 148 minutes so far in 2019-20. In terms of chances created, it was every 49 minutes for the Brazilian frontman in 2017-18, every 61 minutes in 2018-19 and every 66 minutes so far in 2019-20.

Fatigue has undoubtedly played a part. Having both played at the World Cup in 2018 and then either the Africa Cup of Nations or the Copa America last summer, neither has had a proper break for two and a half years.

Salah has also been carrying an ankle injury since early October, when he was hacked down by Leicester City's Hamza Choudhury, and has been on a specially-adapted training programme. Yet the fact he only has six Premier League goals to his name, two of which were penalties, has to be cause for concern. Having missed only two league games across his opening two seasons at Liverpool, the Egyptian has already sat out three this time around and has been subbed off in seven of his 12 league outings.

Two years after scoring the majestic goal against Everton which earned him FIFA's Puskas Award, Salah remained rooted to the bench throughout. It will be intriguing to see if Salah and Firmino are recalled for Saturday's trip to Bournemouth. Origi and Shaqiri have certainly given Klopp food for thought.

How Everton must be sick of the sight of Origi. Since Ramiro Funes Mori was sent off for an X-rated challenge on the Belgian striker in this fixture in April 2016, which inflicted serious ankle ligament damage and derailed his career, Origi has been making them pay. He now boasts five goals in six outings against them.

The former Lille frontman tormented Marco Silva's fragile back line. He held the ball up expertly and darted in behind intelligently. The 24-year-old opened the scoring by tucking away Mane's pinpoint pass and then, his second, from Dejan Lovren's lofted through ball, almost raised the roof. His first touch was impeccable and Origi's lifted finish over Jordan Pickford was even better. His name was chanted vociferously and there was a standing ovation when he was replaced by Firmino late on.

"Div was brilliant and he gave us a different dimension," Robertson says. "We know what Bobby gives us – he's world class. But sometimes even Bobby needs a rest, especially with the amount of work he gets through. The manager looked at it, decided to give Div a shot, and he gave us something a wee bit different. Maybe we caught Everton off guard as maybe they prepared for Bobby dropping into the No 10 position. Div gave us that option in behind and I don't think they knew how to deal with that. It's all about surprising the opposition and I think we did that. The composure he showed for both goals was outstanding. He's a big-game player."

Shaqiri's contribution was all the more eye-catching considering that he had played just 11 minutes of Premier League football so far this season due to a troublesome calf injury. The Swiss attacker, who has been back in full training for a fortnight, had no right to look so sharp and menacing but he caused Everton a stack of problems with his creative spark and bag of tricks on the right flank.

In firing home Liverpool's second goal, Shaqiri scored in the top flight for the first time since last December. What a huge asset he will prove to be for Klopp if he stays fit over the coming weeks and months.

"We train at a high intensity and that was why Shaq was up to the level he needed to be," Robertson explains. "For Shaq to last 90 minutes after such a frustrating start to the season was amazing. He's got so much quality and it was a big step forward.

"It all comes from the environment the manager has built. Credit to all the staff as well for helping to create that atmosphere. Melwood is a great place to work just now. Everyone loves coming in every single day. That's the kind of environment the manager has created. That's why it was so easy for the likes of me, Virgil (van Dijk) and Mo to step into it.

"We all love coming into work. Sometimes, you see Melwood more than you see your own house with the way the schedule is, but it feels like a home from home."

While Salah and Firmino had their feet up, it was no surprise that Klopp unleashed Mane from the off once again. The Senegal international is in the form of his life. Ballon d'Or winner Lionel Messi was on to something when he cast his vote for Mane to win FIFA's World Player of the Year.

Like Salah and Firmino, Mane has also had a relentless schedule since the summer of 2017 but somehow, he appears to be getting stronger. Recently asked about the demands being placed on him, he replied: "Tiredness is all in the head."

Having contributed a goal every 221 minutes in 2017-18, that was reduced to 140 in 2018-19 and 137 so far this season. In terms of chipping in with either a goal or an assist, it was

130 minutes in 2017-18, 134 minutes in 2018-19 and just 95 minutes so far this season. He created a chance every 45 minutes in 2017-18, every 69 minutes in 2018-19 and that is down to every 41 minutes in 2019-20.

Mane's battle with Everton wing-back Djibril Sidibe was such a mismatch that the blundering Monaco loanee was hauled off inside 35 minutes. Having created goals for Origi and Shaqiri with inch-perfect passes, Mane scored Liverpool's fourth himself with a clinical finish from the edge of the box. Trent Alexander-Arnold had led a devastating breakaway to provide his 18th assist since the start of last season, more than any other Premier League player.

If there was a blot on the night it was the fact that Liverpool's wait for a first clean sheet since September continues. At 2-0 and then 4-1, Michael Keane and Richarlison punished some hesitant defending. But when Klopp's men attack with this kind of flair and intensity, the occasional slip at the other end isn't going to cost them points. If Mane hadn't squandered two clear chances in the second half, Liverpool would have been well and truly out of sight before Georginio Wijnaldum bagged their fifth late on, after being teed up by the substitute Firmino.

By then, it was party time. The jubilant Kop goaded their neighbours with chants of "going down" before breaking into a booming rendition of "Liverpool, top of the league".

Their relentless march continues. How does it feel to put together the longest unbeaten league run in the club's history?

"It's amazing, especially when you consider all the great teams this club has had over the years," beamed Robertson. "We're trying to make our own history at a club with a huge history. But I'd rather the 32 games without defeat were all in the same season because then, we'd undoubtedly be champions!

"It's all about trophies rather than records for us but this is another step in the right direction."

It was an ominous sign for their rivals.

"ALL YOU NEED IS... ALISSON BECKER" – THE VIDEO ANALYSIS BEHIND SAVE THAT PROVED LIVERPOOL'S KEEPER IS BACK TO HIS BEST

JAMES PEARCE

DEC 19, 2019

They headed in the direction of the touchline arm in arm. No wonder Jurgen Klopp saved the warmest embrace for his goalkeeper after Liverpool unconvincingly booked themselves a showdown with Flamengo in Saturday's Club World Cup final. On a difficult night for the depleted European champions in Qatar's Khalifa International Stadium, Klopp's £65 million goalkeeper stood tall.

"All you need is Alisson Becker," beamed Klopp, who regularly sings that song about his goalkeeper to the tune of Queen's *Radio Ga Ga*. "He was there in the decisive moments."

Roberto Firmino, on as a substitute, rescued Liverpool with a classy close-range finish from Trent Alexander-Arnold's low cross in stoppage time to finally see off Monterrey. However, it was Alisson's agility, reflexes and commanding presence behind a makeshift back line that helped avert what would have been an embarrassing defeat against Mexico's combative Central and North America champions.

Goalkeeping coach John Achterberg was waiting to greet the

smiling 27-year-old as he strolled off the pitch. The conversation between them that followed would be best summed up by the phrase 'I love it when a plan comes together'.

Achterberg had tailored Alisson's training sessions since Liverpool arrived in Qatar on Sunday after studying hours of footage of Monterrey in action. They had analysed closely the free-kicks of the dangerous Dorlan Pabon, which made the flying save to claw the captain's curling effort to safety early in the second half all the sweeter.

Alisson was well-prepared. He knew Monterrey would unleash shots from distance whenever they got the chance and that he would have to be alert to deal with balls in behind the back four for lone frontman Rogelio Funes Mori to chase. He knew exactly what was coming. There was no element of surprise and that attention to detail paid off.

Liverpool have had an array of heroes en route to establishing a 10-point lead at the top of the Premier League table and reaching the last 16 of the Champions League.

With Klopp's men dominant, Alisson has been a spectator for long periods since he returned to action in late October after 10 weeks on the sidelines with a torn calf muscle. But over the past week, when Liverpool have truly needed him, he has showcased why he's the best goalkeeper on the planet.

Without his brilliance, Liverpool could easily have tumbled out of the Champions League in their all-or-nothing showdown in Salzburg. There was that smart double save early on from Hwang Hee-chan and Takumi Minamino, who Alisson will have as a team-mate from January 1.

When the nerves were jangling at home against rock-bottom Watford last weekend, Alisson ensured that a narrow lead was protected before Mohamed Salah wrapped up the points. Similarly, without the keeper's faultless display against Monterrey, Klopp could have been facing the nightmare scenario of hanging around in Qatar to prepare for a meaningless third-place play-off against Al Hilal on Saturday.

The debate over the merits of the Club World Cup will rumble on and this was hardly an occasion to savour with the atmosphere as flat as Liverpool's disjointed performance. However, losing on Wednesday would have unleashed an unwelcome torrent of negativity, especially after fielding what was essentially a youth team in the 5-0 defeat by Aston Villa in the Carabao Cup less than 24 hours earlier.

What a year 2019 has been for Alisson, who was so instrumental in Liverpool winning the Champions League and Brazil the Copa America. On a personal level, he landed the Premier League Golden Glove with 21 clean sheets, before being crowned UEFA and FIFA Goalkeeper of the Year and collecting the Yashin Trophy for the best performing shot-stopper in the world.

Without Alisson's stunning last-gasp save to deny Napoli's Arkadiusz Milik at Anfield 12 months ago there would have been no magical night in Madrid, no Super Cup, no shot at this world title in Qatar.

Ray Clemence, arguably the finest goalkeeper Liverpool have ever had, has watched his progress with admiration. "Alisson has everything that a goalkeeper needs to have – size, presence, great reactions and a commanding manner," he told *The Athletic*. "He's also mentally strong and good with his feet. It gives everyone confidence having a keeper like that. He makes difficult things look easy. I played there for 20 years. I know what he does isn't easy, believe me, but great goalkeepers make it look that way.

"Great keepers make big saves in big moments whether it's at 0-0, 1-0 up or 1-0 down and Alisson does that. He could be Liverpool's No 1 for another 10 or 12 years and become a real legend at the club. He's as good as anything around and certainly the best we've had for many, many years."

The upgrade in class compared to predecessors Loris Karius and Simon Mignolet is vast. Alisson has certainly lived up to the billing from Roberto Negrisolo, his former coach at Roma, who described him as "a phenomenon… the Messi of goalkeepers… a goalkeeper who can define an era".

Achterberg knew exactly what Liverpool were getting, having tracked Alisson's development closely since being advised by former Anfield keeper Alexander Doni in 2013 to keep an eye on a gifted youngster who was coming up through the ranks at Internacional in Porto Alegre.

When negotiations with Roma initially proved problematic, Klopp refused to lower his sights to another target as he felt that the Brazil No 1 would be "a game-changer". It proved to be an astute assessment. Alisson was always likely to be busy against Monterrey after Virgil van Dijk was ruled out because of illness. With Dejan Lovren (hamstring) and Joel Matip (knee) both back on Merseyside undergoing treatment, Klopp was down to one fit senior centre-back in Joe Gomez.

The situation has been further compounded by injuries to Fabinho and Georginio Wijnaldum, who have both deputised in that department previously. Instead, it was left to captain Jordan Henderson to move back from midfield and fill the void in an unbalanced team that struggled to play with any kind of tempo or fluency.

Alisson was let down by some slack marking, which enabled Funes Mori to cancel out Naby Keita's opener after the goalkeeper had denied Jesus Gallardo. It was the first time he had conceded in nearly five hours of action and he couldn't hide his frustration. But he simply refused to be beaten again. His concentration levels and positional play were immense. Alisson's speed to narrow angles and his hulking presence has the effect of making the goal appear smaller when attackers are trying to pick their spot.

He punched the air in delight when Firmino sent Liverpool into Saturday's final. Once again, Klopp's men had wobbled before ultimately finding a way to win.

"What a match, it was incredible!" roared the stadium's over-enthusiastic MC. It wasn't. In truth, it had the feel of an exhibition game as fans entertained themselves with Mexican waves before Klopp's substitutes made the difference late on.

This competition has always mattered more to South Americans than the Europeans – underlined by the 15,000 passionate Flamengo fans who have descended on Qatar. Saturday will certainly be livelier and standing in the path of the Brazilian champions will be a familiar face – a countryman who's undeniably the best in the business.

Alisson is finishing 2019 the way he started it, operating at the peak of his powers, instilling calm in those around him and propelling Liverpool towards silverware.

"PARTYING? NO, I THINK A RECOVERY RUB WILL BE MY CELEBRATION." RELENTLESS LIVERPOOL ARE CHAMPIONS OF THE WORLD

JAMES PEARCE

DEC 22, 2019

As the Flamengo manager Jorge Jesus conducted his post-match press conference and spoke about his pride in defeat, you could hear the Liverpool dressing-room party in full swing. The noise grew louder and louder. There were booming renditions of *Allez Allez Allez* and *Campione*.

The usually reserved Pep Lijnders, Jurgen Klopp's trusted assistant, was right at the heart of the celebrations in Qatar's Khalifa International Stadium. After the lap of honour the Dutchman came bounding in with Andreas Kornmayer, the head of fitness and conditioning, with the trophy and his medal around his neck. The place erupted. Banging the table in the middle of the room, dancing and then throwing his arms in the air after passing the silverware to Mohamed Salah, Lijnders led the sing-song as players and staff embraced.

Try telling Liverpool that the Club World Cup doesn't matter. For a team which is making a habit of rewriting the Anfield record books, here was another slice of history. Jurgen Klopp triumphed where Bob Paisley, Joe Fagan and Rafael Benitez had fallen short, clinching the only major accolade to have previously eluded the club.

The champions wall in the foyer at Melwood, which illustrates the club's array of honours, will undergo a facelift for the third time in the space of seven months. No English team has ever previously won the Champions League, the Super Cup and the Club World Cup in the same calendar year. The Klopp juggernaut rolls on.

"It's special," Joe Gomez, who excelled alongside Virgil van Dijk, told *The Athletic*. "We knew coming here that we hadn't won it as a club before and that was something we wanted to achieve.

"You don't get here without winning one of the biggest trophies in the world. The consequence of that is you come here and play top teams. We played two good teams this week and you can't underestimate that. The atmosphere in that dressing room just shows you how positive this competition can be.

"It's another trophy and that's what we're here for. We're so hungry as a team. That's the crucial mindset we've got. We want to be relentless."

In comparison to Madrid in June, the post-match scenes were decidedly low-key. There were no tears of joy this time, no all-night party. The squad got back to the luxurious St Regis in Doha's West Bay at around 2am local time.

"It was food, a couple of drinks and then bed," one staff member told *The Athletic*. "Nothing crazy, nothing like the Champions League final. This is a busy period and the boys know there's still so much to achieve."

By midday Qatar time on Sunday the players were in the air and on their way back to Merseyside. Klopp has given them Monday off and they will report back on Tuesday to prepare for the Boxing Day clash at Leicester City. Liverpool's preparations for the trip to the King Power Stadium started in Doha, with head physio Lee Nobes and long-serving masseur Paul Small getting to work on weary limbs. On the seven-hour flight more treatment was given out, while the club's analysts pored over footage of Leicester's recent matches.

"Partying? No, I think a recovery rub will be my celebration," joked Gomez before he left the stadium on Saturday night. "It's not long before we're back at it."

Glory vindicated Klopp's decision to take his entire senior squad on a 6,000-mile round trip to the Middle East and field a youth team in the Carabao Cup defeat to Aston Villa. Forget the flak that came his way, this was the much greater prize – both financially and in terms of prestige. Victory was worth around £4 million in prize money but the commercial benefits of being crowned world champions will significantly inflate that figure.

For the next year Liverpool will proudly wear the gold FIFA world champions badge on their shirts, although bizarrely, as things stand, it's only allowed in Champions League rather than domestic matches.

The Premier League leaders return home with their position of strength in the title race only enhanced during their absence. Their 10-point lead remains intact after Leicester lost to Manchester City on Saturday and Klopp's men now have a game in hand over both those clubs. The only downside from Qatar was the sight of Alex Oxlade-Chamberlain leaving on crutches wearing a protective boot after damaging ankle ligaments. A scan will reveal the extent of the injury with Klopp admitting it had cast "a big shadow" over the occasion.

But what a week for Roberto Firmino. Having endured a barren run of just one goal in 16 appearances, the Brazilian frontman followed up his last-minute winner in the semi-final against Monterrey with the extra-time goal that broke the hearts of his fellow countrymen. Briefly, the fanatical 15,000-strong army from Rio de Janeiro was silenced. Firmino, who provided the cool finish to a sweeping move involving Sadio Mane and the outstanding Jordan Henderson, epitomises the selfless team ethic that Klopp has created.

Similarly, Salah will be energised by his Doha experience. The Egyptian picked up the Golden Ball for player of the tournament – and at least half of the 45,000-strong crowd appeared to be there to watch him alone.

Both FIFA and the hosts should be thankful for Liverpool's extraordinary fitness levels and their mental resilience in the face of adversity, because the fact that Klopp's men ultimately triumphed relegated the shambolic performance of referee Abdulrahman Al-Jassim to a mere footnote. The Qatari official was hopelessly out of his depth and made a succession of bewildering decisions – none more bizarre than in stoppage time at the end of the 90 minutes. He initially awarded Liverpool a penalty after Mane was brought down by Rafinha. Encouraged by the VAR to take a look at the pitchside monitor, he spent an age watching replays that showed the cynical offence took place just outside the box. It should have been a free-kick and a red card – even the giant screen in the stadium displayed the message 'free-kick outside the box' – but Al-Jassim instead decided the challenge was fair and gave the ball back to Flamengo. FIFA subsequently insisted that the message on the screen had been a mistake. Liverpool were rightly incensed, but to their credit they channelled that frustration in the right way. As Flamengo faded, Klopp's men grew stronger.

"I think that shows the mentality of the team," Gomez says. "Our heads could have dropped. We could have felt sorry for ourselves after that decision but credit to the boys for staying focused and keeping the standards high."

Firmino walked away with the man-of-the-match award but it really belonged to Henderson. This was a true captain's performance. He's had so much practice in 2019 that he's been able to perfect the art of the trophy lift.

During the lap of honour, Klopp lifted the Club World Cup above his head and patted the Liver Bird on his chest. "It feels sensational," was his verdict as he gathered his backroom staff together for a group photo.

What a year 2019 has been for Liverpool. Three trophies, a record Premier League points haul, the longest unbeaten league run in their history and establishing a commanding lead at the summit as they look to end a 30-year title drought.

"It's been an incredible time," Andy Robertson told *The Athletic*. "Winning the Champions League was a big step for us and we've kept building momentum. Coming away from here as world champions only adds to the positivity but there's a long way to go this season. Hopefully 2020 has a couple more trophies for us."

Liverpool are champions of Europe and champions of the world. They've got the taste for success. Now it's all about clinching the prize that their fans covet more than any other.

ALEXANDER-ARNOLD DOESN'T NEED MIDFIELD ROLE TO BE CENTRE OF ATTENTION – HE'S THE BEST RIGHT-BACK ON THE PLANET

JAMES PEARCE

DEC 26, 2019

The debate has long since raged over where Trent Alexander-Arnold's prodigious talent is best utilised. There's a school of thought that his career path at Liverpool will mirror that of his boyhood hero Steven Gerrard and he will make the leap from dynamic right-back to commanding centre-midfielder. Yet the idea that the 21-year-old needs a change of position to truly maximise his influence on Jurgen Klopp's swashbuckling side has never been shared by his manager.

Liverpool's ruthless Boxing Day demolition of Leicester City showed why. Here was further proof, if any was needed, that Alexander-Arnold doesn't need to be in the middle to be the centre of attention. At the King Power Stadium, the club's academy graduate produced a masterclass in the art of being a modern full-back.

It's the most physically demanding role in Klopp's blueprint. There is no let up: Alexander-Arnold and Andy Robertson are expected to deliver at both ends of the field. Defensive duties must be twinned with rampaging forward at regular intervals to provide quality from wide areas. And Alexander-Arnold has embraced these expectations and developed to the point where on current form there isn't a finer exponent in world football.

"We're not looking for one," Klopp quipped as he neatly side-stepped whether there was a better right-back on the planet.

This was a night to cherish for Liverpool fans. One of the biggest hurdles standing between Liverpool and a first top-flight title for 30 years was cleared in emphatic fashion.

Top-of-the-table clashes aren't supposed to be this one-sided. Leicester City were outclassed and outfought as Klopp's men extended their lead at the summit to 13 points.

So much for fatigue being a factor after that 6,000-mile round trip to the Middle East to be crowned club world champions. Liverpool were fitter, faster and hungrier.

And what made it all the sweeter was the fact the youngster leading the charge grew up a short walk from the club's Melwood training ground in the West Derby area of the city. He used to peer through the holes in the wall to watch Gerrard, Fernando Torres and Xabi Alonso train.

"He's Alexander-Arnold, the Scouser in our team," crowed the 3,300-strong group of Liverpool supporters, serenading the England international as he received the man of the match award after the final whistle.

It was richly deserved. He provided two assists for Roberto Firmino before completing the rout himself with a sweetly-struck right-footer into the bottom corner, after being teed up by Sadio Mane.

Alexander-Arnold, who has been on the club's books since the age of six, had 105 touches – more than any other player on the field. Some 37 of his 60 passes were made inside Leicester's half and he delivered a remarkable 17 crosses.

He covered 10.64km over the course of the 90 minutes – a distance only bettered by team-mates Georginio Wijnaldum (10.92km) and Roberto Firmino (11.31km).

Liverpool's pre-game analysis had pinpointed that James Maddison has a habit of drifting inside and leaving left-back Ben Chilwell exposed. It meant Alexander-Arnold was always likely to have plenty of space to exploit. Klopp told his players to repeatedly switch play to his right-back and he took full advantage.

Back in August 2015, Brendan Rodgers gave Alexander-Arnold his first taste of senior football in Liverpool's pre-season friendly against Swindon Town. He was just 16 at the time, but the potential was clear. Four-and-a-half years later, on a chastening night, Rodgers was left in no doubt about how far he's come under the guidance of the man who succeeded him at Anfield.

"When I see him, he plays full-back like a midfield player," says the Leicester boss. "His range of passing is phenomenal and he was a midfielder of course as a youngster. His quality, the experience he has gained, for Jurgen he has been absolutely amazing. Trent is up there and is very much England's No 1 (right-back) and playing consistently at a high level."

It was midway through the 2015-16 season when Alexander-Arnold was reinvented as a right-back following a heart-to-heart with academy director Alex Inglethorpe and youth coach Neil Critchley. He had previously been a winger and then a centre-back before playing as a holding midfielder in the youth section. Inglethorpe and Critchley convinced him that right-back represented his best chance of making it in the senior ranks given the glut of midfielders – and the fact that Joe Gomez and Jon Flanagan were both injured and there was precious little cover for Nathaniel Clyne. It proved to be an inspired piece of advice.

Alexander-Arnold has always been a student of the game and he studied hours of footage of Philipp Lahm and Dani Alves in action to pick up tips.

Klopp, who gave him his competitive debut in October 2016, recently described Alexander-Arnold as "a big surprise". The Liverpool boss was in no doubt about his technical ability when they started working together but questioned whether he had the robustness to succeed at the highest level. "He was a big talent, but we were not sure he could do it physically. Now he is a machine," Klopp admits.

All those academy days when he would stay so late for extra tuition with Pep Lijnders – then his youth coach and now Klopp's assistant – that the floodlights at Kirkby would get switched off proved invaluable. He retains that same work ethic and thirst for learning.

So many talented kids struggle to handle fame and fortune but Alexander-Arnold has been fortunate to have a loving, supportive family unit around him who have always kept him humble and grounded. In 2020 he plans to invest a significant chunk of his earnings from a lucrative sponsorship deal with Under Armour into football facilities for the next generation to use on Merseyside. His work serving others on the pitch is outstanding, too. He has registered 20 assists in the Premier League since the start of last season, more than any other player.

Alexander-Arnold is emerging as a serious contender for Liverpool's Player of the Year award, alongside Sadio Mane and Virgil van Dijk. He would be the first Englishman to win it since Gerrard a decade ago. If he maintains his current standards, the PFA Player of the Year award is also a realistic target.

The one criticism of Alexander-Arnold has been that his prowess going forward isn't replicated in terms of his defensive work.

"Defensively at times he can be suspect and the opposition may think they can get at Liverpool there because he pushes forward so much," former Liverpool centre-back Jamie Carragher remarked recently.

But against Leicester he didn't put a foot wrong as Liverpool kept a third successive Premier League clean sheet. He was always alert to danger, he made some crucial interceptions and also cleared his lines.

His crossing ability is increasingly Gerrard-esque. He can fizz it at pace, but he still retains full control over exactly where the ball is heading. The delivery for Firmino's headed opener was inch-perfect and after James Milner's spot-kick, Alexander-Arnold put another one on a plate for the Brazilian, who coolly dispatched it into the top corner.

When Alexander-Arnold drilled Mane's pass past Kasper Schmeichel, he stood in front of the delirious away end with his arms across his chest and a beaming smile on his face. It's the goal celebration favoured by France's World Cup winner Kylian Mbappe.

"Anything Mbappe can do…" Alexander-Arnold later tweeted. He belongs in that kind of company.

At the age of 21, he's already a 'Champions League, Super Cup and Club World Cup winner. He's represented his country at a World Cup, been named in the PFA Team of the Year and been shortlisted for the Ballon d'Or.

He's the Scouse heartbeat of this record-breaking Liverpool side. He's undoubtedly a future captain, but he doesn't need to make the leap into midfield to make his presence felt. Being the best right-back on the planet is more than enough.

DECEMBER RESULTS

Premier League, December 4 2019
Liverpool 5 Everton 2
Liverpool scorers: Origi 6, 31, Shaqiri 17, Mane 45, Wijnaldum 90

Premier League, December 7 2019
Bournemouth 0 Liverpool 3
Liverpool scorers: Oxlade-Chamberlain 35, Keita 44, Salah 54

Champions League, December 10 2019
RB Salzburg 0 Liverpool 2
Liverpool scorers: Keita 57, Salah 58

Premier League, December 14 2019
Liverpool 2 Watford 0
Liverpool scorer: Salah 38, 90

Carabao Cup, December 17 2019
Aston Villa 5 Liverpool 0

Club World Cup, December 18 2019
Monterrey 1 Liverpool 2
Liverpool scorers: Keita 12, Firmino 90+1

Club World Cup, December 21 2019
Liverpool 1 Flamengo 0 (AET)
Liverpool scorer: Firmino 99

Premier League, December 26 2019
Leicester 0 Liverpool 4
Liverpool scorers: Firmino 31, 74, Milner 71 pen, Alexander-Arnold 78

Premier League, December 29 2019
Liverpool 1 Wolves 0
Liverpool scorer: Mane 42

JANUARY

JANUARY HAS BEEN LIVERPOOL'S NEMESIS BEFORE. SURELY NOT THIS TIME?

JAMES PEARCE

JAN 3, 2020

Liverpool have been prone to a bout of the January blues during Jurgen Klopp's reign. It is the time of year when injuries seem to stack up, fatigue takes its toll and form dips after the gruelling demands of the festive schedule.

Rewind to Klopp's first winter in English football and Liverpool won only three of their nine matches in all competitions in January 2016, taking four points out of a possible 12 in the league. A year later they kicked off 2017 with only one victory in nine matches. With Sadio Mane away at the Africa Cup of Nations, Liverpool wilted without their most potent attacking weapon as they were knocked out of both domestic cups and collected only three points from four league games.

Klopp, who had been used to a mid-season break during his time in the Bundesliga, learnt valuable lessons about the need to rotate more and placed a greater emphasis on recovery, rather than training, during such energy-sapping periods.

The opening month of 2018 was better but far from perfect. Buoyed by the signing of Virgil van Dijk from Southampton,

Liverpool started brightly with four wins, before losing their way as a chastening league defeat at lowly Swansea City was followed by crashing out of the FA Cup at the hands of struggling West Brom.

Twelve months ago, Liverpool endured a new-year wobble that ultimately proved decisive in the Premier League title race. There was the narrow defeat by rivals Manchester City at the Etihad, before a much-changed line up lost to Wolverhampton Wanderers in the FA Cup. Two points were thrown away on an icy night at home to Leicester City after nervy wins over Brighton and Crystal Palace.

For those desperately searching for a chink in the armour of the Premier League leaders, Liverpool's habit of stumbling in January has provided a glimmer of hope that they could yet be denied the glory of a 19th top-flight crown.

Yet the opening chapter of 2020 only served to fuel the growing belief that Klopp's men are now a different beast. Victory over Sheffield United at Anfield was secured with an absolute minimum of fuss. A third game in the space of a week isn't physically draining when you enjoy dominance and control to this extent. Liverpool's total of 969 passes was the highest ever recorded by a team in the Premier League. Once Mane had doubled the lead given to the hosts by Mohamed Salah, Klopp's men were able to conserve energy while re-establishing their 13-point lead at the top. At times it was akin to a training exercise.

"We never laid a glove on them," confessed Sheffield United manager Chris Wilder. "The first balls, second balls, running forward, tackling, defending, being aggressive, Liverpool showed all those qualities. Not only technically, but tactically, they are a fantastic side."

Liverpool have gone an entire year unbeaten in the league – securing 32 wins and five draws. They have also kept five successive league clean sheets for the first time since 2007 under Rafael Benitez.

January remains far from straightforward. On Sunday there's the small matter of a Merseyside derby in the FA Cup at Anfield, before league games with Tottenham (away), Manchester United (home), Wolves (away) and West Ham (away). If the cushion at the top is still in double figures come February then Liverpool fans really will be in dreamland.

Just like in previous Januarys, Klopp's squad is heavily depleted. After Naby Keita limped out of Thursday night's warm-up complaining of discomfort in his groin, Liverpool were left with only 12 fit and available senior outfield players. However, new signing Takumi Minamino will boost that total when he makes his debut against Everton on Sunday. The Japan international watched on wide-eyed against Sheffield United from his seat behind Liverpool's bench – filming the rousing rendition of *You'll Never Walk Alone*. The Anfield press box is already over-subscribed for Sunday as a result of the influx of requests from Japanese media looking to attend.

Joel Matip, Dejan Lovren, Fabinho, Alex Oxlade-Chamberlain and Xherdan Shaqiri will all be on the comeback trail over the coming weeks and there are some gifted youngsters ready and waiting to grasp their opportunity.

Klopp will make wholesale changes for the visit of Carlo Ancelotti's side, risking Liverpool's proud unbeaten record in derby games at Anfield that stretches back to 1999. Adam Lallana and Divock Origi look certain to start, while rookies Neco Williams, Nat Phillips, Ki-Jana Hoever, Yasser Larouci, Harvey Elliott, Curtis Jones and Rhian Brewster are all in contention to feature.

"I will do what I think is right to do," says Klopp. "Some things I can decide by myself and some things the medical department will tell me. The only advantage we have is Anfield. We need support from the first second."

It will be a selection gamble based on the understanding that the FA Cup is a distant third in the list of priorities for Liverpool after the Premier League and the Champions League. A far bigger game than Everton is the following Saturday's trip to Tottenham when, if Liverpool triumph, they will have made the best-ever start to a top-flight campaign in the history of English football – surpassing the Manchester City side of 2017-18. Nothing is more important than ending that 30-year title drought.

Jordan Henderson, who continued his outstanding form against Sheffield United, recently told *The Athletic* how Klopp has adjusted his regime to help Liverpool deliver more around the midway point of the season.

"I think the manager has changed a little bit in dealing with this time of year, in terms of recovery days and when to give people a rest," Henderson says. "Bringing in doing treatment and recovery stuff at home during a really intensive period worked really well. It helps the freshness of the players."

In terms of playing minutes, there hasn't been a major difference among key personnel. For example, in December 2018, Salah played 640 minutes, Mane 528 minutes, Roberto Firmino 593 minutes and Virgil van Dijk 720 minutes. In December 2019, Salah played 639 minutes, Mane 592 minutes, Firmino 556 minutes and Van Dijk 660 minutes. But it's between games where Klopp has altered his approach and sought to lighten the load.

"During this period of the season, recovery is the main thing," assistant boss Pep Lijnders tells *The Athletic*. "As Jurgen always says, recovery starts in the mind. We have to speak with them and discuss what the next game looks like and how we can recover better depending on whether we have two or three nights of sleep between games. You have to make the players aware that the recovery process is so important because with the way we play we need that freshness and spontaneity. Without that, our game doesn't look the same way."

Time and time again this season when Klopp has rotated, players on the fringes of the Liverpool squad have stepped up when required and kept standards high. Liverpool's rivals believed a trip to Qatar for the Club World Cup might knock Klopp's men out of their stride. Now they will cling to the hope that an unwanted FA Cup derby could dent momentum. But whatever the outcome at Anfield on Sunday, physically, tactically and mentally, the current crop look to have all the tools to succeed where Klopp's Liverpool previously fell short.

"JURGEN SURPRISES ME EVERY DAY. HIS BRAIN WORKS DIFFERENTLY TO OTHER PEOPLE" – EXCLUSIVE INTERVIEW WITH KLOPP'S NO 2 PEP LIJNDERS

JAMES PEARCE

JAN 7, 2020

Pep Lijnders is in full flow. Liverpool's articulate assistant manager is eulogising about the tempo and intensity of the training session he has just overseen at Melwood. These are the words of a coach with complete job satisfaction.

"The passion and ambition of these players is from another planet," Lijnders tells *The Athletic*. "Their self-confidence, their self-criticism, that is what makes us consistent. These boys have the ability to make even a simple rondo competitive.

"People talk about going game to game – no, we commit session to session. Small things make big things happen. You have to focus on doing the small things right constantly.

"The passion and ambition I see, especially on the rainy and windy days here, that for me is what separates us from the others."

Over the course of two hours in his company, Jurgen Klopp's trusted lieutenant provides a fascinating insight into Liverpool's stunning rise to the heights of European and world champions, as well as runaway Premier League leaders.

The Dutchman's own personal journey has been no less

spectacular. He opens up for the first time about the circumstances surrounding his short spell away from Merseyside in 2018, when he went to manage NEC Nijmegen in his homeland.

Lijnders made player development his life's work after seeing his own hopes of a professional career wrecked by a serious knee injury as a teenager. From coaching in the youth ranks at PSV Eindhoven and Porto, to being responsible for the entire training programme of a Liverpool team who are rewriting the Anfield record books with their dominance, it's been some ride. Lijnders is still only 36 but his expertise is vast and he commands the respect of the dressing room. Owners Fenway Sports Group regard him as a pivotal cog in this winning machine. Like Klopp, he recently signed a contract extension to keep him at Liverpool until 2024. The pair enjoy a close bond.

"There's a super dynamic between us," Lijnders says. "It's much more than just assistant and manager. I believe you need 100 per cent trust in this job because we have to make so many decisions on a daily basis. I love working for him. He sees who I am, and respects that. We know what to expect from each other.

"Jurgen is a true leader. He's inspirational and motivational. He still surprises me every day with something he says. His brain works differently to a lot of other brains! He sees through situations and processes. There is a saying that people don't care how much you know until they know how much you care. And I think everyone who works with Jurgen has the feeling he really cares about you and your development. There is no ego, he purely searches for the right thing to do."

Klopp's famed man-management skills are undoubtedly one of his greatest assets. He has fostered a cherished unity and spirit in the squad which has propelled Liverpool towards glory. On a daily basis, Lijnders witnesses the manager's knack of finding the right words at the right times to get the best out of people.

"When Jurgen speaks to the players, he speaks from the heart and it goes directly into the hearts of the players," he says. "He has this remarkable capacity to touch people with the words he selects. That's not easy, especially with this level of players. I find that intriguing, how it's possible, the convincing way he has and that ability to touch people. You are dealing with a lot of egos in football, but in our club it looks like there are no egos.

"Jurgen has created an environment where everyone has bought into it. He solves problems before they arise. He has this capacity of making sure that certain things won't happen because he speaks about them. The level of respect the players have for him is huge.

"No written word, no spoken plea, can teach our team what they should be, nor all the books on the shelves, it's what the coach is himself. Do you know what I mean? The character of the coach becomes the character of the team. You can see it throughout the club. That's the power of Jurgen's personality."

Klopp's fiercely competitive edge extends to the paddle tennis court that he had installed at Melwood. Most days before training, Lijnders and Klopp lock horns. If training is at 3pm then they will arrange to meet for an 11am showdown. They can be noisy affairs.

"The staff hear the shouting – me probably more than him," laughs Lijnders. "I don't know how he does it but Jurgen is actually quite reserved on the court. He can control his emotions. We put our character into these games and there's a lot of passion.

"It's usually a doubles sport, but we play one v one. We like the fact we have to run more and fight more. He always says his players are mentality monsters, well he's a mentality monster at paddle tennis! He never knows when he's beaten. He's won the past two games and that hurts a lot. There have been many times when he's won without deserving it, but I've got to admit he's deserved the past two wins."

Lijnders enjoys parity with fellow assistant boss Peter Krawietz, whose association with Klopp dates back to his role as chief scout at Mainz nearly two decades ago. Whereas Lijnders' time is largely spent planning and delivering training sessions, Krawietz's area of expertise is video analysis. They complement each other well.

"It's about constantly giving each other information and working together," Lijnders says. "It's always easier with a good leader but still, life is a team sport. We support Jurgen in our best way possible. We know that we have to use each other's strengths to be able to accomplish great things.

"Pete is one of the world's best analysts and knows Jurgen's way very well. He puts his mark on each game's preparation. He supports me and Jurgen with information to include in our exercises and searches for weakness to exploit. The best football analysts simplify instead of complicate.

"There's a culture of preparation and perfection here, but with a lot of freedom. It's a complex job, being manager of such a big club. You need people around you and under you to focus on specific things. Jurgen tries to collect good ones, ones he can trust, he's very strong on that."

Klopp doesn't tolerate yes-men. He wants his viewpoint to be challenged. How much input do Lijnders and Krawietz have on team selection?

"Jurgen makes the decisions," he says firmly. "In the end he's the one who decides but we try to support him with all the information we have and with all the opinions we have. Everyone is encouraged to say exactly what they think. You might not always agree with each other but it's about always thinking together. Six eyes see more than two eyes. Three brains with a common idea can come up with different things and different insights compared to just one.

"The best meeting of the week is always the day before a game when Jurgen, Peter and I are in the office and we go through the video analysis and the plan for the game. Always in this meeting there's a moment when we have full conviction in what we're going to do. We speak about team selection and tactics. It's a beautiful moment."

—————————— **A** ——————————

Lijnders grew up in the small village of Broekhuizen in the Dutch province of Limburg. He was a promising central midfielder on the books at lower league outfit SVEB, before his dream of a pro career was dashed by a ruptured cruciate ligament at the age of 17. He studied sports in the city of Sittard and when a single coaching apprenticeship at PSV Eindhoven was advertised, he won the dogfight over it. At the end of his teens, he was combining youth coaching with PSV and leading the academy of SVEB.

"Everything I learned at PSV, I tried to implement at SVEB. My dad worked as a creative designer at a printers and I designed two big flipovers (flip charts) with our playing formation on and 15 different principles. One flipover for when we had the ball, one for when the opposition had the ball. It was implemented so that all teams from the youngest to the oldest age groups trained and played in this way."

By the time he was 24, Lijnders had become one of the chief architects of a PSV academy voted the best in Holland, and was recruited by Porto, and specifically Vitor Frade, the coach he credits with crystallising his own ideas. There, Lijnders was tasked with restructuring the academy.

"I was an individual coach but Vitor Frade made me look at the collective," says Lijnders. "For me, he's in the category of Cruyff and Coerver."

The gifted youngsters Lijnders helped to develop during his seven years at Porto include Joao Felix, Ruben Neves, Andre Gomes, Andre Silva, Diogo Dalot and Goncalo Paciencia.

"To explain the culture of Porto in one sentence, you go into the complex and written in big letters are the words 'we love the ones who hate to lose'," says Lijnders.

By the summer of 2014, Lijnders was looking for a new challenge. He was on the brink of leaving Porto for Ajax when a phone call from then Liverpool academy coach Michael Beale changed everything. He was offered the job of Under-16s coach.

His impact at the club's Kirkby academy over the course of the 2014-15 season was immense. The squad of youngsters he inherited included Trent Alexander-Arnold and Rhian Brewster. Alexander-Arnold, now arguably the most complete right-back in world football, told *The Athletic* earlier this season about the importance of the role played by Lijnders in his rise through the ranks.

"Trent developed as a guy incredibly that season," Lijnders says. "He was my captain and our No 6, with only three players behind him in a three-diamond-three, so he had to do everything well. You have leaders by talking, but Trent was a leader very naturally. After sessions, Trent and I would stay out there for another 20 minutes doing some skills until the lights went out. Trent would always be like 'again, again'.

"That was one of my favourite years of coaching. I must have said 50 times, 'Guys, I thought you couldn't play better than yesterday, but today you proved me wrong again'. We trained for two hours each day and every session ended with three teams of seven. Goal on, goal off. The better you played, the more you played. With the streetwise Liverpool boys, that was the way to push them.

"I really believe that if you want to play quick then it starts in the mind and you have to train like the game. I do it a lot now with the first team. One team attacks, one team defends. They have 40 seconds to score, if they can't then they're out. If they score then they play against the third team who are waiting. You split the pitch in two and we call it the 'wave' game. If the team defending win the ball, they have to break the halfway line.

"That's how we want to play. We're not defending our goal, we defend the halfway line first. And if you lose the ball, it has to be intense with maximum concentration."

Lijnders was invited to Melwood by then boss Brendan Rodgers on a number of occasions to talk about his counter-pressing methods. He blew Rodgers away with his tactical insights and in the summer of 2015, he was promoted to the Northern Irishman's backroom staff as first-team development coach. He became the key link between the club's two bases in Kirkby and Melwood.

However, just four months later, results nosedived and Rodgers was sacked. Lijnders feared that his own job was in jeopardy, but Fenway Sports Group president Mike Gordon made it clear to both the young coach and the man FSG selected to replace Rodgers that Lijnders would remain as part of the new coaching staff. Almost immediately, the two men were walking in step.

"You need to know exactly what the manager wants. To coach is easy but to know what to coach is much more difficult. Jurgen had a way of coaching and exercises which were close to my own. It was so nice to find someone so good."

— **A** —

Lijnders walked away from a job, a club and a city he loved when he accepted the opportunity to become manager of NEC Nijmegen in January 2018. His mission was to get them promoted back to the Eredivisie.

It was a decision based on professional ambition but also personal anguish. His dad Leo was battling cancer and, as the oldest child, Lijnders felt guilt about his absence at a time of crisis. But just as his father fought his way back to health, Lijnders' experience as manager was over after only five months.

NEC Nijmegen finished third and missed out on automatic promotion, then lost in the play-offs to Emmen.

"I knew it would take time," he adds. "I went to a very traditional, historic club, one of the bigger ones in Holland, who weren't in a good moment and had a lot of problems. As the manager, you have much more communication with the team and in the beginning that worked really well. I think one of my strengths is explaining things. The problem then as the main man was to guide and manage expectations of the people around you when things don't go well. When you have a few bad results, you have to keep everyone in the same direction and convince them that the way you are setting up is still the right way.

"A lot of times with development, first there's a period of instability because you ask players to do things that they aren't used to. I asked a lot, that's my nature. As a manager, you really need to learn from the mistakes that you make and the situations you have to deal with.

"In the back of my mind, I was always thinking: 'How would Jurgen approach this?' That half a year was really important for me. I wouldn't be able to support Jurgen in the way I do if I hadn't had that short time away. I respected him a lot already but I respected him even more having been in that job and seen what comes at you."

Lijnders parted company with NEC by mutual consent in the middle of May 2018 and a fortnight later he accepted Klopp's invitation to attend the Champions League final against Real Madrid in Kyiv. The perceived wisdom is that his return to Melwood was sealed during discussions in the Ukrainian capital. However, the truth is that Lijnders had long since agreed to re-join Klopp's staff.

Klopp needed a new assistant after Zeljko Buvac's surprise exit in the April and he had turned to Lijnders immediately. The Dutchman explained that he had to focus on gaining promotion with NEC, but he made the decision there and then that he would return to Liverpool, whatever the outcome of his rookie season as a manager.

The day he signed the contract to become Liverpool's assistant manager was especially poignant. "My dad got the test results back to say that he was completely clean. He had been sick for two years. There was a lot of emotion. Thankfully, he's still good now. He lives in my hometown, but he comes over for some games. He never stops watching football. He knows a lot – well he thinks he does! He's become a big Liverpool fan."

———————————— **A** ————————————

The role Lijnders came back to was very different from the one he left behind. More demanding, but also more rewarding as he was tasked with filling the void created by Buvac's departure. Where before he had executed sessions planned by others, now he had full responsibility for how Liverpool trained.

"My time away from Liverpool was good for self-reflection," he says. "I became much clearer about how I wanted to work and what is decisive to become successful. I know exactly what I would do differently now. No more concessions, we do it like I want in training, nothing else, convincing each day, create happiness in the players, a clear week plan and we play everywhere we go in the same manner, full energy."

What does a normal day in the life of Pep Lijnders look like?

He says: "My alarm is my youngest one. My two boys are three-and-a-half and five-and-a-half. When they come into our bed, sleeping is done!

"Early in the morning, I usually call Vitor Matos (elite development coach), I'll text Jurgen and then come into Melwood. I have a meeting with Jurgen in his office to talk about training. What are we going to do? Who is delivering what and how is it going to look? Do we want to have Sadio (Mane) on the left wing or as the striker? Things like that.

"When the training is planned, I explain what the ideas behind it are to Andreas (Kornmayer, head of fitness and conditioning), Pete, Vitor, John (Achterberg, goalkeeping coach) and Jack (Robinson, assistant goalkeeping coach).

"Then I go out and put everything on the pitch. Normally Jurgen has a meeting with the players either in the dressing room or outside to give some details about the sessions. We train always in the same intensity as the game, same concentration and tempo. This is the secret of training in my opinion.

"Everything is designed around the training. The day basically starts when the training ends. I'll watch the session back on the video and try to get as many opinions as possible from the people around me. Then the planning starts for the next session. We make decisions about how tomorrow will look. What do we want to do? What players will we have?

"I have to speak with the medical department and try to plan the session in more detail and I'll put it in the tactics planner and work everything out in terms of how it relates to our next opponent. Pete will also give input. Then the plan is clear for the next day and I'll go home. In the evening when the kids have gone to bed, I'll watch footage of our opponents."

During Lijnders' time as assistant manager, Liverpool have collected an extraordinary 155 points out of a possible 174. They have gone to the next level since winning the Champions League in Madrid last June and find themselves 13 points clear at the top of the Premier League as they close in on a first domestic title since 1990.

"Winning something big puts more conviction, more trust into everything; subconsciously you feel stronger. There's a real hunger to fight for more prizes," he says.

"But for me it's about the journey and how the team developed. The trust I got from keeping things simple, never giving up on our way, believing in training and video meetings to improve, clear messages with a lot of conviction from Jurgen, Pete or myself, repeating that process over and over again.

"Trusting the players to always look at our best games and think about what steps won us those games. Was it our full-backs being constantly ready to jump? Was it the centre-backs coming in front of offensive players rather than stepping back? Was it our midfielders being always connected, rather than just searching for it? It's about doing it our way again, becoming better and searching for perfection. We know it doesn't exist but you still have to search for it.

"Our main strength is that we're always together. By that I mean on the pitch, the distances, the organisation, the way we are. That's the only way to be an aggressive, pressing team. If the distances and the organisation are not right, then you have no chance. That's where we've made the biggest improvement. Wherever the game is on the pitch, we are there together. A compact team, an intense team, both on and off the ball. Jurgen talks about the principle that everyone is responsible for everything. It's easy to say, it's harder to put it into practice on the pitch for 95 minutes but that's what these players have been doing a lot. If we recover well and have freshness in our game, we go into every game with a common idea of chasing them all over the pitch."

The style of the team has certainly evolved. Game-management has been a feature of this record-breaking season which has seen Liverpool drop just two points. They put themselves in winning positions and then play with real maturity and control.

"When you become European champions, when you become more dominant on the ball, you don't rely as much on defensive organisation and counterattack, which is a very attractive part of our game. We've become better on the ball as teams have set up differently against us. I'd say 75 percent of teams in the Premier League, even the bigger teams, changed their system or approach to play against us this season – lines much closer together, dropping deeper. Can we then expect to have attack, attack, attack? No, we can't. We have to respect that and find a new way against them. What I like about our game is that we have so many different weapons and that makes us unpredictable. It's not about playing it from A to B to C to D. That's not the game we want. Even our defensive principles aren't like that. That makes us very difficult to read.

"Teams can't just drop deep against us and try to stop us playing through them because Trent and Robbo will get down the wings and then you've got the centre-backs bringing it forward and creating space. There's a lot of freedom because we focus on principles rather than exact plays. We know that if all this is present then the mentality of Jurgen and the boys will put us above the other team. But all this has to be right."

Lijnders' stock has risen to the point that he's been mentioned as a potential successor to Klopp one day. But such talk is far from his thoughts. He's too busy savouring every second of the here and now.

"It makes me proud but it's not realistic because it's not important at this moment in time," he adds. "My only ambition is to support Jurgen and our project in the best way possible. Mike Gordon and Jurgen have been the most important people in my career. They gave me the chance and the belief to lead the process of training and methodology with the first team.

"This is my life. I feel passionate about this club and I feel blessed to work with passionate colleagues. I feel that what we have here in this period we will never experience again in our lives.

"I believe each football project is like the sun rising up and going down, and for our project it's not even noon. That's the reason why we committed for another four years."

Like the team he has helped to shape, Pep Lijnders is relentless.

NINETY MINUTES WATCHING VIRGIL VAN DIJK, THE WORLD'S BEST DEFENDER

JAMES PEARCE

JAN 12, 2020

Before kick-off . . .

As captain Jordan Henderson tossed up with Toby Alderweireld, Van Dijk made a point of walking around the pitch to embrace every single one of his team-mates. On each occasion there were words of encouragement.

He had paired off with fellow centre-back Joe Gomez for the passing drills during the warm-up. The England international, who describes his senior partner as "like a big brother", had seen the funny side after being playfully nutmegged. They are close on and off the pitch. Gomez and Van Dijk share a love of basketball and often shoot hoops together at the Melwood training ground. Dejan Lovren sometimes joins in but gets accused by Van Dijk of lowering the standard.

Aside from his quality, Van Dijk is incredibly durable. He's been ever-present in both the Premier League and the Champions League so far this season. Van Dijk's mental toughness is underlined by the fact he hasn't missed a Premier League game for Liverpool since January 2018. He should have done – he played through the pain barrier with two cracked ribs last season.

1st minute: There's danger when Paulo Gazzaniga's long punt goes over the head of Gomez. However, Van Dijk is alert and reacts quickly to cover before Lucas Moura can capitalise and he hooks the ball to safety. He's then perfectly placed to nod away Harry Winks' cross as he urges Trent Alexander-Arnold to get tighter to Serge Aurier. His leadership is evident from the off.

7th minute: Decision making is one of his biggest strengths. He's able to perfectly assess situations in the heat of battle. When these clubs met at Anfield last March, he was lauded for how he handled a late two-on-one breakaway. Sensing that Moussa Sissoko was desperate to pick out Son Heung-min, he blocked the angle for the pass, forced Sissoko to take the shot on and the Frenchman lashed horribly over. Here, he opted to track the run of Moura rather than close down Son, who curled wide from the edge of the box.

15th minute: With Tottenham dropping off inside their own half, there's little pressure on Liverpool's centre-backs. Remarkably, Van Dijk has already made 25 passes. He's constantly talking to Gomez and the two full-backs either side of them. When attacks are building, he's pointing exactly to where the ball should go next. He barks at Gomez to move wider to give him a better angle for a pass.

He's so vocal, constantly organising and cajoling team-mates. When Henderson and James Milner were both out injured last season, Jurgen Klopp asked his players to vote for a new captain and vice-captain who would then be third and fourth in command in the dressing room. Van Dijk was the overwhelming winner with Georginio Wijnaldum in second place.

21st minute: When Henderson is caught in possession, there's a let-off as Christian Eriksen's finish is weak. "Hey!" screams Van Dijk, who gestures for Liverpool to wake-up. The skipper already has his arm in the air apologetically.

22nd minute: Van Dijk should open the scoring. When Andy Robertson's corner isn't cleared, Henderson hooks it invitingly towards the far post. Van Dijk is unmarked four yards out but nods too close to Gazzaniga, who parries to safety.

27th minute: When Aurier tries to pick out the run of Moura down the inside-left channel, Van Dijk has to really stretch his legs for the first time. He showcases both his pace and strength as he gets there first, makes the tackle and puts Liverpool back on the attack. It all looks so effortless. As Robertson sizes up his options, Van Dijk rolls his arms, urging him to move the ball quicker, demanding that he knocks it inside to Gomez. The Scotsman duly obliges.

29th minute: Moura threatens to latch on to another long punt forward. However, Van Dijk cuts across him, causing him to stumble and Alisson dashes out of his box to nod away. Cynical? You bet. Clever? Undoubtedly. The home fans are howling for a free-kick but Martin Atkinson isn't interested.

Son and Moura change positions to give Van Dijk something different to think about but he remains unruffled. They get no change out of him. Van Dijk credits the daily "nightmare" of facing Mohamed Salah, Roberto Firmino and Sadio Mane in training as helping him go to the next level as a defender.

37th minute: Firmino latches on to Salah's pass and finishes emphatically to break the deadlock. A jubilant Van Dijk runs from the halfway line to join the celebrations, mimicking the

Brazilian's trademark kung-fu kick celebration before patting the goalscorer on the head.

45th minute: When Salah fires wide, Van Dijk has both hands above his head applauding the Egyptian for the mazy run that took him clear. He then apologises to Robertson for over-hitting a lofted pass. Van Dijk has had 79 touches in the first half – more than anyone else on the pitch. He has completed 65 passes, including 33 inside Tottenham's half. It's a sign of Liverpool's dominance that Alderweireld leads the hosts' passing stats with just 12.

55th minute: There's a change of approach from Tottenham after the break and a greater show of ambition. As Moura, Son and Dele Alli start to press, there's suddenly some pressure exerted on Liverpool's backline. Van Dijk remains cool. When Gomez is hurried and misplaces a pass, which goes straight out of play, he doesn't react. He simply gestures for Robertson to drop deeper alongside him.

57th minute: Van Dijk is scared of spiders and snakes but not match-saving tackles. When Gomez slips, Liverpool are left exposed as Alli races forward. Van Dijk initially backs off, assessing the situation carefully. Then at full stretch he makes a perfectly-timed challenge with his left boot. As Alli tumbles, there are howls for a penalty but it's a top-class piece of defending. Van Dijk is so alert to what's around him as he reacts quickly and gets to the loose ball before Moura.

66th minute: Robertson is fortunate to avoid a card after over-stretching and catching young debutant Japhet Tanganga with his studs. During the break in play, Van Dijk is deep in conversation with Gomez and then Henderson and Wijnaldum about providing cover and tracking runners. Tottenham throw caution to the wind with the introduction of Erik Lamela and Giovani Lo Celso off the bench.

75th minute: Van Dijk puffs out his cheeks after Son skies a golden chance to restore parity. Lo Celso is then equally wasteful. It's all getting increasingly frantic as Liverpool cling on to their narrow advantage. The Liverpool centre-back calls for calm and a greater show of composure.

86th minute: Van Dijk riles the home fans by taking an age over a free-kick close to halfway. Jose Mourinho fumes on the touchline but he's no stranger to the dark arts himself. Van Dijk then intervenes with a crucial interception to prevent Lo Celso from releasing Son. His positional play is so good that it feels like he rarely has to break sweat. He hasn't put a foot wrong all night.

90th minute: Tempers get frayed at the death as Gomez and Lamela square up to each other. Van Dijk steps in to pull them apart. He doesn't lose his rag – one booking in 30 starts this season is testament to that. "It's almost perfection to watch him play," was the verdict of former England international Martin Keown in the build-up to the game and he certainly lives up to that billing. He has 129 touches in total and completes 116 passes with an accuracy of 94 per cent.

Post-game

At the final whistle, Van Dijk has both arms aloft. He embraces Gomez and then Moura before shaking the hands of the officials. He walks to applaud the away end but his celebrations are understated compared to Henderson, Robertson and Alexander-Arnold, who toss their shirts into the travelling Kop.

Van Dijk walks off deep in conversation with Gomez. He's the first visiting player to leave the field. Liverpool haven't conceded a league goal since their partnership was rekindled last month. Klopp's men have set a new club record of 38 league games unbeaten – surpassing the previous best set in 1894. They have also become the first team across Europe's big five leagues to ever take 61 points from the first 21 games of a season.

The players' reward is two days off but Van Dijk isn't in the mood for partying. In the away dressing room there's a sense of frustration rather than elation over what was a gritty but scrappy performance.

"We want to analyse this game and do much better," Van Dijk tells the waiting media. "Especially in the second half, they were pressing us and made it very difficult for us. We should have done better. There is still room for improvement. We're in a good situation but there's still so much work we can do to make it easier at times."

LIVERPOOL ALSO TOP THE SET-PIECE TABLE – AND IT'S ALL DOWN TO THE UNSEEN WORK OF THE 'TEAM BEHIND THE TEAM'

JAMES PEARCE

JAN 20, 2020

Jurgen Klopp felt Liverpool were missing a trick. At the start of pre-season in the summer of 2018, he sat down with assistants Pep Lijnders and Peter Krawietz and ordered a complete overhaul of the club's set-piece routines.

Klopp had been busy trying to pinpoint where gains could be made on the back of the club's fourth-place finish in the Premier League and a chastening defeat to Real Madrid in the Champions League final. The stats told him that in terms of making set-pieces count, Liverpool were distinctly mid-table. They had a habit of wasting them at one end and looking vulnerable dealing with them at the other.

With the aerial prowess of Virgil van Dijk – coupled with the pinpoint accuracy of dead-ball specialist Trent Alexander-Arnold – Klopp was convinced they should be a much more potent weapon in Liverpool's attacking armoury. He also knew that with opponents desperately trying to come up with plans to nullify the threat of attacking trio Roberto Firmino, Mohamed Salah and Sadio Mane, his team needed to keep evolving to ensure they

coherent boardroom vision from US owners FSG has fuelled success on and off the field since the appointment of Jurgen Klopp in 2015, steered by key figures such as former chief executive Ian Ayre (far left) who left in 2017, principal owner John W. Henry (centre left), chairman Tom Werner (centre right) and president Mike Gordon (far right). *Getty Images*

Fabinho dominated the midfield as Liverpool equalled a club record of 12 successive league wins with a 3-1 victory over Arsenal at Anfield in August 2019. Against the same opponents less than a year earlier, in his second start for Liverpool, 'The Lighthouse' had been overwhelmed by the intensity of the Premier League. *Getty Images*

Sadio Mane receives a calming hand on the shoulder from team-mate Joe Gomez after an outburst following his substitution in the closing stages of their 3-0 win over Burnley on August 31 2019. The Senegal international had been furious when Mohamed Salah failed to pass to him in front of goal. *Getty Images*

However, the two remain friends as well as team-mates and by November both were on target in a pivotal win over Manchester City. Salah celebrated his strike with Jordan Henderson and Roberto Firmino (below left) before embracing Mane as the forwards focused on their common goal (below right). *Getty Images*

A group of Sadio Mane's extended family po
outside the huge mansion the Liverpool strik
built for them in his home village of Bamba
Senegal, while a young relative watches the gam
inside. *The Athletic*'s Oliver Kay travelled to th
village in a remote part of Senegal to watc
Liverpool's 3-1 win over Manchester City i
their company. Mane did not disappoint, scorin
Liverpool's third goal to spark wild celebration
among the watching family. *The Athletic*

The teeth and the talent. The arrival of Roberto Firmino from Hoffenheim in a £29 million deal in June 2015 has been one of the club's masterpieces in recruitment. The creative forward also has a big personality: when asked what shade he would like his teeth whitened, he answered "*maximo*". *Getty Images*

Red Bull Salzburg was a crucial staging post in Sadio Mane's journey to Liverpool. He enjoyed a very productive spell in Austria, scoring 23 goals in all competitions during his second season. Mane also adapted to life off the field and once wore lederhosen to a friend's wedding. *Getty Images*

Goalkeeping coach John Achterberg first started tracking Alisson Becker in 2013 as he rose through the ranks at Internacional and his arrival from Roma in 2018 for £65 million has been transformative. After missing 10 weeks at the start of the 2019-20 season, he returned to help inspire his team to the title. *Getty Images*

ent Alexander-Arnold took the most famous corner in Liverpool's history in their 4-0 win over Barcelona in the Champions League semi-final second leg in 2019 (above). The right-back made decisive contributions throughout the title-winning season, including the final strike in a 4-0 win over Leicester City on Boxing Day, after which he imitated Kylian Mbappe's celebration, with his arms across his chest. "Anything Mbappe can do . . ." Alexander-Arnold later tweeted. *Getty Images*

The Athletic's James Pearce sits down with Liverpool manager Jurgen Klopp for an exclusive interview in November 2019. "When we start a team meeting the only thing I really know I am going to say is the first sentence," Klopp told Pearce. Below, Klopp delivers some final words to his team ahead of kick-off at the 2019 Champions League final. *The Athletic* and *Getty Images*

The Athletic covered the remarkable rise of Jurgen Klopp from his playing days at FSV Mainz (top, right) to his successful spell as manager of the club (middle, seated with Zeljko Buvac, the assistant who followed Klopp to Liverpool before leaving in 2018). Klopp got Mainz promoted to the Bundesliga in 2004 for the first time in their history, and the self-styled 'carnival club' partied for a week. *Getty Images*

When Liverpool scored late to salvage a 2-2 draw with West Brom in 2015, Klopp led his team in front of the Kop to thank the fans for the support they had shown. It was a move that drew criticism, but proved a key turning point in turning Anfield into a fortress. *Getty Images*

Klopps's conviction that true happiness is a social emotion is best conveyed in the image of his autograph card, which doe not show his face at all but rather captures him from behind, lifting the Champions League in front of thousands of fans.

Jurgen Klopp prepares to lift the Champions League trophy in 2019 after beating Tottenham in the final, before his players throw him in the air in celebration of the club's sixth European Cup. *Getty Images*

Pep Lijnders was at Liverpool before Jurgen Klopp arrived and the club's US owners were insistent that he should form part of the German's staff. The Dutchman has developed a close relationship with Klopp. 'Jurgen surprises me every day. His brain works differently to other people', Lijnders told *The Athletic*'s James Pearce. *Getty Images*

Michael Edwards' journey from frustrated IT teacher to Liverpool's sporting director has been remarkable. It was Edwards who identified Jurgen Klopp as the successor to Brendan Rodgers and his vision that helped bring a roster of world-class talent to the club. Edwards is happy to remain in the shadows and refuses all media requests. *Getty Images*

Mona Nemmer, Liverpool's head of nutrition, poses with the FIFA Club World Cup alongside Andreas Kornmayer (left) head of fitness and conditioning, and first-team physiotherapist Christopher Rohrbeck. Nemmer has revolutionised the players' refuelling habits by bringing in individual diet plans. *Getty Images*

Klopp has frequently praised the contribution of his backroom team in contributing to his marginal gains strategy. (Left to right) Jack Robinson, assistant goalkeeping coach, assistant manager Peter Krawietz, goalkeeping coach John Achterberg, Jurgen Klopp, elite development coach Vitor Matos and assistant Pep Lijnders. *Getty Images*

Andy Robertson screams at team-mate Mohamed Salah during the shock 3-0 loss to Watford in February 2020, which end Liverpool's Premier League record 44-game unbeaten run. The result did not derail their title ambitions. *Getty Images*

Social distancing regulations prevented fans attending matches after the Premier League restarted in June, but 15 fan were allowed into Anfield to make it feel more like home for the players and Liverpool crushed Crystal Palace 4-0 on June 24. "The best behind-closed-doors, counter-pressing football ever," was Jurgen Klopp's verdict. *Getty Images*

iverpool's 2019-20 Premier League title was as much a triumph for the city as the football club. The social and political history of the city – and its famous docklands – has been inextricably linked to the football club, exemplified by the celebrations after their Champions League win in 2019. *Getty Images*

Jordan Henderson ends Liverpool's 30-year wait by lifting the Premier League trophy after their 5-3 win over Chelsea in July, and the players celebrate in the dressing room. The club's status as champions had been confirmed the previous month when the Stamford Bridge side beat Manchester City 2-1. *Getty Images*

retained an element of surprise. "We need to be unpredictable," is a message the manager regularly reiterates to players and staff alike.

Around the same time that Lijnders and Krawietz were tasked with improving set-pieces, Klopp brought specialist throw-in coach Thomas Gronnemark on board after reading about his work in a German newspaper. The transformation in that area over the past 18 months has been remarkable. For all the focus on Klopp's force of personality and man-management in turning Liverpool into Champions League winners and Premier League champions-elect, his attention to detail is often overlooked. The planning for every mission is meticulous.

When Van Dijk soared highest to power home a header from Alexander-Arnold's corner against Manchester United at Anfield on Sunday, it cemented their status as the top-flight's set-piece kings. Liverpool have scored 14 league goals (including penalties) from set-pieces so far this season, more than any other team. Last season, they topped that table with 29 set-piece goals. Bournemouth and Manchester United were joint second on 21.

At set-plays – from free-kicks, corners and throws – in the Premier League, Liverpool managed just eight goals in the entire 2017-18 season. That figure leapt to 14 for 2018-19 and they are on nine so far this term.

Krawietz, who is nicknamed 'The Eye' by Klopp, works closely with the club's team of video analysts to find weaknesses they believe Liverpool can exploit. The 48-year-old German coach then discusses their findings with Klopp and Lijnders before a decision is made on what set-pieces to work on with the players. To help reinforce what they are trying to achieve, the squad are shown examples on a big screen before they head out on to the training field to put the theory into practice. The day before a game is always when Liverpool focus on set-piece routines.

"Our record in that area is credit to all the boys and the analysts who do so much of the work," Lijnders tells *The Athletic*.

"We always come up with a clear plan in how we can make our set-pieces count against a particular opponent and then we implement those ways in training. We really spend time on it. It's a good weapon, especially against a deep defending team as when you're always trying to create you're bound to have more corners. There's a strong emphasis on making set-pieces decisive.

"Offensive teams don't usually have this mentality. It's more the teams who aren't dominant in games, but we really have the mentality to be a set-play team."

The opening goal against United was especially satisfying for Liverpool staff because they had worked on pinpointing that area during training at Melwood on Saturday. "We wanted to target that near post and we managed to do that," confirmed Van Dijk, whose eight-goal haul in the Premier League since joining Liverpool two years ago is more than any other centre-back in the division. "It was a perfect corner from Trent. It was a good feeling. We have players who can be very dangerous in those situations, including myself."

Alexander-Arnold has assisted five league goals from dead-ball situations this season, more than any other player across Europe's top five leagues. His total tally of 21 Premier League assists since the start of last season is more than any other top-flight player. His development since being handed his full league debut by Klopp against United three years ago has been astonishing. He's following in the footsteps of his boyhood hero Steven Gerrard with his dead-ball prowess, as well as providing the Scouse heartbeat to this trophy-winning machine.

He's already taken the most famous corner in Anfield history, when his quick thinking put the killer fourth goal on a plate for Divock Origi as Liverpool pulled off a miraculous fightback against Barcelona en route to European glory last season. On that occasion, Lijnders had relayed a message to the ball boys at the academy on the day of the game urging them to recycle the ball quickly as they had spotted that Barcelona had a habit of switching off and could be caught off-guard.

"The team behind the team here are fantastic," left-back Andy Robertson tells *The Athletic* shortly after victory over United sent Liverpool 16 points clear with a game in hand. "They really examine an opponent's strengths and weaknesses and work out good plans. The day before every game, we do 11 v 11 at Melwood and try to make the set-piece routines work. Peter takes the leads on it in team meetings and talks us through everything with the video analysis. Credit to him and the analysis team. When we score goals from that area, it feels good because we're repaying them for all their hard work.

"Sometimes, it's a routine we've used to our advantage in a previous game or a routine that another team has had joy with. It's about having the right delivery and ensuring that the right man is on the end of it. Trent's delivery was right on the money and Virgil did so well to get on the end of it. They tried to mark him out of it but his movement was phenomenal. Set-pieces are a massive part of football, so why not try to take advantage of them?"

That Van Dijk opener gave Liverpool the platform to dominate. But for a questionable VAR decision, some poor finishing and inspired goalkeeping, Klopp's men would have been out of sight before United rallied. When the points were finally secured at the death, the second goal followed from another set-piece. Van Dijk won the initial header from a United corner, Alisson claimed and then expertly released Salah, who finished in style to spark scenes of delirium inside Anfield.

Since Klopp ordered that set-piece overhaul 18 months ago, Liverpool have taken 161 points out of the last 180 on offer. There's nothing lucky about this team. There's expertise and hard graft in abundance. No stone has been left unturned in Klopp's quest for excellence.

THE PLAYERS' MEETING THAT HELPED TURN 'LONELY' ANFIELD INTO A GENUINE FORTRESS

OLIVER KAY

JAN 20, 2020

It had been coming for months. Tongues had been bitten, powerful urges suppressed. Finally, at 6.19pm on Sunday evening, after Alisson released Mohamed Salah to secure victory over Manchester United, Anfield exploded into euphoria. Liverpool's supporters could resist no longer.

'And now you're gonna believe us,' they chanted. 'We're gonna win the league.'

It wasn't only based on a calculation – that Liverpool were now 16 points clear of Manchester City, having played a game fewer, and their Premier League title-winning chances are now rated above 99 per cent by various predictive models. It was a release of tension, an outpouring of joy. 'We're gonna win the league.'

The statistics back up those supporters' optimism. Liverpool have won 21 and drawn one of their first 22 Premier League games, the best start in top-flight history in England. They have gone 39 Premier League matches unbeaten since losing to Manchester City on January 3 last year. Since March 10 they have taken 91 points out of a possible 93. Since drawing with

Leicester 12 months ago, they have won 19 consecutive home games in the Premier League, one short of Manchester City's record. They have not lost in the Premier League at Anfield since April 2017.

Jurgen Klopp smiled afterwards when it was put to him that this was the first time all season that Liverpool's supporters had dared to declare – so publicly, so rapturously – that their 30-year wait was nearly over. "I'm not here to dictate what they sing," the Liverpool manager said. "If our fans were not in a good mood now, that would be really strange. Of course they're allowed to dream, to sing whatever they want. We will not be part of that party yet but it's no problem."

He might have chosen to put it a different way: that "we decide when it's over." Remember that phrase? Possibly not. But Klopp does. It constitutes one of several significant moments in the restoration of the crumbling fortress he walked into just over four years ago.

———————— **A** ————————

November 8, 2015: Liverpool 1 Crystal Palace 2

Four weeks had passed since Klopp breezed into Liverpool, pledging to energise the club's players and supporters in the same way he had at Borussia Dortmund. From a distance, he had detected that "at this moment, all of the LFC family is a little bit too nervous, a little bit too pessimistic, a little bit too much in doubt. Nobody is really enjoying themselves. They don't believe at the moment. It's a really important thing that the players feel the difference from now on. We have to change from doubters to believers".

He had already secured a 3-1 win away to Chelsea, but a week later against Palace they were labouring. At 1-1 the mood inside the stadium was frustrated. The moment Palace's Liverpool-born defender Scott Dann scored to put his team 2-1 up in the 82nd minute, Klopp was bewildered, then shocked, then appalled to see thousands of home fans streaming towards the exits. "I turned around," he said, "and I felt pretty alone in that moment. *We* decide when it's over."

Klopp had come from Dortmund, where he felt the bond between his team and the supporters was unique. If he was to be able to replicate that anywhere, folklore, along with a powerful sales pitch from Fenway Sports Group, told him that Liverpool was the place. But this was nothing like the brochure. Anfield was a miserable, angst-ridden place where, as he had detected, nobody was really enjoying themselves. Something had to change. He wasn't going to put up with a team or a crowd who made each other anxious.

Five weeks later they were 2-1 down again, this time at home to West Bromwich Albion. In response to the manager's exhortations, the crowd stayed put. Klopp kept gesticulating, demanding that they pumped up the volume to help his fragile team. The noise increased and Liverpool pushed forward, equalising through Divock Origi in the fifth minute of stoppage time. At the final whistle, Klopp responded by walking onto the pitch and leading his players towards the Kop, where they lined up, looking a little sheepish, and held each other's arms aloft to thank the fans for the support they had been shown.

Rival fans found it hilarious. Celebrating a 2-2 draw! At Anfield! Against West Brom! Liverpool's supporters were divided between those who understood the gesture, which was the kind of thing that is common among German teams, and those who felt he had misjudged the climate spectacularly. But Klopp thought that an important message had been sent out that day. *We decide when it's over.* It was going to take time to restore a feelgood factor, but that, he felt, was an important step

— **A** —

February 6 2016, Liverpool 2 Sunderland 2

"This has been glossed over by a lot of people," Neil Atkinson, presenter of *The Anfield Wrap* podcast, says. "There's almost a hint of shame about it, but I think it changed everything."

Liverpool were 2-0 up against Sunderland when around a quarter of the crowd walked out. This was not an attempt to beat the post-match traffic. This was a symbolic gesture designed to highlight opposition to the club's new ticket pricing policy. The policy included plans for a £77 ticket in the new Main Stand, so, on 77 minutes, at least 10,000 fans walked out in protest, singing "You greedy bastards. Enough is enough".

Inside Anfield they share Atkinson's belief that it was another significant moment. Only five years had passed since the infighting that had blighted the period under the ownership of American investors Tom Hicks and George Gillett. "There was no trust at that time," one Liverpool official says. "There was no trust in the players and no trust in the club. The relationship was broken and desperately needed to be fixed."

It had been broken for years. There had been two very different types of title challenge – under Rafa Benitez in 2008-09 and under Brendan Rodgers in 2013-14 – but Anfield was a fractious place, a world away from what Klopp had imagined. "In 08-09 it was the height of the battle with Hicks and felt as if everyone in the ground hated each other," Atkinson recalls. "There was one game where we beat Portsmouth 1-0 to go top and, although we won, all I can remember from the whole of the second half is anxious fans screaming at each other to stop making everyone so nervous. 'CALM DOWN, YOU.' 'SHUT UP, WILL YER.' The first caller on *606* that night was someone saying Benitez should be sacked. It was ridiculous. We were top."

Liverpool rode on the crest of an emotional wave in the 2013-14 season, coming so close to landing that elusive Premier League title, but by early 2016 Steven Gerrard, Luis Suarez and

Raheem Sterling had gone and the relationship was at breaking point once more. So much goodwill towards FSG was shattered by the ticket scheme. Liverpool's supporters felt as if, for all the club's attempts to trade on the notion of the '12th man', their support was being taken for granted.

Spirit of Shankly, the Liverpool supporters' group, warned that pushing ticket prices higher, when clubs were already benefiting from increased Premier League broadcast revenue and prize money, would alienate the fanbase further. On that day against Sunderland, the fans walked out in protest. With the ground emptying, in what was now an eerie atmosphere, Sunderland turned a 2-0 deficit into a 2-2 draw. Did the Liverpool hierarchy think they could just name their price? The message here was that they would be making a terrible mistake.

Klopp was absent from that game, undergoing an operation to remove his appendix, but he appeared to side with the supporters, suggesting that the walk-out was a "sign" and that it was down to the club to "find a solution".

FSG had already reached the same conclusion. Within days, they announced that the £77 ticket had been abolished and the most expensive match day ticket would remain at £59. Rather than risk widening the gap between the club and the fanbase, they pledged to preserve the "unique and sacred relationship between Liverpool Football Club and its supporters".

It felt like a significant victory for the Anfield crowd. It seemed to mark a change in the relationship between the board and the fanbase. "No fan wants to walk out on their team," Atkinson says, "but that was significant – not just to Liverpool but in a wider sense. If you look at it since then, almost every club in the Premier League has frozen ticket prices at some point."

On the pitch, things had been starting to pick up under Klopp and the feelgood factor started to return with a stirring run to the Europa League final, beating Manchester United, Borussia

Dortmund and Villarreal on nights that seemed to live up to a certain Anfield tradition.

"Coming back to beat Dortmund 4-3 was massive," Atkinson says. "That was only a few weeks after Sunderland and it really helped bring everyone together. But the atmosphere against Villarreal was great too. It felt almost feral that night. It felt like the Europa League run really brought everyone together again. It also felt like that was the moment that Klopp really became Liverpool manager in the eyes of the fans. And I'm sure it was also the moment where he thought, 'Yes, this is Anfield'."

Doubters – severely disgruntled doubters – were starting to become believers.

———————————— **A** ————————————

January 14 2018, Liverpool 4 Manchester City 3

By the dawn of 2018, Liverpool were going places under Klopp. They had finished fourth in the Premier League the previous season, playing some exciting football, and forced their way back into the Champions League. Players such as Sadio Mane and Salah were now on board. There were some neurotic moments on the pitch, when goalkeeping or defensive errors saw them drop points carelessly, but Anfield was now an optimistic place. Liverpool hadn't lost there since a 2-1 defeat by Palace at the back end of the previous season.

One Sunday in January, Manchester City rolled up on Merseyside having gone 22 Premier League games unbeaten since the start of the season. They were already firmly on course for the Premier League title, but that day were served a warning that Liverpool's resurgence was real. It was a performance in keeping with Klopp's demand for the kind of intensity which, he believes, is impossible to produce without drawing on the energy of the crowd. In an eight-minute spell in the second half, Liverpool scored three times to go 4-1 up.

"That was an unbelievable occasion," Atkinson says. "City seemed to be rattled by the atmosphere. The whole '12th man' thing, if we're honest about it, is mostly bollocks, but that day it really was the case. This brilliant, brilliant City team, who had passed teams off the park all season, suddenly couldn't string five passes together. Our lads were snapping into tackles and you could see them thriving off the adrenaline."

The mood had been set the moment the Liverpool team arrived to fanfare from the supporters who lined Anfield Road, waiting to welcome the team bus. That has become another modern-day tradition. It dates back to a show of solidarity with Rafa Benitez before a game against Tottenham during the troubled 2009-10 season, but really took hold when Liverpool were challenging for the title under Brendan Rodgers four years later. The fervour is at its greatest before a big game; it went way beyond acceptable levels on the day missiles were thrown at Manchester City's bus before the Champions League quarter-final first leg a few months later, which was angrily condemned by Klopp. These days every game is a big one.

Stirring victories over City and Roma took them to the Champions League final. They lost to Real Madrid in Kyiv, but supporters look back on that whole trip with a sense of wonder. The whole Champions League run had been an intoxicating adventure: the victories over City and Roma at Anfield, the fans' takeover of Shevchenko Park in Kyiv, new chants and a burgeoning relationship between the fans and a group of players who, in many cases, had been viewed with suspicion on arrival. *Allez, Allez, Allez.*

--------------------------------- **A** ---------------------------------

January 30 2019, Liverpool 1 Leicester City 1

On a freezing cold night last January, Liverpool extended their lead at the top of the Premier League to five points. It was only the second time all season that they had dropped points at

Anfield, their 33rd home Premier League game without defeat since April 2017, but nobody who was there that night saw it in such positive terms.

Manchester City had lost at Newcastle United the previous night and there was the strong feeling that this game represented a window of opportunity for a Liverpool team chasing the club's first league title since 1990. On a hard pitch, against awkward opponents, they produced their worst performance at Anfield in a long time. They looked nervous.

Words that can be found in just about every match report that night include "tension" and "anxiety". For much of that season, Liverpool's supporters were indeed believers, but the Leicester game confirmed something unsettling: that, among players and supporters, the doubts were still there underneath the surface. "There was a level of anxiety that hadn't been there all season," Atkinson says.

The players recognised it too. The more nervous they had got, trying to recover from a poor spell in the first half, the more nervous the crowd had got. Debates raged afterwards on social media.

It was a conversation in the Liverpool dressing room that night and at their Melwood training ground over the days that followed. The players talked about it in much the same way they would have done if, for example, they felt an opponent had exposed a weakness at set-pieces. They had even felt that tension from the crowd during the pre-match warm-up. Led by Jordan Henderson, James Milner and Adam Lallana, they decided they were going to have to try to do something about it because, if there was a Premier League title to be won, they couldn't afford for the atmosphere to be so fraught over the months ahead.

There were only 10 days before the next home game against Bournemouth. A 1-1 draw at West Ham United in the meantime didn't help one bit. Neither did Manchester City's victory over

Everton, which took them to the top of the table. But there were a few subtle steps taken in the build-up to the Bournemouth fixture to try to ensure that the atmosphere was different.

It wasn't a coincidence that, on the eve of the Bournemouth game, Sir Kenny Dalglish, the last man to lead Liverpool to a league title, sent a message of unity in an interview with the *Liverpool Echo*. "There's no problem with nerves," he said. "I think it's normal to feel nervous. It's anticipation. We have been brilliant this season, the support has been brilliant. For us, we've never, ever won a trophy in my time here without the help of the fans. When it gets towards the finishing line that's when you need them most of all. If we can all stick together collectively that will give us a chance to move forward. The fans can get them over the line with their support."

On the same day, Liverpool's official website published an interview with Lallana in which they asked how atmosphere can affect a team – positively or negatively. "It's probably not just us they can have an impact on. It's probably the opponents too," the midfielder said. "I've played at grounds where it can feel intimidating and the noise is that loud and they're getting behind the home team.

"Although I never came here many times as an away player, [the atmosphere] can have a negative effect on the opposition. As well as helping the players out, it probably has an adverse effect on the opponents. The season before I signed for Liverpool, 2013-14, I was aware of Liverpool's interest in me so I was paying close attention to their matches. The atmosphere at Anfield in that run-in was epic. You just wanted to play for that team at that ground. It would be great if we can get similar atmospheres and a similar vibe around Anfield, during the warm-ups. They do really act as a 12th man."

Klopp said something similar, urging "whoever wants us to succeed in this game and in general … to shout your soul onto the pitch".

The Spion Kop 1906 group, which organises the flags and banners at Anfield, was on-message too. "Let's get inside the ground early tomorrow and show the players we're behind them from the warm-up," the group said on Twitter. "We'll be in from 2pm and we'll need all the help we can get in the corner, so if you're on The Kop, come down and give us a hand. Let's get the ground bouncing. Unity is strength."

One other thing Liverpool's players did in the build-up to that game was talk about the music that should be played in the stadium during the warm-up. *You'll Never Walk Alone* was sacrosanct, but some of the players wondered whether, during the warm-up, there should be more emphasis on the type of upbeat, powerful music they had in the dressing room. Players were invited to come up with alternatives to pass on to the club.

One player proposed *This is Me*, as sung by the bearded lady in *The Greatest Showman*. There was laughter, but then they went through the lyrics and they felt it struck the right note: "We're burstin' though the barricades and reachin' for the sun. We are warriors." That went on the list, along with an acoustic version of the fans' *Allez, Allez, Allez* chant and Dua Lipa's *One Kiss*. George Sephton, the club's stadium announcer and DJ since 1971, welcomed the requests and executed the players' plan to the letter. It was considered a resounding success.

It was precisely the kind of low-key Saturday-afternoon fixture when talk of Anfield's legendary atmosphere can often seem wildly misplaced. On this occasion, the noise seemed relentless as Liverpool surged to a 3-0 win. Trent Alexander-Arnold said: "I've never seen it like that at a Saturday 3 o'clock game. The scarves, the flags, the banners. It was something I hadn't really experienced. This is what we need to push on."

If this all sounds like Liverpool's players were still playing to the gallery, saying things for effect, it is worth looking back at what the Bournemouth defender Steve Cook said unprompted that day. "You could see that the crowd were going to play a major part in the game," he said. "I haven't quite heard an atmosphere like it."

For the remainder of that season, Liverpool powered on. They beat Watford 5-0, Burnley 4-2, Tottenham Hotspur 2-1 (thanks to a last-minute own goal from Toby Alderweireld which seemed to conform to the old cliche of the Kop "sucking the ball into the net"), Chelsea 2-0 and Huddersfield Town 5-0 to take the title race into the final week. For all the talk about how the Anfield atmosphere might suffocate Liverpool, it was only in the away games, notably in draws at Manchester and Everton and fraught victories at Fulham, Southampton, Cardiff and Newcastle, that tension was apparent.

They reached another Champions League final, overpowering Barcelona 4-0 in the semi-final on what will go down as possibly Anfield's greatest European night of all. A few days later they played Wolves on the final day of the Premier League season, hoping and praying for Manchester City to slip up away to Brighton. Liverpool won their game, but their rivals prevailed on the south coast. The end of the dream? It didn't feel like it that day. The atmosphere at the final whistle was one of defiance as the fans sang about winning the European Cup, which they duly did, before setting their sights back on the prize the supporters covet most of all.

— **A** —

January 19 2020, Liverpool 2 Manchester United 0
Seven minutes had gone inside Anfield when the Manchester United supporters started asking, "Where's your famous atmosphere?"

It was not, in fact, a classic Liverpool v Manchester United atmosphere. There were times when it was extremely loud – when Virgil van Dijk headed Liverpool in front and, perhaps more so, when Roberto Firmino curled home what appeared to be a second goal before the VAR intervened – but other times during the first hour when it was simply contented. The home crowd were just enjoying the performance. For long periods, there was more noise from the away end as United's supporters tried to keep their spirits up.

It would be plain wrong to suggest that every Liverpool home game is played to an ear-splitting soundtrack. There are games where that seems to be the case – Barcelona last May was perhaps the ultimate – but there are also spells when it falls quiet, sometimes for long periods.

The Anfield mythology drives rival supporters mad. Then again, when expressing frustration with the lack of noise when he was managing both Chelsea and Manchester United, Jose Mourinho spoke of the "beautiful" atmosphere at Anfield. Pep Guardiola spoke about it last season, saying, "The motto 'This is Anfield' is no marketing spin. There's something about it that you will find in no other stadium in the world. They score a goal and over the next five minutes you feel that you'll receive another four. You feel it, smell it, and the rival players seem to be all over you."

Ultimately, though, this isn't about the difference between Anfield and other grounds. It is about how different it is to the Anfield that Klopp walked into in late 2015, when he and his players felt "pretty alone", or the Anfield of the late 2000s, when the club was in the grip of a power struggle and, as Atkinson puts it, "it felt like everyone in the ground hated each other". Right now, it feels like everyone in that ground loves each other.

Liverpool have now gone 52 Premier League games without defeat at Anfield. They are closing in on the club record of 63, set by Bob Paisley's team between 1978 and 1981, even if Chelsea's record of 86 games, between 2004 and 2008, remains a long way off. Perhaps the most striking thing about Liverpool's record since April 2017 (42 wins and 10 draws) is the number of times they have won tight games, often in the closing stages. Confidence breeds confidence. Success breeds success.

There have been times over the past decade when talk of Anfield as a fortress has been laughable. The 2010s saw three Anfield victories apiece for Crystal Palace and West Brom as well as wins for, among many others, Blackpool, Wolves, Wigan and Fulham. The nadir was a League Cup defeat at home to Northampton Town in September 2010. The attendance that night was just 22,577 and, in the grim final weeks of the Hicks-Gillett regime, with the unpopular figure of Roy Hodgson on the touchline, it really was a case of fear and loathing.

What Liverpool have right now, with Klopp, is the precise opposite of that. Is that simply the difference that top-class players make? Perhaps, but it is hard to avoid the feeling that this Liverpool team and this crowd, under the guidance of this manager, are propelling each other to new heights. There have been times in the not-too-distant past when new signings were regarded with distrust and more established players, with few exceptions, were tainted by previous failures. It was not a happy or positive place.

Henderson is one of those players who struggled, for years, to win the affection and the trust of the Anfield crowd. These days he thrives on it. During that tense final period against Manchester United, he was the one who was leading the way, chasing down opponents, making tackles, determined to snuff out any hint of an equaliser. His team-mates fed off that and so did the crowd. They love Henderson now, just like they love Alisson, Andy Robertson, Roberto Firmino, Mane and the rest. Trust and affection, lacking for so long, now appear total.

It is not unique to Liverpool; Atkinson says he sees something similar at Sheffield United under Chris Wilder, Wolves under Nuno Espirito Santo and even Southampton under Ralph Hasenhuttl. It was certainly something that was said of Dortmund under Klopp.

Klopp felt that, if he was to have any chance of his success on Merseyside, he and his players were going to have to connect with and energise the crowd in the same way. There have been a few bumps in the road – it certainly hasn't happened overnight – but that connection now seems every bit as powerful as the one his Dortmund team thrived upon.

"I don't take that atmosphere for granted," Klopp told *The Athletic* afterwards. "At the moment, even in the living rooms in front of the television, there is a lot of passion around the world based on LFC and we can take the energy from that.

"They carried us through the difficult period. It is exceptional. The atmosphere is absolutely exceptional. Everybody is on their toes – everybody. I really love that relationship. The atmosphere in the stands and the relationship between the two is incredible."

There was still some tension in the air in the final stages when United pushed forward in search of an equaliser – a few groans and shouts when Lallana gave the ball away deep in Liverpool territory and then Alisson hit the ball into touch when he was seeking out Robertson. But how tense can supporters really be when their team are already 13 points clear at the top of the Premier League, when Van Dijk is getting his head to every cross and Henderson is fighting for every loose ball?

Finally, in stoppage time, Alisson pounced on the ball in his own penalty area and, rather than run down the clock, he sought out Salah, left alone near the halfway line as United threw caution to the wind. Salah raced clear to score and Alisson, the goalkeeper, raced 100 yards to slide on his knees in front of the Kop in celebration. Anfield could no longer hold it in. "People piling on one another, everyone at the top of their voice, the thing no one has wanted to say, the unspoken truth," Atkinson wrote afterwards on *The Anfield Wrap*. "We're gonna win the league."

And now just about everyone believes them, that by May – and perhaps considerably sooner – Liverpool will be champions of England for the first time in three decades. Anfield feels like a fortress once more.

JANUARY RESULTS

Premier League, January 2 2020
Liverpool 2 Sheffield United 0
Liverpool scorers: Salah 4, Mane 64

FA Cup, January 5 2020
Liverpool 1 Everton 0
Liverpool scorer: Jones 71

Premier League, January 11 2020
Tottenham 0 Liverpool 1
Liverpool scorer: Firmino 37

Premier League, January 19 2020
Liverpool 2 Manchester United 0
Liverpool scorers: Van Dijk 14, Salah 90+3

Premier League, January 23 2019
Wolves 1 Liverpool 2
Liverpool scorers: Henderson 8, Firmino 84

FA Cup, January 26 2020
Shrewsbury 2 Liverpool 2
Liverpool scorers: Jones 15, Love 46 OG

Premier League, January 29 2020
West Ham 0 Liverpool 2
Liverpool scorers: Salah 35 pen, Oxlade-Chamberlain 52

FEBRUARY

THE SECRETS OF FORTRESS ANFIELD AND "A PITCH AS FINELY TUNED AS THE ATHLETES WHO PLAY ON IT"

JAMES PEARCE

FEB 2, 2020

Many dismissed it as a lame excuse when Jurgen Klopp lamented the dryness of the Anfield pitch after Liverpool were held to a dour stalemate by Southampton in May 2017.

"I know nobody wants to hear it but I am brave enough to say it. The pitch was really dry," he declared. "We gave it all the water we had but after 15 minutes it was really dry again with the wind. You could see it… a lot of passes you thought 'why are they playing this?' But it was difficult.

"In a possession game you need to have the best circumstances, in a home game especially, but we couldn't have this. That's nobody's fault. It is not what I want. To be successful you have to have a fortress at home."

Klopp felt that Liverpool's ageing playing surface was holding them back. It was too slow and inhibited their attacking play. Fenway Sports Group (FSG) took action, sanctioning a multi-million pound investment in the club's infrastructure that summer. To say that the owners have had a decent return on that outlay would be something of an understatement.

On Saturday a resurgent Southampton suffered at the hands of Klopp's juggernaut. A dazzling second-half blitz secured a 4-0 triumph as Liverpool equalled Manchester City's Premier League record of 20 successive home league wins. "Wow, the Kop was in full voice today," declared FSG president Mike Gordon as he greeted reporters waiting to speak to the players post-match.

Klopp has built an imposing fortress and these days Anfield brings out the best in the Premier League champions elect. The array of improvements made to the playing surface are a key part of that.

"A lot of teams come to Anfield and play compact and that means there isn't a lot of space," Liverpool goalkeeping coach John Achterberg tells *The Athletic*. "In the past we struggled against teams who sat back with 11 men behind the ball and we'd drop points. But the owners made the pitch so much better with the new surface and the water system they had installed. We always have a wet pitch now and that helps the speed of the game so much.

"I always used to be worried that on a sunny day we'd struggle because the pitch was too slow to move the ball quick to create things. Now the players know how to break teams down and where to find the solutions."

Liverpool had a new state-of-the-art GrassMaster pitch installed; a hybrid field consisting of 97 per cent organic grass combined with three per cent of artificial fibres. Some 25,000 miles of artificial fibres were stitched into the pitch – the equivalent of the earth's circumference.

Anfield became the first stadium in the UK to fit the Permavoid irrigation system to speed up drainage and allow for the entire surface to be watered in less than three minutes. A new undersoil heating system made up of some 19 miles of pipeline was also put in place to help aid growth and prevent the pitch from freezing.

Work was completed in time for the start of the 2017-18

season. Since then Liverpool have played 51 home league matches – winning 42 and drawing nine. It's now been more than a year since any top-flight team left Anfield with something to show for their efforts.

Maintenance of the turf is the responsibility of grounds manager Dave Roberts, who joined the club in April 2016. He previously carried out the same role at Southampton before working for public school Charterhouse in Surrey. Klopp's attention to detail means that he's in regular dialogue with Roberts to ensure the pitch is exactly how the manager wants it.

"Dave is one of the unsung heroes," Geoff Webb, chief executive officer of the Institute of Groundsmanship, tells *The Athletic*. "Pitch technology has moved on massively over the last 10 years and Dave has been ahead of the game on that. He's a brilliant groundsman and is well-respected by his peers. There aren't many around with the skill he's got.

"He's got a very good working relationship with Klopp and that communication is very important in terms of creating a surface that the players really trust and feel safe and comfortable on."

At Melwood, Roberts is tasked with ensuring Liverpool train ahead of home games on a pitch that replicates Anfield in every possible way, but at other times he has to adapt.

Towards the end of last season, Klopp anticipated Cardiff City boss Neil Warnock would do everything in his power to slow Liverpool down. He therefore asked for the training pitch not to be cut or watered to prepare his players for what they might face in the Welsh capital. His hunch was right. Cardiff's sprinkler system appeared to have been given the day off but Liverpool ran out 2-0 winners.

Anfield is now pristine all-year round. Eight heat and moisture sensors help monitor the best growing environment, while ground staff use 15 grow lights to cultivate the grass. Temperature and humidity can be controlled to speed up growth.

"It's about 10 per cent soil, 90 per cent sand and that pitch is as finely tuned as the athletes who play on it," Webb adds. "Even the technology behind grass seed is huge. It's genetically modified for each particular stadium, taking into account the environment and things like shade tolerance.

"Tests are done regularly and everything these days is data driven. Areas are flagged up and work is carried out. It's about getting the balance right in terms of stability and drainage. The lighting rigs have made a massive difference as they give you the opportunity to create sunlight and help grow the grass, no matter what time of year it is."

Premier League rules state that match delegates must measure pitches before every game to ensure the grass is no longer than 30mm (1.2in). Anfield is around 23mm (0.9in) – "just about the perfect height for football", according to Webb.

There was no slowing Liverpool down on Saturday as they zipped the ball around at pace and turned defence into attack in devastating fashion during that second-half onslaught. "When my team starts rolling, the power we create in these moments is really incredible," beamed Klopp.

Ten passes and 25 seconds after Danny Ings had stumbled over in the box appealing for a penalty, Alex Oxlade-Chamberlain fired home the opener. There were nine seconds between Alisson having the ball at his feet and Mohamed Salah converting Liverpool's third after a pinpoint pass from the outstanding Jordan Henderson, which skipped perfectly off the turf. The slick exchange between Salah and Roberto Firmino in the build-up to the fourth had Anfield on its feet once again. It was another good day at the office for Roberts and his staff.

Liverpool have taken 100 points out of the last 102 on offer and have equalled Nottingham Forest's 42-game unbeaten league run in 1977-78. Now they have Arsenal's record of 49 from 2003-04 in their sights.

Shrewd recruitment has been at the heart of the transformation Klopp has overseen. But FSG have also committed £200 million into the club's infrastructure with the Main Stand redevelopment, the pitch, the retail store and the new training complex in Kirkby, which will open its doors in July.

Where once their surroundings held them back, Liverpool now have everything in place to flourish.

FEBRUARY RESULTS

Premier League, February 1 2020
Liverpool 4 Southampton 0
Liverpool scorers: Oxlade-Chamberlain 47, Henderson 60, Salah 71, 90

FA Cup replay, February 4 2020
Liverpool 1 Shrewsbury Town 0
Scorer: Williams 75 OG

Premier League, February 15 2020
Norwich City 0 Liverpool 1
Liverpool scorer: Mane 78

Champions League, February 18 2020
Atletico Madrid 1 Liverpool 0

Premier League, February 24 2020
Liverpool 3 West Ham United 2
Liverpool scorers: Wijnaldum 9, Salah 68, Mane 81

Premier League, February 29 2020
Watford 3 Liverpool 0

MARCH

HOW LIVERPOOL REACT TO DEFEAT AT WATFORD WILL DEFINE THEIR SEASON

JAMES PEARCE

MAR 1, 2020

There was no inquest or angry tirade in the away dressing room at Vicarage Road. Jurgen Klopp always prefers to let the dust settle and give the players his considered verdict the following day, rather than speak at length when emotions are running high. Even Liverpool's proud, unbeaten 44-game Premier League record biting the dust in such alarming fashion at the hands of lowly Watford didn't alter that approach.

"I'd say he was just honest when he spoke to us for a few minutes afterwards," midfielder Georginio Wijnaldum tells *The Athletic*. "He talked about how we've had an unbelievable run but we can't close our eyes to what happened in this game. He said we have to take it on the chin, assess where it went wrong and then work to put things right.

"It's really painful and difficult to take. Losing hits you a lot harder when you haven't lost in the league for such a long time. Nothing seemed to work for us. We have to learn from it and do better."

The Liverpool boss did most of his talking – aided by video

analysis – when the squad reassembled at Melwood on Sunday to do their recovery work. Footage was dissected to try to understand why a day which was expected to yield a historic 19th successive league win went so spectacularly wrong. It had been a long time since Klopp's team had failed to function in every single department and been swept aside in this manner. You have to go back to October 2017 and the wretched 4-1 defeat by Tottenham Hotspur at Wembley for the last time Liverpool performed this poorly in the top flight. That was also the previous occasion when they lost a Premier League fixture by more than one goal.

Their hopes of emulating Arsenal's Invincibles may have been dashed, but in the context of the title race, the consequences are minimal. Liverpool go into March with a 22-point cushion at the summit. It's still simply a question of when, rather than if that 30-year drought is ended.

Saturday wasn't a complete shock. Liverpool's performances have been disjointed since their two-week hiatus due to the inaugural Premier League break. Rhythm has been lost.

A scrappy win at Norwich City a fortnight ago was followed by a nervy journey home. The team's flight was delayed on the runway due to high winds making it unsafe to take off. As a result, a handful of players decided to get off and travel back to Merseyside by road instead. There has been plenty of turbulence since: an insipid defeat away to Atletico Madrid in the first leg of their last-16 Champions League tie and an unconvincing win over West Ham at Anfield. Then they found themselves bullied by Watford.

Dejan Lovren was a lightning rod for criticism on Saturday and the Croatia international certainly came off second best in his battle with Troy Deeney. Rusty and erratic, he spread a degree of panic with his errors and poor decision-making. However, it would be wrong to scapegoat Lovren, who hadn't started in the league since December 7. The reality is that a collective malaise cost Liverpool. Even the usually unflappable Virgil van Dijk was way off the pace.

"No-one in the dressing room was pointing at any individuals," says Wijnaldum. "We win as a team and we lose as a team. We all know that we can do much better than that. I wouldn't blame the winter break because I actually think that was good for us as players. You have to give Watford credit as they defended pretty well. They dropped quite deep and they stopped us from creating chances. We were not close to our best.

"Sometimes as a team you have days like that. There have been times this season when we haven't played at our level but we've still been able to find a way to win. This time we weren't able to do that but we're still in a great position."

It was the first time Liverpool had fired blanks in the Premier League since the stalemate at Goodison Park a year ago. Mohamed Salah, Roberto Firmino and Sadio Mane failed to muster a single key pass or shot on target between them. The service to them was non-existent.

Defensively, Klopp's men have conceded five goals in two games – as many as they had leaked in their previous 14 league matches. Joe Gomez was sorely missed after being ruled out due to a minor muscle problem.

The past two matches have also served to underline the importance of captain Jordan Henderson, who is back running as he steps up his recovery from a hamstring injury. Liverpool simply aren't the same force without his drive and leadership at the heart of the midfield. There were no complaints, for example, to referee Michael Oliver after Trent Alexander-Arnold was chopped down by a reckless challenge from Deeney in the first half. Henderson would have demanded action. Life without their skipper hasn't been helped by the fact that Fabinho has been nowhere near his commanding best since returning from an ankle ligament injury in late January. The team's defensive shield no longer looks impregnable. Klopp has work to do to help the Brazilian rediscover his swagger. The imminent return to fitness of James Milner will at least bolster the midfield options, while more will be expected from Naby Keita, who missed the weekend with a sore hip.

Having somehow negotiated FA Cup ties against Everton and Shrewsbury with youthful line-ups, it will be intriguing to see how Klopp approaches Tuesday's trip to Stamford Bridge in the same competition. Will he stick with the plan to hand starts to the likes of Adrian, Takumi Minamino, Adam Lallana, Divock Origi, Joel Matip and Curtis Jones? Or will he give more of the personnel smarting from events at Vicarage Road the chance to make amends? There's a strong case to be made that the tie with Chelsea is more important than Bournemouth at home on March 7, given Liverpool's cushion at the top of the Premier League.

Klopp suggested on Saturday night that all the talk of going the entire league season unbeaten had heaped pressure on his players. "From now on we can play free football again," he said.

Yet it's hard to believe that was a factor here. Complacency, the absence of key personnel and Watford's perfectly executed tactical plan were more significant.

This was a throwback to Klopp's first visit to Vicarage Road in December 2015, which ended with the same chastening scoreline. Back then the players were convinced that their Christmas Party at Formby Hall that evening would be cancelled after such an inept display. Instead, they all received a text message from the manager that read: "Whatever we do together we do as well as we can and tonight that means we party." They were informed they all had to stay until at least 1am.

Liverpool have come a long way since then. They didn't hit the dance floor on Saturday night but that message of unity from Klopp remains the same.

HOW LIVERPOOL ARE HELPING THEIR PLAYERS AND THE COMMUNITY DURING PANDEMIC

JAMES PEARCE

MAR 26, 2020

Liverpool have extended their shutdown of Melwood as the players prepare to start training together again via video link. Jurgen Klopp's squad were told that the training complex in West Derby would be off-limits for an initial two-week period when the Premier League season was suspended on March 13 due to the coronavirus pandemic. However, it quickly became clear the champions-elect would be kept apart for much longer than that. Only the club's injured players were allowed to visit Melwood last week for treatment but in the wake of the UK government bringing in more stringent rules about social distancing to combat the spread of the virus, a full closure has been implemented.

Alisson (hip) and Xherdan Shaqiri (calf), who were given different physios to work with and different time slots to keep them apart, will complete their recoveries on their own at home. They have been given the equipment they require as well as guidance from club medical staff.

With each of Klopp's players having kept to individual training programmes over the past fortnight, Liverpool are now in the process of co-ordinating team sessions, which are likely to be conducted over Zoom, the video communications platform.

"The manager initially treated it like an international break, with players given their own work to do," a senior Anfield source tells *The Athletic*. "But there was also an acceptance at the time that this situation was always likely to get worse before it got better. There's no timescale on returning to Melwood because the situation is so fluid.

"Now the plan is to move on to daily group sessions, with all the players doing their gym work at the same time via smartphones or smart TVs. It's a period of real uncertainty but it's important to retain that team spirit and camaraderie and guard against players feeling lonely and isolated.

"Jurgen is in touch with all the players two or three times a day via WhatsApp and data from their individual workouts is collected by the sports science team. The contact remains really regular."

Before they went their separate ways, the players were given a list of what they would require for use at home. Deliveries were arranged for those who indicated they didn't have access to certain weights and cardio equipment.

The players were also advised not to head overseas in the knowledge that borders could be closed and that it would be easier for the club to provide assistance if they remained local. Instead it was recommended that arrangements were made for close family members living abroad to come to Merseyside, with club staff helping to sort out travel plans.

Club doctors Jim Moxon and Sarah Lindsay have been giving advice to minimise the threat of catching the virus and are on call if any of the players have concerns. The same goes for sports psychologist Lee Richardson, who is helping them cope with the mental side of isolation and the change in lifestyle. There are breathing exercises to help players deal with anxiety.

The players have been following guidance from head of nutrition Mona Nemmer, too. Food parcels are regularly dispatched to the homes of those in need of assistance, especially players who live on their own. First-team operations manager Ray Haughan has been co-ordinating the help given to the senior squad.

As well as retaining fitness levels and eating healthily, players have been analysing footage from matches over the course of this season and pinpointing areas of potential improvement. Netflix and PlayStations are also proving popular to pass the time.

Liverpool's discussions with agents and rival clubs regarding their summer transfer plans are currently on hold. Sporting director Michael Edwards, head of recruitment Dave Fallows and chief scout Barry Hunter are continuing to consider various options in consultation with Klopp. They are examining the array of data at their disposal and gathering as much information as possible about potential targets. However, there is little prospect of any real progress being made on deals during the current hiatus.

"The truth is there are just too many variables currently," the Anfield source adds. "We don't know if this season is going to end in June or September. We don't know when next season will start. We don't know whether the summer transfer window will be moved or extended. We don't know the financial situation of clubs when we come out the other side of this.

"With so many things up in the air, it would be ludicrous to try to push on with anything practical to do with recruitment. For now, it's just a case of assessing what's needed and looking at what might be achievable. Thankfully, as a club we have brilliant strategists in place with Michael and his team."

Privately, Liverpool's owners have welcomed the collective desire shown across the Premier League for this season to be completed when it is deemed safe for football to resume, rather than declared null and void. Klopp's side require just six points from their final nine games to be mathematically certain of ending the club's 30-year wait to be domestic champions again.

However, no senior figure has spoken publicly since Klopp's thoughtful statement to supporters on the day of the shutdown a fortnight ago, and that's set to continue. Liverpool believe it would be inappropriate for players or staff to be talking about football and their prospects of still lifting the Premier League trophy at a time of crisis across the world.

Work on Liverpool's new £50 million training complex in Kirkby ground to a halt earlier this week after contractors McLaughlin and Harvey took government advice and temporarily closed the site, while parents of the 170 youngsters on the books at the club's academy have been sent an email stating it will remain shut "for the foreseeable future".

'Unity Is Strength' reads one well-known banner on the Kop and behind the scenes Liverpool have embarked on a wide range of measures designed to help reduce the devastating impact of the virus on their wider community and help those in need. The club have vowed to pay all casual match-day workers at Anfield for the three home matches until the end of April which have been postponed so far. That goodwill gesture will cost them around £750,000.

Concerned about the shortfall facing North Liverpool Foodbank, which relies heavily on match-day collections, captain Jordan Henderson stepped up and vowed that the first-team squad would help plug the gap. Together with the LFC Foundation, £40,000 has been donated to ensure it can still function as normal.

Liverpool have since launched the LFC Emergency Foodbank Appeal in aid of the Trussell Trust Foodbank network, which provides emergency assistance to families and vulnerable people living in food poverty across Merseyside. Donations from fans are being made via Facebook.

"It's important during these difficult times that we continue to help the people who need our support the most," says Matt Parish, director of the LFC Foundation.

Having been forced to suspend their usual array of school and community programmes, the club have launched a new initiative called LFC Connect, which is designed to reduce feelings of social isolation among older and vulnerable neighbours in the north Liverpool and Kirkby communities. Staff have been manning the phones to call around those who usually attend their sessions and have "a virtual cuppa" with them. They are checking they have sufficient food at home as well as offering to collect prescriptions. The club have also sent out postcards letting fans know about the support that's available during this difficult time.

Chair-based yoga sessions for the over-50s, as part of the Red Neighbours scheme, are being delivered online. Videos to download have also been made available for those who normally attend activities such as walking football and youth coaching sessions to keep them involved.

The club already have close ties with local hospitals, which find themselves under increasing strain due to the pandemic. Players and staff regularly visit Alder Hey Children's Hospital, which is close to the training ground and is an official charity partner of the LFC Foundation. Some £225,000 was donated to the new research, innovation and education facility. Members of the club's Red Neighbours team also attend the Royal Liverpool University Hospital and local care homes, although those trips are currently on hold.

Chief executive Peter Moore has reached out to supermarket chiefs after the club's match-day stewards offered their time and expertise to help with crowd control and queue management. "They are truly the best in the business and would be delighted to help in whatever way you would deem appropriate (and safe) on your premises," Moore tweeted.

Support and advice is also being given to the array of former Liverpool players who regularly work at Anfield in the executive lounges on match days. Former Liverpool scout Arthur Edwards is currently ill in hospital and the 81-year-old's spirits were lifted by phone calls from Steven Gerrard and Jamie Carragher, while Kenny Dalglish sent a video message.

In a time of crisis, Liverpool have stayed true to their iconic anthem. Nobody has been left to walk alone.

MARCH RESULTS

FA Cup, March 3 2020
Chelsea 2 Liverpool 0

Premier League, March 7 2020
Liverpool 2 Bournemouth 1
Liverpool scorers: Salah 24, Mane 33

Champions League, March 11 2020
Liverpool 2 Atletico Madrid 3 (AET)
Liverpool scorers: Wijnaldum 43, Firmino 94

APRIL

INSIDE LIVERPOOL'S U-TURN: A 'LEAK', A TOXIC BACKLASH AND REAL MONEY WORRIES

JAMES PEARCE

APR 7, 2020

Liverpool had not planned to make an announcement on Saturday afternoon regarding their controversial decision to utilise the UK government's Coronavirus Job Retention Scheme. "Our hand was forced," one senior club source told *The Athletic*.

The Anfield hierarchy believe details were leaked by another Premier League club after what Liverpool understood to be confidential discussions involving top-flight sides about how they intended to handle the effects of the pandemic.

Liverpool's plan was to wait until Monday to release their statement, to ensure that every impacted employee was made aware by the club directly via letter before any public announcement was made. Little did owners Fenway Sports Group know that the publication of a hastily-constructed statement on the club website confirming that some non-playing staff had been placed on furlough would trigger a furious backlash that culminated 48 hours later in a dramatic U-turn and public apology.

In an open letter to supporters on Monday, chief executive Peter Moore said the club was "truly sorry" for coming to the "wrong conclusion" after initially deciding to furlough about 200 employees. Liverpool will no longer seek taxpayers' money to cover 80 per cent of the wages of staff who are currently unable to work with no matches going on. They would have been claiming about £500,000 per month.

The Athletic understands principal owner John W Henry, chairman Tom Werner and FSG president Mike Gordon were "shocked" by the torrent of criticism and stung by what they regard as unfair accusations of greed. During a series of conference calls on Monday, they were in full agreement that back-tracking was the best solution to limiting the damage caused by the fallout.

Gordon, who is FSG's second biggest shareholder after Henry, runs Liverpool on a day-to-day basis and is a popular figure at both Melwood and in the club's Chapel Street offices. The Milwaukee-born businessman, who divides his time between Merseyside and FSG's home in Boston, has the final word on everything from sanctioning transfer deals to making senior executive appointments.

Managing director Billy Hogan and Moore answer to him and the trio spoke extensively before the initial decision to furlough was taken last week. From a business perspective, they felt it was crucial to help ease the current cash-flow issues. All revenue streams have dried up in the current crisis but overheads remain huge and even for a club the size of Liverpool that's a major headache. As well as an annual wage bill of £310 million, there are payments on previous transfers due in the coming months. There's uncertainty over whether TV money will need to be repaid and if the next instalments from global sponsors will be forthcoming, given that with no games being played Liverpool are currently unable to fulfil their side of the bargain.

The Athletic has reported there are significant fears that Premier League sides may yet need to repay £762 million to broadcasters should the 2019-20 season not be completed, while the determination to finish the campaign even led to one idea of taking games to China.

The collective commitment to find a way to complete the Premier League season when it's safe to do so is good news for Liverpool, with Jurgen Klopp's side on the brink of sealing the title. However, just when football will return remains unclear. Mid-to-late June, with matches initially played behind closed doors, is currently regarded as the most optimistic scenario. Meanwhile, the financial toll will keep growing.

Liverpool's latest accounts may have shown a pre-tax profit of £42 million, but FSG insists those figures are almost a year old and all money generated is reinvested into the club as it constantly looks to balance the books.

There has been no public announcement, but *The Athletic* understands more than a dozen executive staff, including Hogan, Moore and chief operating officer Andy Hughes, voluntarily took a 25 per cent pay cut last week. It was kept quiet as they didn't want to place the players in a difficult situation as their own discussions over wage reductions continue.

As a major UK taxpayer and one of the biggest employers in the city with a staff of around 800, FSG felt it was entitled to utilise the coronavirus fund to help safeguard jobs.

Bigger companies than Liverpool FC have turned to the government for help and they currently have hundreds of operational, hospitality and catering staff who have no work to do in the continued absence of Premier League football.

Liverpool had already promised to cover the wages of casual Anfield match-day staff for the postponed games in April, which will cost them about £250,000 per match.

The club hierarchy believed criticism of their furlough decision would be mitigated by the fact that, unlike Tottenham Hotspur, they would be topping up the 80 per cent coming from the government with the remaining 20 per cent to ensure that no employee would be left out of pocket.

They were wrong. And the backlash over the weekend was so toxic that *The Athletic* understands a number of other Premier League clubs who had intended to announce the furloughing of staff have since decided to shelve those plans.

"That kind of thing was almost expected of Daniel Levy and Mike Ashley but you don't expect Liverpool to go down that same route," one Liverpool staff member, who asked to remain anonymous, told *The Athletic*.

"We're always told we're part of a family here and that working for Liverpool is different. 'This means more' is the marketing slogan. Surely part of that is looking after your own rather than taking government money which would be better spent elsewhere with so many businesses struggling?"

Former Liverpool players including Jamie Carragher and Stan Collymore led the fierce criticism on social media and as one FSG executive in Boston admitted, "the bullets really started flying".

The fact that it became national headline news, with government ministers wading into the debate as Liverpool took a battering, led to a series of urgent trans-Atlantic calls and a swift rethink. It had been a decision driven by data, but the emotion it triggered hadn't been properly considered.

Influential supporters' union Spirit of Shankly (SOS) submitted an open letter to Moore via email on Sunday afternoon, demanding a full explanation and expressing concern for "the damage this is causing to our club's reputation and values". On Monday, Moore and Tony Barrett, Liverpool's head of club and supporter engagement, conducted a series of phone discussions with respected figures in the community. Feedback was collated and then presented to Gordon. There were three separate conversations with Joe Blott, the chair of SOS.

"It wasn't clear at that stage that the decision would be reversed, but I genuinely felt they were listening," Blott tells *The Athletic*. "They wanted to gauge where the fanbase was on this. We told them it went right to the heart of the values of the club. I'm thankful we got to this position in the end but it all could have been avoided if supporters had been involved from an early stage."

Moore also rang the Mayor of Liverpool Joe Anderson and the region's Metro Mayor Steve Rotheram, as well as local MPs Ian Byrne and Dan Carden. Byrne, a lifelong Liverpool fan, tells *The Athletic*: "Peter asked me what I thought and I told him that I'm in favour of using furlough if it means retaining jobs, as the overriding priority has to be that staff members get paid.

"Everyone was delighted when British Airways went into furlough as it saved jobs, but the reality is that football gets judged by a different set of rules. With football clubs, there is a moral side to this. If Liverpool were saying, 'We're going to furlough for three months, we're going to get X amount from the government and then we're going to pay it back further down the line' – that's a different argument. The shame for me was that this decision has overshadowed a lot of the great work the club is doing in the local community at this difficult time.

"Football is an easy target for the government and some people are always looking for a reason to give Liverpool a knock. The club gave them an open goal on this one. It's caused some damage but they've done the right thing in the end."

Manchester City and Manchester United subsequently announced they would not be furloughing staff.

Having assessed all the feedback from Merseyside and done plenty of soul-searching, Gordon sanctioned the U-turn on Monday afternoon as he concluded there had been "a misjudgement" which needed to be reversed. He fed back to Henry and Werner. It was decided that Moore would write an open letter to fans.

There are parallels with February 2016, when FSG scrapped plans to increase ticket prices after 10,000 supporters walked out of Anfield in protest during a game against Sunderland.

On Monday, Moore wrote that Liverpool would find "alternative means" to cover wages rather than furlough during this "unprecedented period". In the short-term that means dipping into cash reserves, but concerns within the club about the impact of this crisis going forward are genuine and growing.

A glaring mistake has been rectified and the damage done has been reduced if not erased.

It's a fine line between running Liverpool FC as a business and embracing the principles and values that the club's supporters hold dear. After a torrid 48 hours, FSG acknowledged they fell on the wrong side of it.

LIVERPOOL'S PLAYER OF THE YEAR: MANE, SALAH, HENDERSON, TRENT, VAN DIJK...?

JAMES PEARCE

APR 22, 2020

There has been a chasm between Liverpool and their Premier League rivals over the course of this season. The 25-point cushion at the summit is testament to the exhilarating brilliance and unprecedented consistency of Jurgen Klopp's side.

The records books were rewritten as they moved to the brink of sealing the club's first domestic title for 30 years prior to the season being suspended due to the coronavirus pandemic.

It was a procession – but the race to be crowned Liverpool Player of the Year has been a great deal more competitive. Sadio Mane, the African Footballer of the Year, has undoubtedly been the standout performer in Klopp's potent three-man attack. On the other flank, Mohamed Salah became the first Liverpool player since Michael Owen, nearly two decades ago, to reach the 20-goal mark in three successive seasons. Virgil van Dijk, the runaway winner a year ago, has maintained his imperious form and expertly marshalled a miserly backline. Alongside the Dutchman, Trent Alexander-Arnold has cemented his status as the best right-back in European football – equalling his own top-flight record for assists from a defender, set in 2018-19. But for the time they spent on the sidelines earlier in the campaign, Alisson and Joe Gomez would also have been part of the conversation given the calibre of their displays.

However, judged on August right through to April, there is one man who deserves the accolade more than any other – a man whose contribution puts him at the head of that stellar cast. His name is Jordan Henderson. The Liverpool skipper's ninth season at Anfield has been the best of his career. He has grown in stature since he triumphantly hoisted the Champions League trophy into the Madrid sky last June.

Having fought a seemingly endless battle to win over his army of doubters, the 29-year-old is now the beating heart of this special Liverpool team. He's a model professional with a social conscience who commands the respect of his peers and leads by example – both on and off the field. That was epitomised by the manner in which he responded to the pandemic by contacting his fellow Premier League skippers and becoming the driving force behind the 'Players Together' fund which is raising money for NHS charities.

Klopp is indebted to Henderson for the dressing-room unity and spirit that has helped carry Liverpool so far. He's selfless, ensures there are no cliques and demands the highest of standards from everyone around him.

After Liverpool beat Tottenham 1-0 in the capital back in January to register the best ever start to a season in Europe's top five leagues (20 wins and a draw from 21 games), the TV cameras picked up on Henderson's comments to Klopp after the final whistle.

"Not good enough. It was shit," he told his manager. It was typical of the mentality of a player who banned talk of winning the title in the dressing room and repeatedly warned his team-mates there could be no easing off – despite their mammoth lead.

"You can see how much being captain of this football club means to Hendo," says Alexander-Arnold. "Anyone who isn't pulling their weight gets a bollocking off him. He's a role model for all the lads. He's someone who is incredibly passionate about the game, about this club and about the fans.

"He doesn't care whether someone like Mo or Sadio or Virgil is getting all the praise. He's not bothered about being in the spotlight, he's happy to go under the radar and just go about his job. He always puts the team first. It's incredible to see on a daily basis."

Yet for all the plaudits that rightly come his way about his leadership, character and mentality, his quality on the pitch is still underestimated by some. Make no mistake, this award is based on performance levels – the other stuff simply strengthens his claims.

Henderson, who lifted both the UEFA Super Cup and the Club World Cup, has repeatedly set the tempo with his energy and dynamism in the centre of the Liverpool midfield. When Fabinho was trusted to play the No 6 role on his own and Henderson was let off the leash in a more advanced role, he relished the freedom.

When the Brazil international was sidelined by an ankle injury, Henderson dropped back into the holding role and pulled the strings – the transition was seamless. He even did a job at centre-back when Klopp was faced with a defensive crisis in the semi-final of the Club World Cup against Monterrey in Qatar.

The £16 million signing from Sunderland back in 2011 has always been a fine athlete, but with greater belief his decision-making has improved markedly.

"The natural quality was always there," says Klopp. "I knew Hendo before I came here as a proper box-to-box player, who can make the difference with power, his speed, as well as the stuff like this, the desire he puts on the pitch. He was 25 when I came here, the best age to make the next steps. He is now calmer in certain situations. His self-awareness, self-confidence grew."

Once derided by some for favouring the sideways pass and not making an impact in the final third, this season Henderson has been a valuable creative force. As well as his reading of the game and ability to shut down space and win back possession, he has given Liverpool an added dimension with his pin-point long-range deliveries.

There was the equaliser at home to Tottenham, when he tucked away Fabinho's cross in front of the Kop; and the assist in the victory over Manchester City at Anfield, when he burst away from Ilkay Gundogan down the right and put a glorious cross on to Mane's head. Away to Bournemouth, he created something out of nothing – collecting the ball off Dejan Lovren deep inside his own half and picking out the run of Alex Oxlade-Chamberlain, who volleyed home an inch perfect 60-yard pass. At Wolves, in January, he opened the scoring with an emphatic header and then laid on the late winner for Roberto Firmino. When Southampton were routed at Anfield in February, Henderson emphatically converted Firmino's cut-back, before creating the third for Salah with a gloriously weighted pass from close to the touchline. The Egyptian didn't even need to break stride as he gleefully accepted the gift. A horribly scrappy contest at lowly Norwich City was settled by Henderson's vision and the finishing prowess of Mane late on.

His stats of three goals, five assists and 26 chances created in 25 Premier League appearances this season don't do justice to his influence on Klopp's juggernaut. Look instead at how sorely he was missed when a hamstring strain kept him out from mid-February until mid-March and Liverpool suffered a wobble.

When Salah raced away to score the goal that killed off Manchester United at Anfield back in January, Henderson dropped to the turf. Both emotionally and physically, he was spent. He was immense on a day when the Kop unveiled a new giant banner in his honour and chanted his name repeatedly.

Klopp described following in the footsteps of Steven Gerrard as "the most difficult job in the last 500 years of football". Unfair comparisons were made, but now no-one questions Henderson's suitability to wear the armband. He has made the job his own.

"He's outstanding," adds Klopp. "If anybody who is with us still doesn't see the quality of Jordan Henderson then I cannot help them.

"Is Hendo the perfect football player? No. Do I know anybody who is? No. Is he unbelievably important to us? Yes."

The back story makes Henderson's Anfield journey all the more compelling, from the baptism of fire after being signed by Kenny Dalglish, to the tears when Brendan Rodgers told him he could leave for Fulham and the debilitating heel injury which wrecked his first year under Klopp.

He has certainly triumphed in the face of adversity, but this is no sympathy vote. Henderson has been more instrumental than anyone in a season like no other for Liverpool.

JUNE

CONTROLLED AGGRESSION, COLLECTIVE DEFENCE: LIVERPOOL ARE LEAGUE'S CLEANEST TEAM

JAMES PEARCE

JUN 10, 2020

It was once used by some as a stick with which to beat Jurgen Klopp. During his first two full seasons at Anfield, Liverpool finished top of the Premier League Fair Play table, but won nothing else. They were a long way off the summit in the standings that truly matter – 17 points behind champions Chelsea in 2016-17 and 25 adrift of Manchester City a year later. Too nice.

The argument went that a more combative, spiky, cynical edge would be required if Liverpool were going to progress to the next level and become serious contenders for the top-flight crown. Yet the exhilarating rise of Klopp's side to the brink of ending the club's 30-year wait for the title has not been accompanied by an increase in their transgressions. Having taken 179 points out of a possible 201 since the start of the 2018-19 season, they remain the cleanest team in the Premier League and are on course to top the Fair Play table for the fourth successive season.

Liverpool have accumulated just 26 yellow cards and one red in their 29 league matches so far, and even that solitary dismissal was for Alisson's rush of blood which saw the goalkeeper handle the ball outside the box during November's home win over Brighton. Leicester City (30 yellows, one red) have the next-best disciplinary record. At the other end of the table, Arsenal and Tottenham have collected 62 yellows and three reds apiece.

Klopp's men have also conceded fewer fouls (242) than any other Premier League team. Southampton lead the way on 355, followed by Watford (350) and Everton (346).

The amount of possession Liverpool enjoy is undoubtedly a factor. They have had an average of 63 per cent in league games this season – only Manchester City (66 per cent) have had more. Of course, the more ball you have, the less chance there is of conceding fouls and picking up cards. However, it goes much deeper than that. After all, Pep Guardiola's side have had 49 yellows and three red cards (two of them for a second booking) and conceded 283 fouls.

It comes down to the culture that Klopp and his coaching staff have created at Melwood. There's a strong tactical element behind those numbers but it's also about the discipline the manager has instilled in the squad and the character of a group of players who are able to keep their heads in high-pressure situations.

Pep Lijnders, Liverpool's assistant manager, never subscribed to the idea that topping the Fair Play table in those early years of Klopp's reign was somehow a sign of weakness. Liverpool had finished ninth in the Fair Play table in 2014-15 and were seventh in 2015-16. "It's how Johan Cruyff said it: you are stupid until you are a genius," Lijnders tells *The Athletic*. "That's exactly how it is. What other people thought was a problem is, for us, the solution."

Of the 26 yellows Liverpool have collected in the Premier League so far this season, none have been for showing dissent towards officials. Twenty-one have been for fouls and the vast majority have been committed in the middle third of the field. Three have been for time-wasting by Adrian, Trent Alexander-

Arnold and Sadio Mane late on in matches when Liverpool have been winning narrowly. Mohamed Salah was booked for taking his shirt off after scoring to wrap up victory over Manchester United at Anfield, while Mane was penalised for simulation away to Aston Villa. Replays showed there was contact from Frederic Guilbert, but Mane did go down theatrically in the penalty box. Fabinho leads the way for Liverpool with five yellows, followed by Alexander-Arnold on four and James Milner and Joe Gomez on three.

Mane (38) has conceded more fouls than any Liverpool player this season, followed by Jordan Henderson (26) and Roberto Firmino (24). Remarkably, frontman Firmino, who so often sets the tone for Klopp's side with his work rate and intensity, has given away 119 free-kicks in the Premier League over the past three seasons, but has been booked just once – for taking his shirt off after scoring in a thrilling 4-3 win over Manchester City in January 2018.

Mane is consistently the most-fouled Liverpool player – 33 times already this season and 147 times in total over the past three seasons. Over the same period, Salah has been fouled 76 times.

Given Liverpool's high-pressing game and the manner in which they swarm over opponents, it's a remarkable stat that they concede an average of just eight fouls per Premier League match. Based on the percentage of opposition turnovers ending in a foul, Klopp's side have the best record in the top flight with just four per cent. Arsenal are at the other end on eight per cent.

The reason? Preparation, organisation, structure and timing. Liverpool hunt in packs. You don't need to launch yourself into challenges if you shut down space, block passing lanes and force your opponents to panic and cough up possession.

Klopp often speaks to his squad before matches about producing shows of "controlled aggression". "I understand aggressiveness in only one way: being prepared to hurt yourself, not someone else," he says. "It's a ball we fight for and not a bone. We always want to be very aggressive in the best football way."

Klopp doesn't tolerate indiscipline. Behind that beaming smile, there's a ruthless streak. Just ask defender Mamadou Sakho, who was sent home from the pre-season tour of America in disgrace in 2016 after repeatedly breaking the rules with his attitude and poor timekeeping. He never played for the club again.

The manager's messages are always reiterated by captain Henderson and vice-captain James Milner – two model professionals who command the respect of their peers and ensure that nobody steps out of line. Milner is in charge of the dressing room fines.

Having Virgil van Dijk, the finest defender in world football with the composure and capacity to read the game so well, certainly helps to keep Liverpool's foul and yellow card count down. He's conceded just 10 free-kicks in the Premier League this season and has been booked once – for dragging down Anwar El Ghazi to halt a counter-attack at Villa Park in November. Fans roar their approval at the sight of Van Dijk making a perfectly timed last-ditch tackle, or Henderson tracking back to snuff out danger when Liverpool have been left exposed, but for Lijnders, the Liverpool assistant manager, it is the team's ability to keep such scenarios to a minimum which has been crucial to their success. It comes back to the structure and playing as a unit.

"We want a team fully concentrated in playing the game our way," he says. "One of Jurgen's principles is that we want to be aggressive but legally aggressive, and here lies the key in our approach to win the ball back.

"Good defending is associated with tackling and heading but for us, it means avoiding certain situations. For example, good individual defending means a lot of bad collective defending beforehand. Good collective defending gives us the chance to be on time. Most yellow and red cards come from being too late. The key is to be on time, so you have to start earlier and that's only possible with good organisation and distances."

Liverpool's playing style has certainly evolved under Klopp. They have become less gung-ho and take fewer risks. Over the past two seasons, they have played with much greater control. With experience and maturity, they have also become more streetwise in terms of their game-management.

They aren't paragons of virtue. At times, they have dabbled in the dark arts to get over the line – taking the sting out of proceedings by slowing games down at every turn when in front. It's a similar story on the touchline, where Klopp isn't averse to venting his spleen at the officials.

When needs must, Liverpool can be cynical – Fabinho's late booking at Stamford Bridge in September for hauling down Michy Batshuayi when Chelsea were bursting away in search of an equaliser is the perfect example; Milner's three yellows in the league this season have all been for similar offences.

Occasionally, the rules of the game have been bent and broken to get the job done but for the most part, Klopp's men have operated firmly within them.

Not since Manchester United in 2002-03 have the champions of England also finished top of the Fair Play table. Klopp has turned Liverpool into champions-elect without having to compromise on the principles he holds dear.

RESISTANCE, PRIDE AND RELIEF: WHAT LIVERPOOL'S TITLE WILL MEAN TO A CITY

SIMON HUGHES

JUN 20, 2020

Jordan Henderson should have been lifting Liverpool's first league trophy in 30 years when, on May 9, I stood on Falkner Street and looked down into the lungs of the city.

The Belvedere pub was just a couple of cobbled steps away and that was closed, so too the Caledonia and the Blackburne Arms. Hope Street, the starting point of many a fine night, possessed an end-of-days sort of quality. In the middle distance, the huge gothic-style doors of the brooding Anglican Cathedral were bolted. The Mersey river shimmered in the afternoon sun, but its waters were unusually still. Further away, there seemed to be fewer ships in the Irish Sea and barely a breeze near the distant wind farms.

I imagined a life without lockdown. Concert Square is not my place but it would have been bouncing. Bedlam would otherwise have been a place called Bold Street. For mayhem there was Mathew Street; for chaos, Castle Street; a degree of seed on Seel Street; maybe disorder on Duke Street but even more chance of that at The Dispensary over on the increasingly raucous

Renshaw Street, given its history. The old manager has retired but the TripAdvisor reviews are still worth checking out...

I longed for the sights and sounds of outrageous normality. Liverpool's entire urban population seems to disgorge into the same space in moments of celebration, because there is no break from the pandemonium. It has been described as a Catholic Calcutta for good reason. Yet Protestantism remains a strong but subtle feature of feeling and this cannot be denied when you consider Jurgen Klopp's role and his faith.

For what it is worth, he spent his first Friday night as Liverpool manager in the outside drinking area of what used to be the Old Blind School bar and restaurant on Hardman Street.

His appointment had felt momentous. I had met a man of 70-something earlier that day in October 2015, who told me he had waited since the crack of dawn at the gates of Anfield for Klopp to arrive for his press unveiling. Nobody, including me, thought he was mad because it was in line with the surrounding excitement, which bordered on a hysteria. Liverpool is a fanatical place and it does not suit or react well to being quelled. Yet it has had to become like anywhere else at this time, in a state of pause, waiting and waiting.

When people claim the pandemic reduces delight at the imminent sense of triumph, it is difficult to argue otherwise. With pubs, bars and restaurants shut, winning the title will not be marked in the same way. Yet that doesn't mean the scale of Klopp's sporting achievement also recedes.

Speak to anyone from Liverpool who supports Liverpool and you remember why winning the Premier League still matters.

———————————— A ————————————

When police closed off roads in Liverpool's Georgian Quarter, Tony Nelson was fuming. He walked out of the front doors of the Casa and asked a copper what was going on. "Blame him," came the reply, as he pointed down the road towards the Hope Street Hotel, where a huge crowd had gathered before a Liverpool home game; Klopp was there, signing autographs.

With that, Nelson calmed down. He is the landlord of the Casa, the pub he opened 21 years ago initially as a place of refuge for sacked dockworkers. He is a Liverpool supporter as well, though lapsed in terms of attending matches. That routine ended at some point in the 1980s when other things in his life seemed to become more important. His working life had been spent on the docks and that meant he was fighting for his own survival as well as others, given his role in the union.

Pretty much anything you need to know about Liverpool can be traced back to a location by its phenomenal dockside. The city was once the second most significant, behind London, in the British empire, built from the wealth generated by the slave trade, then bringing imports from the new world as well as mass immigration.

It grew rich at the expense of huge suffering but the slums were largely written out of the story of a city once divided on religious grounds. This had separated the working class but the Second World War changed everything, forcing families out of the devastation of the inner-city and into a vast relocation programme that involved new estates in places such as Kirkby and Speke. Living together for the first time, workers began to appreciate they had more in common and this resulted in industry bosses feeling greater pressure than ever before.

Such unity, however, also arrived in a period where Liverpool's significance as a port dwindled due to the dismantling of empire and the rise of the European Community. Now on the wrong side of the country for trade and with newer ports in England's south-east not having anywhere near the same level of operative-discord, while also possessing newer technology able to deal with the rise of containerisation, a

Conservative government led by Margaret Thatcher advocated 'managed decline' for Liverpool in 1981 and this accelerated a population slump. Opposition towards her political cause has gurgled ever since.

Though Liverpool's problems were growing in the 1970s, Nelson remembers the decade as a simpler age, filled with excitement and journey because it was his entry point to working life as well as Anfield. In 1973, Liverpool were on the verge of winning the league for the first time in seven years when he was recruited by Victorian firm Harrison Line just before his 16th birthday. He had the night shift and his tasks initially included keeping a check on timekeeping and wages. This brought him into close contact with the dock workers, and these were men with formidable opinions, personalities hewn out of Mersey limestone.

Barely into his apprenticeship, Nelson can remember the reaction when Chilean leader Salvador Allende was ousted by Colonel Augusto Pinochet and a number of sailors from that country refused to return home from Liverpool, fearing Pinochet's death squads. A campaign to secure their stay proved successful and one of the sailors, Julio Arellano, contributed towards Liverpool's rich cultural tapestry by running a restaurant named after the Chilean port city Valparaiso on Hardman Street for nearly 25 years.

It is this background and these sorts of stories that make Nelson and many others in Liverpool feel more of a connection with the rest of the world than the rest of England.

Canada was another place of interest because of the amount of timber that arrived at the accordingly named Canada Dock. Nelson used to drink in the Dominion pub, where there was a statue of a lumberjack on its primary exterior turret. The lounges of the Dominion were also where the conversations started with other workers, who encouraged him to attend

Liverpool away matches at faraway and mysterious sounding venues like the Dell.

Being from a Bootle family of dock workers, the port was a "natural progression" and Nelson uses the same term to describe the pathway to Anfield. He remembers returning seafarers showing up triumphantly in the pubs that lined Walton Breck Road. Five weeks earlier they'd been sailing on the Amazon. "There were more conversations about what it is like working in cities like Manaus than there were St Helens," he says. "By extension, Liverpool became an exotic sort of place."

He'd previously stood on the ledge at the back of the boys' pen but was now just about old enough to blag his way onto the Kop, mainly because he was accompanied by men who tended to be almost twice his age. Though Liverpool has since seemed somewhat more of a politicised football club than others because of Hillsborough, listening to Nelson reminds you political feeling had entered Anfield long before a disaster which still has a profound effect on the city's relationship with authority.

Nelson suggests that dock workers in New York or Mombasa faced similar realities to those in Liverpool and this helped drive unionism in the industry across the old world, the sort that meant those Chilean sailors were in good hands when they arrived in Liverpool. Politicisation between the 1950s and 1970s had risen because of disputes in Liverpool's docks and car factories. He believes such accord between workers transferred into the city's football stadiums at weekends, Everton's Goodison Park included.

He used to clock on at 8am and clock off at 1pm on a Saturday before marching to Anfield by crossing the Dock Road and Derby Road and heading up Fountains Lane or Lambeth Road. "There were thousands upon thousands of us," he remembers.

Nelson thinks the Kop's reputation for song derived from the port, because dock workers liked to sing. "On a match day, it would start in the pub. After a few pints, we'd be merry. Then that would transfer into the ground as well."

There were few women on the Kop then and even fewer children. Black faces were rarer still. "None of this makes me proud but it's the way it was," he adds. "When you have 25,000 working-class men on the Kop and the overwhelming majority are in a trade union, it has an impact on the atmosphere because of the solidarity."

He describes the match as "a full-stop at the end of the week". It was something to look forward to. "When the team is doing well, it makes a difference to the atmosphere in the city. In the 1970s, it helped keep a lot of people sane."

Sanity was in short supply in the 1980s. Liverpool was beset by 40 per cent unemployment rates, racial tension, riots and a heroin epidemic. Football felt like the 'last way' of resisting but not everyone was in a position to enjoy what became the most successful decade in the city's sporting history, considering the dominance of Liverpool and Everton. This is reflected in attendances at both Anfield and Goodison, which dropped in some seasons by as much as two fifths.

"I couldn't justify going anymore," says Nelson. "Not in terms of money or time." And yet, football remained – besides the docks – the most 'important' feature of city conversation and the main source of absolute pride.

"Football felt like the last thing we had to show off," says Nelson. "That's why, I think, we celebrate big when it does go off. There's the Catholic thing, of course, where families have always had big parties. Football ties into that. It's our way of reminding people who criticise us that we're still knocking around; that we're not going to go away."

— A —

Steve Rotheram also has Irish-Catholic heritage through his mum, Dot. He was 28 when Liverpool were last here, on the brink of the title. He can't remember the celebrations because they blurred into previous achievements. It was the club's 11th championship in 17 seasons and he just thought, "We'll do it again next year."

Rotheram's son, also a Steve, is now 28 and quietly, the father compares their experiences of following Liverpool. "He doesn't know what it is like." He means reaching what is considered the Holy Grail: the league title, what Bill Shankly ordained more modestly as, "the bread and butter".

Like Nelson, he thinks the 1980s was a defining decade in the history of Liverpool as a city. It finished with Hillsborough, where 96 supporters were crushed to death. Authority lies and false coverage of the event had a lasting impact, affecting the way many outsiders felt about Liverpool. Liverpool people, knowing what had really happened, defended the truth.

While Rotheram can see there has been some change in opinion since the findings of the Hillsborough Independent Panel in 2012 and an unlawful killing verdict in subsequent inquests three years later, he is in a position to know that there is some distance left to travel.

Rotheram has a season ticket in the upper tier of the Sir Kenny Dalglish Stand. He is also the metro mayor for the Liverpool city region. Not so long ago, he travelled to Manhattan for a meeting with Michael Bloomberg, the former mayor of New York. Rotheram was hoping to attract investment. He was there with delegates from Greater Manchester, the West Midlands and Tees Valley.

"Everyone wanted to talk about Liverpool," he recalls. "The name of the place itself opens doors because they know about our history. There is a link with New York because of immigration from Ireland. There are the Beatles. There's the football. Liverpool is a very powerful brand internationally. Globally, we're smashing it, but in this country, the name can be toxic in certain places. That's something I'm desperate to try to change, because it limits our options financially."

Why is Liverpool's brand as a city a negative one? Rotheram's office conducted surveys in Manchester and London about perceptions because "if anyone is going to tell us what they really think, it will be Mancunians and Cockneys". It was aimed at boardroom executives rather than people on the street.

"The theme running through the results tended to show that younger people thought of Liverpool being a dynamic place. White men over the age of 45 tended to think differently. They still had their doubts and they were predicated on events like the Toxteth Riots, even though there were riots all over the country." They also talked about the city's support of left-wing politics, and about Heysel and Hillsborough. "Commonly, if a person hadn't been to Liverpool, they had a dim view. Those who have been had a completely different perspective," he says.

While the 1980s shaped opinion about Liverpool, that decade also strengthened the regional identity. "No area was devastated as much as Liverpool was in the post-industrial decline under Thatcher," Rotheram suggests. "There was a clear-out in Liverpool, and people here have got long memories. It has taken us further when we've had to campaign, like with Hillsborough and dockers' strikes. We don't suffer fools gladly. I don't think the Tories will ever be able to repair the damage they caused, because it's passed down by generation. If you are from Liverpool and you are a Tory, you get shunned if people find out."

Voting results support Rotheram's view. Just as Britain swung right in the 1983 general election and Liverpool turned in the opposite direction, the same pattern has followed in the past three general elections. Rotheram is not alone in thinking the

2010s have hardened opinion in Liverpool. Whereas political chanting previously did not have a place at Anfield, it has done more recently. The 1980s remain relevant, he thinks, in part by extension because Liverpool's last title was in 1990, a season which started in 1989 – a year which on Merseyside will forever be associated with one event.

Without justice, Liverpool as a city has not been able to move on, and without league success supporters of both Liverpool and Everton (whose last title was in 1987) have constantly found themselves imprisoned by its past.

Some will read this and claim other places and clubs have moved on, that it is time to let go, but many in Liverpool recognise the country has never been able to escape the 1980s – that the economic measures imposed on Britain are still impacting lives four decades later. That fans of other clubs reliably sing about unemployment and poverty on Merseyside whenever they face Liverpool or Everton, even though some of these clubs come from towns and cities where those rates are now much higher, shows that stigmas from the 1980s carried down through generations still matter elsewhere.

There had been a degree of ownership in Liverpool about the 1980s, where previously only those who lived through it felt comfortable enough to speak about the impact. Now there is a feeling that a younger generation, born in that decade or thereafter, has been energised by confirmation of things their parents long suspected – the 'managed decline' memo from Geoffrey Howe released in 2011, the HIP findings a year later and then the verdicts in the Hillsborough inquests. Sensitivities were then heightened when match commander David Duckenfield was found not guilty of gross negligence manslaughter earlier this year.

"We've also had 10 years of Tory rule," Rotheram reminds. "We had the Cameron coalition, the Cameron government, the May government and now the Johnson government. Liverpudlians are optimists by nature but I wouldn't say we're idealists. I think the Tories have always attempted to dissipate the hope that we have."

There is some sense that history is repeating itself. While Klopp has made Liverpool one of the most feared teams in Europe again and that team is close to one of the most significant achievements in club history, Merseyside has suffered from some of the biggest cuts in funding from central government since 2010, placing extreme pressure on figures like Rotheram.

"It results in people taking an even greater pride in their football team," he says. "When *it* finally happens, the sense of relief will be incredible."

---- **A** ----

Jamie Webster was born in 1994. That means he was aged one when Liverpool won the Coca-Cola Cup, as it was known then. He was two when they lost the FA Cup final. He was 10 when Istanbul happened, though he was at home in Croxteth – unable to grasp the magnitude of what he was seeing from his living-room couch.

Younger Liverpool supporters can relate to his frustrations. "My grandad used to tell me about Liverpool being an unstoppable force," he says. "Best side in the country. Best side in Europe. Then I'd watch Man United win trophy after trophy after trophy. Chelsea got into it. Istanbul happened, but it sort of stands as a one-off event. We weren't particularly a great side. We overachieved.

"Towards the end of Rafa's (Benitez) time, we were close to being a great side. It used to do my head in. Throughout my teenage years, we fell short. We weren't challenging. I was envious of United fans, Chelsea fans and Arsenal fans getting all these boss European away trips. It felt like if we were lucky, we'd get Rabotnicki."

When Brighton took the lead against Manchester City in the final round of fixtures in the 2018-19 season and for a moment Anfield started to believe the title was heading back to Merseyside, Webster was stood in the Main Stand, crying.

"My body was trembling. I was like, 'Oh my god, this is real... We're already going to Madrid and we've got a gig tonight... imagine...' For 50 seconds until City equalised, I felt something I've never felt before. Then it was taken away..."

There have been spine-tingling moments this season including Villa away, City at home, Leicester away and United at home, but Liverpool's relentlessness means Webster thinks he will feel differently when he's close to ending what for him is a 26-year wait. "We've put so much distance between ourselves and the rest there's an expectancy now. I think I'll feel relieved when it happens. The satisfaction will come later."

Webster's rise has followed Liverpool's. Three years ago, he was a singer known only among a collection of match-going Liverpool fans. After big games at Anfield, he'd headline gigs at small venues in the city centre. At one event, following defeat at Old Trafford in 2018, a video of him singing *Allez Allez Allez* went viral and suddenly the club was asking him to perform for them.

He's since been around the world: North America, Australasia, South East Asia, the Middle East, Scandinavia. "This is what Liverpool can do to a person's life," he says. "It's not easy to understand. I'll be on my way to the match now and someone will grab you, 'Alright there, Jamie...' giving you a good shake. I'm like, 'Mate, I've just had me brekkie...'"

Six hours after landing at John Lennon Airport following Liverpool's summer tour of the US in 2019, Webster was at a social housing complex in Birkenhead working with his father Ron, an electrician. This prompted him to think seriously about his career and he has since signed a record deal that in normal circumstances would have sent him around the world again, promoting the album *We Get By*, which is now set for release in August.

He says the first single from it will essentially be about Liverpool as a city – "never forgetting where you are from, no matter where you go in the world or what you do". He recognises some of his biggest challenges now relate to the club he supports. While lots of Liverpool fans want to hear his football-related material, he realises he'll have to work harder to win the confidence of supporters from rival clubs who currently associate him with one thing. Having a huge fanbase and the experience of performing in front of 20,000 people has been a platform but he is wary of it becoming a hindrance.

"Even within the city, Evertonians are sometimes reluctant to get behind you because of the stuff I've done with Liverpool. 'I'm not listening to that shit… Kopite bastard', that sort of thing. If I can build some momentum and get the Blues on first, I'm confident I can win other crowds over as well."

Some of his writing is about Liverpool as a place. It frustrates him that similar social issues face other cities but they have a different way of dealing with it. "I just think, if you're working class you've got to do more to stick together. It doesn't matter if you're a bricklayer in Liverpool or London, you've got more in common than you think. People from outside the city seem to get dead wound up because we create a scene whenever we celebrate. Maybe it's not terribly British."

He thinks there is a misunderstanding about the noise around Liverpool. "For some clubs, I think football is just about the result," he says. "In Liverpool, football is also about the party. I've done plenty of gigs when we've lost and the place has been packed. It's great being with your mates. People don't want to go home and the city swings. Football in Liverpool really can be an escape."

THIS WAS A PERFORMANCE OF CHAMPIONS

JAMES PEARCE

JUN 25, 2020

Jurgen Klopp knew the danger. Sprinters who have blown their rivals away have a habit of easing up when the finish line is in sight. It's human nature to take your foot off the gas when the outcome appears to be a foregone conclusion.

The Liverpool manager told his players in no uncertain terms that he wasn't interested in watching them coast to this Premier League title. "Forget the table. Let's get back to doing what we do best. Remember the things that made us successful," was the message before Wednesday's visit of in-form Crystal Palace.

Klopp talked to them about hunger, tempo, intensity, rhythm and controlled aggression. He talked about the need not only to complete the job in style, but to put down a marker for next season, when Liverpool will be the ones with a target on their backs. "I want to see the best behind-closed-doors football ever," he demanded.

No excuses. Standards had to rise again. Klopp was determined that a record-breaking season wouldn't be allowed to drift during the closing chapters. He spoke about how they owed it to those supporters forced to stay at home to deliver "the highest level" for them.

Sunday's dour stalemate at Goodison had been in keeping with the league performances shortly before the season was halted, when scrappy wins over Norwich City (1-0), West Ham United (3-2) and Bournemouth (2-1) were accompanied by the 3-0 defeat at Watford that ended talk of emulating Arsenal's Invincibles.

Liverpool had stumbled after the February winter break, also exiting the FA Cup and Champions League, leading to some questioning the credentials of Klopp's side. Were they really that special? Hadn't this just been a mediocre top-flight season with the lucky Merseysiders cashing in?

Some have short memories.

The COVID-19 shutdown initially brought talk of a null-and-void season, before the conversation turned to how the lengthy delay and the empty grounds meant an asterisk would need to be placed against their title triumph. What was required now was a show of force, a reminder of why such a chasm at the summit of the Premier League exists.

Here it was. This was Klopp's Liverpool. This was the performance of bona fide champions.

Palace, who arrived on the back of four straight wins, were pummelled into submission. The Londoners failed to record a single touch of the ball in the opposition penalty box – the first side to do so in the Premier League since Opta started collecting that data 12 years ago.

Liverpool were relentless. They swarmed all over Roy Hodgson's side from start to finish, like a ravenous pack of wolves.

"Really exceptional," was Klopp's verdict. "The best behind-closed-doors, counter-pressing football ever. Four-nil up after 80 minutes and (still) four players chasing one from the other team like it's the only ball left on this planet. That's us. If I try to search for a negative, I can't remember one. You should not underestimate how much this team wants it."

The balance of the team was transformed by the return of Andy Robertson and Mohamed Salah. Their passing was slick and their movement intelligent. Liverpool hadn't hit these heights collectively since demolishing Leicester City on Boxing Day. The goals oozed quality. From Trent Alexander-Arnold's curling free-kick to Fabinho's lofted pass which was expertly tucked away by Salah, who moved within two of Jamie Vardy in the race for the golden boot.

Fabinho excelled at the base of Klopp's midfield from start to finish – snapping into tackles and bossing the game, back to the form he was in before being sidelined by ankle ligament damage in November. The Brazilian's second-half thunderbolt was followed by a blistering counter-attack that ended with Sadio Mane converting Salah's incisive pass.

Alisson, who has kept more clean sheets than any other goalkeeper (12) despite missing nine of the 31 league games so far, remained socially distant from Palace throughout.

Match days are different for Liverpool these days. After a light 40-minute session at Melwood on Wednesday morning when they went through their set-piece routines, the squad assembled at Formby Hall Golf Club & Spa, 13 miles north of the city, for their pre-game meeting and meal. COVID-19 and social distancing rules have forced them to break with the long tradition of using the Hope Street Hotel in the city centre.

Parts of Formby Hall have been reopened especially for them and sanitised. Luggage was sprayed with disinfectant on arrival and players and staff wore face marks as they boarded three separate coaches for the journey to the stadium.

Klopp got his players accustomed to the prospect of playing in an empty Anfield by organising a friendly against Blackburn Rovers there, as well as an intra-squad game. The manager wanted as much normality as possible. Despite the absence of fans, George Sephton, the 'Voice of Anfield' since 1971, was on duty. Players have been invited to submit song requests for him to play while they are warming up.

"The most surreal day I've ever had in the job," Sephton tells *The Athletic*. "Usually, it's my task to help build the atmosphere. We had a practice run on Tuesday to get the sound levels right. If I played at the normal level for when there are 54,000 in here the players would have blood coming out of their ears, so we had to tone it down.

"I couldn't announce the subs or the goalscorers because I share my room with the lad who relays the VAR decisions and it's not big enough to stay two metres apart. I had to step aside for him at the start of each half. I can't wait for the day the fans are allowed back in."

The Kop was eerily quiet, but Klopp's players still gazed in wonder at it. That was thanks to the efforts of around 15 supporters who had spent Monday and Tuesday decking the iconic stand out in the usual array of flags and banners. 'Welcome to Wonderland', 'The Kop Spirit Survives' and 'What We Achieve in Life Echoes in Eternity' were among them.

"We'd been talking to the club about what we could do and they said the players wanted it to be authentic," says Andy Hudson, of fans' group Spion Kop 1906. "The club could have made it easy and gone down the route of some generic images or marketing slogans, but credit to them for getting supporters involved. They said, 'The Kop is for the fans, so it's only right that the fans get to deck it out'."

Hudson, a 33-year-old IT systems analyst from Lydiate, normally follows Liverpool home and away. Watching from afar as they scale these heights is bittersweet. "I'd have loved to have been there," he says. "Lads my age have never seen us win the title. Having to stay away is horrible, especially when we're so close to being crowned champions after 30 years. When you dedicate your life to going to the match it feels like we're losing out, but we've got to look at the bigger picture.

"I just hope this period makes the Premier League realise how important fans are. As the banner says, 'Football without fans is nothing'."

Klopp would certainly agree with that assessment. The manager made it clear that this game was for them. "They push us to incredible things and I never missed them more than tonight, but it was so important we showed our supporters the respect they deserve, that we can play like they are here even when they are not," Klopp said.

Despite the absence of their foot soldiers, Fortress Anfield remains very much intact after Liverpool extended their top-flight record to 23 successive home league wins. It puts them on the brink.

"It's our time to win it," beamed Salah.

The destination of the 2019-20 title has long since been known but what will satisfy Klopp more than anything is that the shackles are off. No limping over the finish line.

Liverpool have shown the world once again why they are such worthy winners.

JURGEN KLOPP – THE FIST-PUMPING GENIUS WHO TURNED DREAMS INTO REALITY

JAMES PEARCE and SIMON HUGHES

JUN 25, 2020

Without a meeting on the quiet outskirts of Frankfurt, maybe there is no marriage with Liverpool a decade later.

Jurgen Klopp was a 38-year-old football manager from the Black Forest nobody really thought too much of and Marc Kosicke was a Bremen-born rep for Nike, based in the company's old German headquarters. Klopp had been in charge of Mainz for four years by 2005 and was able to arrange his own clothing deals, separate from the club. Kosicke had been at Nike for much longer and he was considering whether Klopp had the right sort of image to pull off the company's footwear while prowling the touchline.

Mainz was a 40-minute drive away and Klopp arrived with his friend, a lawyer who'd always looked over his contracts. He did not have an agent because he did not think of himself as being important enough.

A desk separated each party and Kosicke leaned back in his leather chair with his arms placed behind his head, considering the view. Klopp was wearing jeans and a hoodie. He did not look like a football manager. Mainz were a Bundesliga club and although they had finished 11th in 2004-05, they qualified for the UEFA Cup on account of their fair-play record. To Kosicke, Klopp seemed a fair and reasonable man, even though he was full of big hand gestures and occasional grand statements.

Another meeting was arranged, this time at a pub out in the countryside. Kosicke liked the guy but wanted to know a bit more. Klopp ordered a round of wheat beer. Kosicke ordered another round of wheat beer. Afternoon turned into evening. Another wheat beer. And another…

Klopp emerged from the toilets and Kosicke passed him as he went in. "I don't care about the money," Klopp told him. "But my lawyer friend…" he explained, had bought a rusting barge and was in the process of making it river-worthy again. The full refurbishment would cost close to €12,000.

"Let's do the deal and he can have his boat," Klopp suggested.

Kosicke laughed and agreed it was a good idea. He could see himself working with Klopp. He thought he was different to the rest of the clients he had dealt with at Nike.

––––––––––––––––– **A** –––––––––––––––––

In the autumn of 2015, Klopp and Kosicke were relaxing in the Lufthansa Lounge at Munich Airport when a steward recognised him despite his attempts at disguise (though on reflection he admits they were meek).

Why was he flying to New York?

In the decade since Klopp and Kosicke had first met in Frankfurt, a lot had changed. By 2006, the demands on Klopp were increasing and he realised he needed someone to help with the day-to-day running of his own affairs.

Mainz were doing better than anyone expected and his image had been projected into the homes of millions of countrymen during that summer's World Cup finals in Germany, following his work as a television analyst. Kosicke was impressed with the way he was quickly able to interpret tactics without coming across like a know-it-all. He got his point across in a memorable way, through the strength of his personality.

Kosicke had left Nike and was setting up alone, dealing only with players initially. Klopp approached him at an event and asked him straight up: "I'd like you to represent me…"

The first big deal was with Borussia Dortmund, where Klopp turned around the fortunes of the second-biggest club in Germany, winning two league titles, a German Cup and a German Supercup before reaching the club's first Champions League final in 16 years.

Though Klopp was officially on a sabbatical in the summer of 2015, Kosicke was working – laying the groundwork for his return to management after leaving his position at Dortmund following seven successful seasons. Though he was not under instruction from Klopp, he was doing what any responsible agent would do: making phone calls, taking phone calls and gathering information from trusted contacts about clubs where his client's future might lie.

One of those was Chelsea. Another was Liverpool. He wanted to know about the owners and the structure of the boardroom. Who, really, was Michael Edwards and what did he do? Edwards was not officially the sporting director, yet Kosicke learned that he had the role in everything but title. Ian Ayre was another figure of interest, given that he was likely to be the first point of contact if Liverpool were to make their move. Material on the internet about Ayre was not positive, given the number of deals Liverpool had failed to get across the line during his time as chief executive. What was he really like?

Not all of the information fed back to Kosicke was positive. Yet both he and Klopp were keen to form their own judgements, especially on the figures whose names had been associated with

Liverpool's failings. While this was an interview for Klopp, it was also an interview for those hoping to give him a new job.

Another part of the ruse that day was the meeting point in Manhattan. Klopp had told the attendant in Munich Airport that he was flying to New York to watch a basketball game. But the NBA season didn't start for another month or so.

He was fortunate that Fenway Sports Group's Mike Gordon suggested they met away from Boston. If Klopp was spotted in FSG's hometown, it would be obvious why he was there. Kosicke knew the least about Gordon, who by 2015 was running Liverpool's day-to-day operation from his home in the Boston suburb of Brookline, not far away from the famous golf course.

Klopp and Gordon hit it off straight away, trading stories about their upbringings in Glatten near Stuttgart and Minneapolis respectively. It was quickly established they were both liberally minded but, most significantly, that any preconceived concerns about Klopp possessing a domineering personality melted away because of the way he listened first and spoke later.

Gordon stands at around 5ft 8in and Klopp is almost 6ft 4in. Gordon is also quietly spoken and usually feels uncomfortable talking about himself, while Klopp is the opposite. Yet Gordon realised there was more to Klopp than his size and charisma. Klopp stressed he was impressed by the structure in place at Liverpool, but he also told the owners what they needed to do to take the club to the next level. Klopp believed there had been too many injuries at Liverpool and one of his first tasks was to ensure this changed.

By the end of the meeting, Gordon told John W Henry, the club's principal owner, that Klopp had the capacity to work as a CEO for any major international company. In football terms, he had the presence and personality to offer on Merseyside what they could not from the other side of the Atlantic.

Carlo Ancelotti had walked through the doors of the law firm Shearman & Sterling a day earlier. Gordon liked him as well, but he figured out quickly that Klopp was more what Liverpool needed at that particular moment. Whereas three years earlier, FSG had to work hard to convince Brendan Rodgers to become manager, that was not the case with Klopp, whose passion for the job meant there wasn't the sort of wrangling that made the process of recruiting Rodgers drag on.

It did not take long for Kosicke to agree financial terms. Klopp left the room at that point, walking around Central Park, across Strawberry Fields and towards The Dakota building, where John Lennon once lived. That was when Liverpool's reach as a city really dawned on him.

A

The canteen at Liverpool's academy had a coffee machine and Klopp spent part of his first afternoon in charge of the club at the Kirkby site. It was a cold October day and strong winds were blowing across the facility. After being photographed talking casually with Alex Inglethorpe and an assortment of youth coaches on the facility's balcony, he retreated and made himself an espresso. It's how Klopp usually likes to start his morning off, along with a cigarette.

Those watching him fiddle about with the buttons remember the sour expression on his face and what he said next. "We need a new coffee machine!" he announced loudly, snorting with the sort of laughter that is now familiar whenever he amuses himself.

Klopp does not visit the academy regularly. He reassured everyone that day they were doing a fine job, that he was aware of some of the players in the production line because Dortmund had scouted them too. Ever since, he has trusted Inglethorpe to run the place as he sees fit.

Yet the next time he was there, he was delighted to find the old coffee machine had been replaced. "Someone was listening!" he boomed several months later, by which point he had already established control of everything that happened five miles away at Melwood, the first team's training centre.

Klopp once took to a stage at an Opel auto factory in Germany in front of 10,000 workers. His talk became more of a performance and, by the end, the audience were chanting his name. He considers first impressions important, the basis of any relationship. An introduction to the squad at Melwood's meeting room included writing the word TERRIBLE in block capitals on a whiteboard, explaining that was how teams would feel after playing against his Liverpool. This would be achieved by running further and quicker and by pressing straight away when possession was lost. From there, Liverpool would hit opponents on the counter-attack.

Klopp asked every member of staff to then introduce themselves, and describe their role at the club in front of the squad. This was designed to remind everyone present that each person had a responsibility to one another. Players were told they needed to learn the name of every employee at the training facility and warned that unless this happened, the sort of togetherness which brings success would be impossible.

Though Klopp lauded the playing talent sitting in front of him, since getting told the job was his he had watched most Liverpool games from the previous 12 months and it was clear to him most players were not performing to their best because of a lack of confidence. He decided to reduce holiday time and, overnight, training sessions became much more intensive.

Klopp was unimpressed with some of the new gear Liverpool's players were made to train in during those early months, identifying quickly that the fabric did not absorb sweat particularly well. This was a problem because he expected players to treat training sessions like they were matches.

It is fair to say that, although Klopp got commitment and performances out of players who a fortnight earlier had needed penalties to beat fourth-tier Carlisle United at home in the League Cup, not all were impressed by the training sessions in those early months. Some of the more experienced figures talked among themselves and quietly agreed that the work was a bit repetitive.

For the time being, though, it did not seem to matter, because Liverpool's results improved dramatically, with away victories at champions Chelsea and 2014-15 runners-up Manchester City in the first six weeks acting as evidence that Klopp's methods were working.

There was no acclimatisation period. From the very beginning, there was only Klopp's way. This was clear from his very first game, a 0-0 away at Tottenham, where Adam Lallana emerged as the key runner in midfield having impressed Klopp in training with his understanding of positioning as well as his lung capacity. Another player who stood out in those early sessions was Daniel Sturridge. Klopp knew he was inheriting a talented player but Sturridge was better than he'd thought: the player his Dortmund stars Robert Lewandowski and Mario Gotze would be if they combined their talents. Klopp is not the sort of person to have regrets, but he wishes he had been able to work with Sturridge when he was injury-free because he could have been, in his opinion, one of European football's great No 9s.

Klopp's staff spent the earliest part of the morning on day one dividing Melwood's training pitches into three sections, preparing for counter-pressing drills. This would be the basis for everything Klopp has since achieved, but players admitted some of the practices seemed alien at first. They arrived with mannequins placed at equal distances from one another, representing the difference between the high, medium and low press.

Before nearly every match since, Klopp identifies what he calls the "pressing victim": usually a defender or midfielder whose ability on the ball is considered dubious. The idea is to ensure the ball arrives at the victim's feet instead of someone else with more talent. This is achieved by pressing in the right areas and funnelling the possession in the victim's direction, then hunting him down in a pack and stealing the ball away.

"The best moment to win the ball is immediately after your team just lost it," Klopp told Liverpool's players. "The opponent is still understanding his bearings and deciding where to pass. He will have taken his eyes off the game to make his tackle or interception and he will have expended energy. Both make him vulnerable."

Regularly in those early weeks and months, Klopp would halt training and remind them of exactly what he wanted to see. He knew that while the tactic increased the pressure on the opponent, it also meant greater risk was taken by his own team. If three or sometimes four players went off to hunt an opponent and were not in the right positions to block off passing angles, the whole Liverpool team would be vulnerable in other areas of the pitch.

— **A** —

It was long after midnight and Liverpool had lost again.

Klopp's debut season finished in Basel, where a rousing second-half performance from Sevilla in the Europa League final allowed the Spanish side to overturn Liverpool's 1-0 lead at the break. The margin of the Spanish side's victory, in the end, could have been greater than 3-1.

The mood inside the Swiss city's Novotel was despondent. Even Klopp had been knocked sideways by Liverpool's collapse. In conversation with the other coaches, he admitted Sevilla appeared stronger, fitter and better organised. He was blaming himself but he also knew this was not really his team and that perhaps Liverpool had overachieved by reaching the final in the first place.

His first season at Liverpool felt like a successful sort of failure because of the starting point. It was a free hit for him in many ways because expectations were so low and it was widely understood a rebuilding job would need time and likely involve some disappointments along the way. Finishing eighth matched their worst league season in two decades, but it also felt like some progress had been made: they had been 10th when he took over.

A League Cup final loss on penalties to Manchester City was also a part of this process, though Klopp found it easier accepting that because of the talent in City's team. What happened in Basel reminded him of the scale of the task at Anfield. It also meant there would be no European football in the 2016-17 season.

He took the microphone and told the players he was still proud of them, reminding them nobody had given them a chance at the start of the competition. "Two hours ago, we all felt shit," he admitted. Yet this was just the start of something. There would be other finals, he said. They should remember this feeling and use the sense of disappointment to drive them further next time. He told the players he could not be any prouder of the way they had listened to him and embraced his ideas – that the season had certainly not been a waste.

A

Klopp became a friend of the players but never their best friend.

Christian Benteke was the first to use the description and was sold six months later. Mamadou Sakho described Klopp's relationships in a similar way before he too was shown the exit door during the 2016-17 season.

Though Sakho was respected in the dressing room and Klopp liked him as a player, he valued discipline more. Sakho was late for the flight when Liverpool flew out for a tour of the United States and it was not his first indiscretion. Sakho had missed the Europa League final against Sevilla because of a UEFA investigation into a failed drugs test. Though he was subsequently cleared, Klopp was furious that Sakho had taken weight-loss supplements without the club's knowledge. Klopp wanted senior players to set the right examples. Sakho never played for him again and moved to Crystal Palace in the winter window.

Key signings were made that summer, though none really felt like it at the time. Sadio Mane, Joel Matip and Gini Wijnaldum would all emerge as Champions League winners within three years. They came from Southampton, Schalke and Newcastle – a relegated club. Of the three, Mane arguably proved to be the most important in Klopp's first full season, as his goals fired Liverpool back into the Champions League. Klopp had once tried to sign Mane for Dortmund, meeting him face-to-face in Germany. The Senegalese was younger then and much quieter. Klopp hesitated, wondering whether he had the personality to play for his team. He would not make the same mistake twice. Though Mane also had a meeting with Tottenham manager Mauricio Pochettino, Klopp's enthusiasm about the future at Liverpool made him want to move to Anfield.

Meanwhile, there were significant additions to the backroom staff. Nutritionist Mona Nemmer joined from Bayern Munich and one of her first decisions was to place a juice station in the first-team changing room at Melwood, so players could refuel as soon as they left the field. Instead of sugary sweets at half-time, players also started drinking apple juice laced with caffeine. The new head of fitness was Andreas Kornmayer, whom Klopp has likened to a drill sergeant.

There was also focus on the players Klopp wanted but did not get. He tried to sign Gotze from Bayern Munich, but Klopp became less keen after he was told that Germany's World Cup 2014 final matchwinner wanted to wait until after the 2016 European Championship to see what offers he had. Then there was a failed move for Leicester teenager Ben Chilwell, which prompted Klopp to use James Milner at left-back for a season.

The pressure on Liverpool sharpened because of what other clubs were doing. Klopp scoffed at the extravagant spending of rivals such as Manchester City and Manchester United. "I want to do it differently," Klopp insisted. By 2017, this stance would change when a run to the Champions League final and advance knowledge of Philippe Coutinho's £142 million sale to Barcelona allowed record-breaking moves for first Virgil van Dijk and then, in 2018, Alisson Becker.

It helped that for the first time since Gerard Houllier's five-and-a-half-year spell in charge, from 1998-2004, there was a clear understanding between boardroom and dugout. When Klopp missed out on the targets he wanted, there were fears that the friction that undermined Rafa Benitez's reign, as well as that of Rodgers, was repeating itself.

Despite an entire ocean separating Klopp and the club's ownership group based primarily in Massachusetts, daily contact with Gordon helped iron out concerns before they ever became problems.

Rodgers would sometimes accept FSG decisions in the moment, before privately venting frustration. The thing Gordon wanted to know most about Klopp was whether they would be comfortable enough in each other's company to express constructive disagreement. "Speaking your mind and disagreeing at Liverpool isn't just allowed," Gordon told Klopp, "it's required."

An example: Henry believed Mohamed Salah was overpriced at nearly £40 million because he had already failed to make a mark in the Premier League with Chelsea. Yet Liverpool signed him from Roma on the recommendation of sporting director Edwards. Klopp had wanted Bayer Leverkusen's Julian Brandt instead, but both he and Gordon were won over by the conviction of Edwards, who had followed the Egyptian's progress since his pre-Chelsea days at Basel.

For so long, there had been division over the recruitment structure: its effectiveness and the break down of responsibility within it. For many, it was refreshing to hear Klopp openly praising Edwards, Dave Fallows (the head of recruitment) and Barry Hunter (chief scout) instead of headlines being created and battle lines drawn by those who were supposed to be working together.

There had initially been some differences of opinion over the sale of Coutinho. In Klopp's first full season in charge, 2016-17, Champions League qualification was only sealed on the final day of the campaign as Liverpool finished fourth. Coutinho had been the team's star performer and that status was rewarded with a new contract in January 2017. Eight months later, Barcelona made their move.

FSG were under pressure. Sanctioning a transfer felt like a surrender, a sign that Liverpool could make progress but not quickly enough for players to stick around and achieve what they wanted at Anfield. This led to Henry deciding that Coutinho would remain that summer. It was a decision which prompted a reaction from the player, who suddenly claimed he was injured – even though scans on his back proved otherwise.

Through conversations, Klopp realised how desperately Coutinho wanted to play for Barcelona. In the changing room, he thought he was sulking. Before the opening game of 2017-18, Coutinho submitted a transfer request, only hours after Liverpool had released a statement confirming he was staying.

Klopp was furious with the player and told Gordon he did not want to work with anyone who didn't believe in him or the team he was trying to build. The manager suggested selling in the current window, but when that message was relayed to Henry, Liverpool's principal owner did not alter his position. Instead of railing against his boss, Klopp saw a different strategy: one whereby Liverpool ended up with a better deal and which protected the development of his team.

Over the course of the next few days, a plan was hatched. Coutinho would remain at Liverpool until the winter window. Return him to fitness and form, sell him for an even bigger fee. Recruit Alex Oxlade-Chamberlain in the meantime. Make sure *he* is ready for January.

------------------------------ **A** ------------------------------

It was just after 6am on Sunday, May 27, 2018. The setting was Klopp's Formby home. The party was in full swing. The beer and wine were flowing. There was the Liverpool manager, baseball cap on back-to-front and with his arms around old friends, leading the sing-song. To his right were his trusted assistant Peter Krawietz and Campino, lead singer of German punk rock band Die Toten Hosen, who had Klopp's silver medal from the Champions League final defeat by Real Madrid the night before around his neck. To Klopp's left was Johannes B Kerner, a well-known German TV personality. Their booming chant was one of defiance.

> *We saw the European Cup,*
> *Madrid had all the fucking luck,*
> *We swear we'll keep on being cool,*
> *We'll bring it back to Liverpool!*

Those words were repeated time and time again. Each rendition was louder than the previous one.

It was typical Klopp. No doom and gloom, no hint of self-pity. He repeatedly reassured his concerned guests that he was OK, adamant that this was the start of something special, not the end.

An hour or so earlier, the message had been similar when he addressed his devastated Liverpool players in the meeting room at Melwood following their return from Kyiv. "You have all made me so proud. The journey was outstanding," he told them, before they embraced and went their separate ways for the summer.

The squad had flown straight home from the Ukrainian capital after the heartache of losing 3-1 to Zinedine Zidane's star-studded side. The atmosphere on the plane had been funereal.

"I was pretty much the only one that was not crying, from all my family," Klopp revealed. "Even my agent was crying, because he felt so much for me. They were only that sad and disappointed because they thought I was. I was of course, but I didn't think it was the end of something. It's only another step. Life is like this.

"We have to accept sometimes that there is someone better, there is someone else with a little bit more luck. I accepted it long ago. I know I will be there again. I will try to go to the next final again and then we will turn it."

Klopp's belief had been fuelled by the second half of that 2017-18 season. Liverpool had exceeded all expectations in reaching their first Champions League final for 11 years and securing back-to-back top-four finishes in the Premier League for the first time since 2009.

They hadn't just coped without Coutinho, they had flourished in his absence. Sanctioning the sale of such a gifted attacker mid-season was a gamble, especially as he wasn't replaced with a new signing. Liverpool had tried and failed in the January window to convince RB Leipzig to bring forward Naby Keita's agreed summer switch to Anfield. They had considered re-igniting their pursuit of France international Thomas Lemar, but were put off by Monaco's £90 million asking price.

Previously, Liverpool had been guilty of panic buying when they lost a top talent. Alberto Aquilani for Xabi Alonso, Andy Carroll for Fernando Torres and Mario Balotelli for Luis Suarez. Klopp was determined that history would not repeat itself. He was happy to wait.

After an impassioned plea to Coutinho from Liverpool's owners to put his dream move on hold until the summer had fallen on deaf ears, the manager felt that keeping the Brazilian against his wishes would have had a detrimental impact on the team.

"My job is always a risk, but I could not decide differently," Klopp insisted. "We are big enough and strong enough to continue with our aggressive progression on the pitch."

Klopp knew that £142 million was an extraordinary sum of money for a player who had cost £8.5 million from Inter Milan five years earlier. In contrast to the negativity outside the club at the sight of Coutinho packing his bags for Catalonia, Klopp saw opportunity. He felt Liverpool could be too predictable at times going forward when so much of their play went through Coutinho. Team-mates looked to him to make something happen. Without him, others would have to take on greater responsibility and Liverpool would be more difficult to stop because they could hurt teams from all angles.

Klopp was proved right, in glorious fashion. Liverpool's tally of 135 goals in all competitions in 2017-18 had only been bettered once in the club's history. Salah rewrote the Premier League record books, setting a new best of 32 league goals over a 38-game season and scoring 44 times in total. As well as the golden boot, he landed both the PFA Player of the Year and the FWA sportswriters' Footballer of the Year awards. The three-pronged attack of Salah, Roberto Firmino and Mane contributed a staggering 91 goals between them. Coutinho watched from afar as Porto, Manchester City and then Roma were dismantled in the Champions League knockout stages.

Oxlade-Chamberlain and Andy Robertson blossomed after difficult starts to their Liverpool careers. "We've bought you for five years not five months," Klopp reassured the pair as he worked with them on the training field to help them make the necessary tactical adjustments.

The biggest change was defensively. Liverpool's total of 17 Premier League clean sheets was their highest since Benitez's reign. Five days before a fee was agreed with Barcelona for Coutinho, Liverpool had secured a £75 million deal for Southampton centre-back Van Dijk. It proved to be one of the most transformative signings of the Premier League era.

Liverpool had lacked a real leader in their backline since Jamie Carragher's retirement in 2013. Buying a player for that kind of money was alien to Klopp. He had always developed elite talent rather than buying the finished article. After his comments about Manchester United's acquisition of Paul Pogba for a world record fee, Klopp was accused of hypocrisy when he made Van Dijk the most expensive defender on the planet. He grinned and said: "Did I change my opinion? Yes. That is true. But it is better to change your opinion than never have one."

The transfer landscape had shifted and Klopp could finally buy from the top shelf. The club's recruitment staff tracked in excess of 30 centre-backs from across Europe over an 18-month period and Van Dijk came out on top in all the metrics. Aymeric Laporte, Kalidou Koulibaly and Jerome Boateng also made the shortlist but Van Dijk was viewed as being in a class of his own. Liverpool had serious competition for his signature from both Manchester City and Chelsea, but Klopp's pulling power helped to win the day.

During their discussions, he left the Holland international in no doubt about his admiration for Van Dijk's defensive qualities, describing him as the "game-changer" who would help Liverpool make the leap from contenders to winners. Van Dijk was won over and in June 2017 he made it clear his heart was set on Liverpool. However, Klopp's joy proved to be short-lived. Reports the pair had met in Blackpool and that the player was Anfield-bound infuriated Southampton. At that time, Liverpool had yet to officially open negotiations over the fee.

Southampton complained to the Premier League and accused Liverpool of making an illegal approach. After a series of emergency meetings, FSG president Gordon felt the club had no option but to climb down and issue an embarrassing public apology. A statement included the line: "We have ended any interest in the player."

The reality was very different. Klopp ignored the clamour from a section of the fanbase to pursue a Plan B. He had no intention of lowering his sights. He knew Van Dijk was worth waiting for. Gordon worked behind the scenes to repair relations with Southampton chairman Ralph Krueger and, six months later than planned, Klopp got his man.

The manager had no doubts about Van Dijk's ability but sought reassurances from the Anfield hierarchy that the club wouldn't be overstretching themselves by sanctioning the deal. Liverpool's transfer record was duly shattered. "The first thing all Liverpool supporters should do is forget the price," Klopp said. At the time, it seemed like wishful thinking but within a matter of weeks, his new defender's impact had silenced that debate.

Klopp had planned to have Van Dijk on the bench for an FA Cup third-round derby against Everton four days after he signed, but changed his mind on the morning of the match after deciding Dejan Lovren and Ragnar Klavan both needed a breather following a demanding festive period. "Are you ready?" Klopp asked him. The response was instant: "Of course." Van Dijk oozed class all night and with six minutes left in his debut he soared in front of the Kop to head the winner past Jordan Pickford. "A fairytale in a world with not a lot of fairytales anymore," beamed Klopp.

Straight after his debut, Van Dijk flew off with his new team-mates on a bonding trip to Dubai. It brought them all closer together.

Commanding in the air, strong in the tackle, ice-cool with the ball at his feet and with an excellent range of passing, Van Dijk provided an injection of composure, organisation and leadership.

What had once been an area of glaring weakness soon became one of huge strength. His presence improved those around him en route to that final in Kyiv.

Van Dijk's arrival had solved one glaring issue for Klopp, but there was another one he was still grappling with.

— A —

"I'm infinitely sorry to my team-mates, for you fans, and for all the staff. I know that I messed it up with the two mistakes and let you all down. I'd just like to turn back the time but that's not possible," tweeted Loris Karius in the aftermath of the 2018 Champions League final.

As Real Madrid celebrated a hat-trick of European crowns, a tearful Karius dropped to the turf at the final whistle, wanting it to swallow him up. When he finally got to his feet, he begged the travelling Kop for forgiveness, as Klopp's wife Ulla comforted the goalkeeper's sobbing mother in the stands.

Liverpool's captain Jordan Henderson emerged from a scene of devastation in the dressing room to tell the waiting media: "It is the worst feeling I have had in football, but I believe in this team, I believe in this manager. I believe we are going in the right direction. It is so difficult to stand here now and say it, but that's the truth. I believe we will be back in the Champions League final again. I believe we will be challenging in all competitions domestically."

For the opening half-hour in Kyiv, Liverpool had more than held their own but then came the skulduggery and the implosion. Salah was forced off with a shoulder injury after being cynically slammed into the turf by Sergio Ramos. The Real Madrid captain struck again early in the second half when he elbowed Karius in the head. Moments later, the goalkeeper inexplicably rolled the ball straight into the path of Karim Benzema, who gleefully accepted the gift. Mane's equaliser briefly gave Liverpool hope, but it was swiftly whipped away by the impact of substitute Gareth Bale. His sensational overhead kick restored the advantage and the Welshman settled proceedings with seven minutes left when his 30-yarder embarrassingly slipped through Karius' grasp.

Liverpool's transfer plans for the coming summer were already well advanced. Keita was arriving from RB Leipzig for £52.75 million and within two days of Kyiv they had completed a £40 million move for Monaco midfielder Fabinho. The combative Brazilian was viewed as the perfect replacement for Emre Can, who was on his way to Juventus after running down his contract.

They were also on the brink of completing a £53 million move for Lyon midfielder Nabil Fekir when the deal collapsed due to concerns over how an old ACL injury had been repaired. The France international, who was viewed as a replacement for Coutinho, had already posed in a red shirt and conducted an interview with the club's in-house media when Liverpool pulled the plug at the 11th hour. Klopp agreed with sporting director Edwards and Gordon that it was too great a risk considering the financial outlay and didn't pursue an alternative. Liverpool had already decided they would trigger Xherdan Shaqiri's £13 million release clause at relegated Stoke City after the World Cup to bolster their attacking armoury.

The big dilemma for the manager was the goalkeeper situation and how to handle a distraught Karius in the aftermath of Kyiv. His compassionate instinct was to wrap an arm around the countryman signed for £4.7 million from old employers Mainz and rehabilitate his Liverpool career, rather than show him the door. Four days after the final, Klopp received a call from Franz Beckenbauer, who alerted him to the possibility that Karius may have been concussed by that blow to the head from Ramos shortly before his first blunder of the night. This set in motion a bizarre chain of events that led to Karius, who by that stage was on holiday in the US, being told to visit specialists at Boston's Massachusetts General Hospital to get himself checked out.

Brain scans showed Karius had 'visual-spatial dysfunction', which can result in an inability to judge where objects are. Out of 30 markers for concussion, Liverpool said test results showed Karius had 26.

"What the rest of the world is making of it, I don't care. We don't use it as an excuse, we use it as an explanation," insisted Klopp, who branded Ramos "a brutal wrestler". "At the time, Loris didn't say a word but that's normal. He thought he was 100 per cent responsible."

Klopp talked about a fresh start for Karius but the player was a bag of nerves the following pre-season as more alarming errors laid bare the scars of Kyiv. His confidence was shot to bits. Klopp simply had to be ruthless.

Behind the scenes, Liverpool had been working on a replacement long before the events of the Champions League final.

Klopp didn't have complete faith in either Mignolet or Karius – underlined by the fact he alternated between the two in domestic and European competition for much of 2017-18 before sticking with the latter from February on. It was an unsatisfactory situation which created uncertainty and a degree of resentment between the two goalkeepers. Even with Van Dijk in front of him, Karius had proved to be a weak link.

Long-serving goalkeeping coach John Achterberg had long since been championing the credentials of Roma's Alisson in recruitment meetings. He had first been alerted to Alisson's potential in 2013 by Alexander Doni, a fellow Brazilian, who had a brief spell at Anfield under Kenny Dalglish and then Rodgers. "Keep an eye on the young keeper at (Porto Alegre club) Internacional. He's a big talent," Doni told him.

Achterberg's analysis stepped up a gear after Alisson joined Roma in the summer of 2016. His performances in the 2017-18

Champions League group stage against Chelsea and Atletico Madrid convinced Klopp he ticked all the boxes and would provide the kind of commanding presence between the posts that Liverpool lacked. "A transformer," was Klopp's description.

Talks were initially opened with Roma sporting director Monchi in February 2018 but broke down as their demands quickly escalated. It was made more complicated by Roma demanding "a Salah tax" in the belief that they had been left short-changed by the Egyptian's move to Anfield a year earlier. After being quoted £90 million for Alisson in May, Edwards walked away and the saga dragged on until mid-July. Just like with Van Dijk, Klopp refused to lower his sights. It was Alisson or no one – despite persistent links with Stoke's Jack Butland and Nick Pope of Burnley.

Roma blinked first and when the asking price dropped significantly, Liverpool pounced to seal a £65 million deal. For three weeks, before Kepa Arrizabalaga went to Chelsea, Alisson was the most expensive goalkeeper in history.

Chief negotiator Edwards, whose office at Melwood is opposite Klopp's, had delivered once again. His ability to drive a hard bargain had also been underlined by the money he managed to generate from selling unwanted fringe players including Benteke (£32 million), Jordon Ibe (£15 million), Sakho (£26 million) and Dominic Solanke (£19 million). It's the reason why, despite an outlay on players in excess of £400 million during Klopp's reign, the net spend stands at around £90 million.

Edwards shuns the limelight. He's a very different personality to the manager but mutual respect abounds. "They challenge each other. It's a very healthy relationship," one senior club source tells *The Athletic*.

In terms of elite personnel, Liverpool had added the final piece of the jigsaw with Alisson. Karius was packed off to Besiktas of Turkey on loan. The upgrade was vast. "Before, the crowd at

Anfield was on edge a lot with the goalies but Ali changed that around," admits Achterberg.

Within 12 months of his arrival, Alisson had lifted both the Champions League and the Copa America. He won the Premier League golden glove for most clean sheets (21) and was crowned both UEFA and FIFA goalkeeper of the year.

No wonder Klopp is regularly heard at Melwood singing, "All you need is Alisson Becker" to the tune of the old Queen hit *Radio Ga Ga*.

"Alisson makes difficult things look easy. He's got everything you want from your No 1. He makes big saves at big times," says Ray Clemence, arguably Liverpool's finest-ever goalkeeper.

That was underlined deep into stoppage time during the final Champions League group game against Napoli, at Anfield in December 2018. Hearts were in mouths when the ball dropped to Arkadiusz Milik, who had a golden chance to equalise and thereby dump Liverpool out of the competition. But Alisson reacted brilliantly to deny him from point-blank range.

"I have no words for that. It was a life-saver," said a relieved Klopp, who joked, "If I'd known he was this good, I'd have paid double."

That save is rightly viewed as one of the pivotal moments of Klopp's reign. Without it, there would have been no miraculous fightback against Barcelona, no night of glory in Madrid. No Super Cup, no Club World Cup, no springboard to the Premier League crown.

A

"We are still Rocky Balboa, not Ivan Drago," insisted Klopp on the eve of last season.

A big fan of the Rocky movies, the Liverpool manager wasn't trying to claim the underdog tag after £170 million worth of talent had been added to his squad in an attempt to bridge the

25-point gap to champions Manchester City. Klopp's point was that Liverpool would need to make sacrifices, would need to work harder than any of their rivals if they were going to triumph like Sylvester Stallone's fictional boxer.

Pre-season had been gruelling with triple sessions at a training camp in Evian, France. Days started with 7am runs, before coaching drills at 11am and 5pm. As the players lay on the ground exhausted one day, shortly before lunch, Klopp told them: "If you think you feel tired now, gentlemen, then just wait until this evening. Then you'll know what tired is."

As well as new signings, there were significant changes to Klopp's backroom staff. Zeljko Buvac, his No 2 for 17 years at Mainz, Dortmund and Liverpool, had walked away the previous April, shortly before the second leg of the Champions League semi-final against Roma. Initially, Liverpool claimed the Bosnian-Serb's absence would only extend until the end of the season due to 'personal reasons' but it was soon clear the man nicknamed 'The Brain' by Klopp wouldn't be returning.

There had been no big bust-up. Buvac had simply become more distant over the course of the season. Players had picked up on the fact that he was playing a reduced role when tactics were discussed in team talks and meetings. "His heart just didn't seem to be in it anymore," one senior player told *The Athletic*.

Buvac felt that his responsibilities had been diluted as Klopp increasingly welcomed the input of other staff members. The influence of Lijnders, the first-team development coach, had grown prior to his exit in January 2018 to manage NEC Nijmegen in the Netherlands. Klopp has always refused to discuss Buvac's departure, insisting it's a private matter.

Some questioned how Liverpool would cope without Klopp's trusted lieutenant. The answer was emphatic. That was in no small part down to the coaching acumen, passion and drive of Buvac's successor. Klopp moved quickly to fill the void with the return of Lijnders, who had initially joined Liverpool as under-16s coach in the summer of 2014 before being promoted to Melwood a year later by Rodgers. The Dutchman, a popular figure among the players and whose enthusiasm for the game is infectious, lasted only a few months at Nijmegen and had agreed to become Klopp's assistant manager a few weeks before the final in Kyiv, but the news was initially kept quiet.

In that summer of 2018, Klopp spoke extensively with Lijnders and Krawietz about making subtle changes to Liverpool's blueprint. They had been exhilarating to watch but the manager felt they needed to evolve and play with more control if they were going to last the pace and be genuine title challengers. "We need more game management," he explained. "Everyone talks about our intensity but sometimes when we run like devils I have to say, 'Come on, please cool down'."

Klopp warned opponents would increasingly look to starve Firmino, Salah and Mane of space, so Liverpool would need more strings to their bow. One key area he targeted was set-pieces. The stats told him that Liverpool were distinctly mid-table in that department. They had a habit of wasting them at one end and looking vulnerable trying to deal with them at the other.

With the aerial prowess of Van Dijk – coupled with the pinpoint accuracy of dead-ball specialist Trent Alexander-Arnold – Klopp was convinced they should be a much more potent weapon in Liverpool's armoury. Lijnders and Krawietz were tasked with coming up with the routines necessary to make them count.

"I wanted it because I never had it before: a proper set-piece team," says Klopp. "It was clear that we wanted to focus on it because it was not a proper strength of us."

By the end of last season, Liverpool sat top of the Premier League set-piece table with 29 goals. Bournemouth and Manchester United were joint second on 21.

Part of the improvement centred on the recruiting of specialist throw-in coach Thomas Gronnemark after Klopp read about his work in a German newspaper. Critics scoffed at the time but the sessions conducted by the Danish former sprinter and bobsledder enabled Liverpool to retain the ball better as well as recapture it more often.

"Before I met Jurgen, it was frustrating for me," Gronnemark tells *The Athletic*. "I had all this knowledge about how to keep possession from throw-ins and create chances, but people didn't really want to listen. They only wanted the long throw-ins.

"The first club that really took it all on board was Liverpool. That was the big breakthrough for me. This is the first club where I've been able to use all my knowledge. That says a lot about the mentality and the culture at Liverpool.

"Jurgen is an innovator. He's a leader who says he doesn't know everything and is willing to listen to people if they have the knowledge to take the club forward."

———————————— **A** ————————————

The order was given for the giant TV screen in the Melwood canteen to be switched off.

It was the morning of Tuesday, May 7, 2019 and the players were sitting down to have breakfast after reporting for duty. They had seen quite enough reruns of Vincent Kompany's 70th-minute piledriver for Manchester City against Leicester City the previous night. It had been a dagger through the heart for Liverpool. The title race was going down to the final day but it was out of their hands and, deep down, Klopp knew it was over.

This wasn't the time to feel sorry for themselves. Klopp had to shift minds to that night's Champions League semi-final second leg against Barcelona at Anfield. The odds were stacked against Liverpool after a 3-0 defeat at Camp Nou. They also had to face Lionel Messi and Co without the injured duo of Firmino and

Salah, who turned up for the game wearing a T-shirt emblazoned with the message 'Never Give Up'.

In the pre-game meeting at the city's Hope Street Hotel, Klopp had told his players: "The world outside is saying it is not possible. And let's be honest, it probably is impossible. But because it's you? Because it's you, we have a chance."

"The manager always finds the right words at the right times," says captain Henderson, the midfielder who had redefined his role in the team after a long conversation with Klopp ahead of a game at Southampton a month before. Henderson had asked to speak to Klopp because he was worried about his future and in those discussions convinced him that he could still shine in his old No 8 role, having been recycled by Klopp as a No 6. A Henderson goal at St Mary's followed in a 3-1 victory and this was another sign of Klopp's managerial strength – that he was willing to have his own opinions challenged.

At the Hope Street Hotel, Henderson remembers the mood: "We all walked out of that room pumped up and believing that we could do it."

What followed was one of the greatest nights Anfield has ever hosted. Divock Origi started the fightback before Wijnaldum's quick double early in the second half wiped out the deficit. Then, with 11 minutes to go, Alexander-Arnold took the most famous corner in Liverpool's history.

His quick thinking was followed by a clinical finish from Origi. It came about because Klopp and his staff had noticed Barcelona had a habit of taking their time to organise at set-pieces so the ball boys, from the club's academy, had been given strict instructions by Lijnders to recycle the ball quickly when Liverpool were on the front foot. Fourteen-year-old Oakley Cannonier, a youth team player, knew what to do when Barcelona conceded a corner with Liverpool, in need of a goal, attacking the Kop.

Talk about attention to detail.

A few weeks earlier, Klopp had described his players as "mentality monsters" after a series of late winners in domestic action enabled them to keep pace with City. "That spirit and unity comes from the manager," Alexander-Arnold tells *The Athletic*. "We've had so many late goals that it can't be a coincidence. We never give up on anything and the fitness levels are so good."

The Premier League title eluded Liverpool by a solitary point. It was gut-wrenching but Klopp provided a sense of perspective.

"That was our first chance to win it, not our last," he reassured his players, before attention turned to a Champions League final showdown with Tottenham in Madrid.

No stone was left unturned during the three weeks Liverpool had to prepare. Lijnders even set up a closed-doors friendly in Marbella against Benfica's B team on the basis that their style and formation was similar to Pochettino's side. In contrast to Kyiv 12 months earlier, there was no sign of nerves in the Spanish capital. Klopp was so relaxed he even had a two-hour sleep in his hotel room on the afternoon of the final.

This was the night when Liverpool finally took the leap from nearly men to winners and Klopp ended his run of six successive final defeats as a manager.

"Let's talk about six, baby," he beamed after Salah's early penalty and Origi's drilled 87th-minute finish sealed the club's sixth European Cup. "Did you ever see a team like this, fighting, with no fuel in the tank? They suffer for me. They deserve it more than anybody. It was an intense season with the most beautiful finish I ever could have imagined."

Moments earlier, the players had repeatedly thrown Klopp into the air – a warm tribute to a man who had believed in them and unlocked their potential.

The celebrations inside the club's private party in Madrid's luxurious Eurostars Hotel went on until dawn. There was a symbolic moment as Klopp and his friends, including German rock star Campino, headed to a side room to record an impromptu follow-up to their initial track in Kyiv a year earlier.

We're sending greetings from Madrid,
Tonight we made it number six,
We brought it back to Liverpool
Because we promised we would do

————————— **A** —————————

More than half a million jubilant supporters lined the streets of the city for the victory parade the day after the final.

"If you could've put all the emotions, all the excitement, all the love in the air that day and bottled it up, the world would be a better place," Klopp says.

Previous Liverpool title challenges in the Premier League era have proved to be false dawns. Rather than kick on, they regressed, as star men jumped ship and mistakes were made in the transfer market. Not this time.

The summer of 2019 was serene, with all of Klopp's key performers having signed new long-term contracts. He had succeeded in his mission to make Anfield a final destination for world-class talent rather than merely a stepping stone to other European giants.

"Let's be greedy" was his message to his players when they reassembled in July. He told them the best was yet to come. This was a group still with plenty of room to develop. The intensity and quality of the training sessions reaffirmed the confidence of the staff that their momentum would be maintained.

Klopp added to his staff with sports psychologist Lee Richardson. He also brought in German surfer Sebastian Steudtner during pre-season to speak to the squad about dealing with stress, panic and breathing techniques. More marginal gains.

Liverpool had stumbled in the 2018-19 title race, squandering the seven-point lead they took into the new year. Anxiety had momentarily crept into both the dressing room and the stands – the fear of something so coveted slipping from their hands. There would be no repeat.

This time, their rivals were blown away by Liverpool's ruthless and relentless consistency. They played like streetwise, serial winners – swashbuckling at times, simply grinding it out on other occasions.

Klopp had considered taking a sabbatical when his contract expired in 2022, but was so enthused by the future at Anfield that much to FSG's delight he signed a two-year extension. "Let's try to make the best time of our lives," he declared.

In ending Liverpool's 30-year wait for their 19th title, this is that time. No wonder fellow club royalty Steven Gerrard has called for a statue of Klopp to be built at Anfield.

It's been a collective effort, but at the heart of Liverpool's thrilling resurgence over the past five years has been one extraordinary individual.

Jurgen Klopp – the fist-pumping genius who turned dreams into reality.

MICHAEL EDWARDS – THE VISIONARY BEHIND LIVERPOOL'S REMARKABLE RISE

DANIEL TAYLOR and ADAM CRAFTON

JUN 29, 2020

Perhaps the best place to start is the story Harry Redknapp tells when he is asked about Michael Edwards and the remarkable chain of events that has taken a frustrated IT teacher from Peterborough to a position of power and influence at the football club whose supporters now have a banner pronouncing, 'Champions of Everything'.

Redknapp had been Portsmouth manager when Edwards – or Eddie, as he is commonly known – got his big break there. A while ago, more than a decade after they last worked together, Redknapp got back in touch to request a favour.

"I'd met a guy who had only a few weeks to live," Redknapp says. "This poor guy was in his early 40s. He had been married only a couple of years and he knew he was dying. Someone had got in touch and said, 'Harry, he'd love to meet you. He's football mad'. So I went round to his house one Sunday and spent a couple of hours with him, his wife and his in-laws. He was an amazing boy, so strong, and he told me it was his dream to go to Liverpool.

"I rang Michael Edwards and, straight away, he went, 'Harry, not a problem'. I arranged a car, I got a driver. Eddie sorted everything else. There wasn't any of the, 'Oh, Harry, I'm sorry, mate, you know how busy I am', that you can get sometimes.

"He put himself out, he organised the full day and treated him incredibly. We have to remember we are in a position where we can make a difference to people's lives. Sadly, this guy died four or five weeks later. Eddie had got him into the directors' box, introduced him to everybody – Kenny Dalglish, Jurgen Klopp – the boy had the best day of his life. Loved every minute of it."

It was all done with no publicity, of course, because Edwards has a strict understanding with Liverpool that, as far as the media are concerned, he would rather keep everyone a long arm's distance away and speak about as regularly as Chief Bromden does in *One Flew Over The Cuckoo's Nest*.

Edwards is the sporting director who identified Klopp as an ideal manager-in-waiting and has been responsible for bringing in, among others, Mohamed Salah, Roberto Firmino, Sadio Mane, Alisson and Virgil van Dijk – the collection of players that has helped Liverpool end their 30-year wait for a league title and turned a drifting giant into the champions of England, Europe and the world.

Edwards is the University of Sheffield graduate who convinced Liverpool about the potential of Andy Robertson at Hull City to flourish at a higher level and become one of the outstanding full-backs in world football. Yet he does not even have a Wikipedia page. Type in his name and, until recently, the first result was that of an ex-pro from Notts County.

Edwards has kept so far under the radar that for a long time the only photograph of him in the media's possession was from a Just Giving fundraising page for the 2018 Manchester half-marathon, for which the list of donations included £5,000 from a certain Mr J Klopp. Edwards' primary concern when he was promoted to his current role, in November 2016, was the extra publicity it might bring. And the paradox is that he can still walk around Anfield without anybody recognising him.

"He isn't the most stereotypical football director," Redknapp says. "You won't often see him in a suit. He isn't a go-getting, big-personality kind of guy. You look at him, he used to have this spiky hair... a very inoffensive, quiet guy. You'd probably think he should be standing behind the goal."

Others talk about a fiercely driven, intelligent and ambitious individual who possesses the streak of ruthlessness that is sometimes required to reach the top in football.

Edwards has upset a few people along the way and was one of the three members of staff from Anfield cited in the alleged hacking of Manchester City's scouting system in 2013. Liverpool offered a £1 million settlement, including a legally binding confidentiality agreement, to stop the matter going any further and Edwards' presence is one of the reasons why relations between the two clubs are so strained at boardroom level. Not that Edwards will have cared too greatly about that detail when he and others from Liverpool's scouting department gathered at a colleague's house last Thursday to watch Manchester City surrender the title with a 2-1 defeat at Chelsea.

Edwards was a youth and reserve-team footballer at Peterborough United who never made the grade and, released at the age of 18, trained to be a teacher before getting his first job in a local high school. He is the lorry driver's son who grew up in Fareham, between Southampton and Portsmouth, in Hampshire and developed a fetish for numbers and statistics. The 'laptop guru', as he was called in one headline.

When the final whistle sounded at Stamford Bridge to confirm Liverpool as Premier League champions, Tom Werner pulled out his mobile phone to get in touch with the relevant people. The first to receive a congratulatory text from Liverpool's chairman was not Klopp, it was Edwards.

—————————————— **A** ——————————————

As Jurgen Klopp flashed that considerable smile, champagne bottles were uncorked and Kenny Dalglish's phone started bleeping with text messages while he was trying to conduct a live television interview, it could feel like a trick of the imagination that Liverpool gave serious consideration to hiring Eddie Howe rather than the German. Howe was on a three-man shortlist with Klopp and Carlo Ancelotti for the manager's position and it was part of Edwards' job, then as Liverpool's technical director, to determine who had the outstanding credentials to replace Brendan Rodgers.

Ancelotti, who now finds himself on the other side of Stanley Park with Everton, passed all the criteria in terms of his record in the Champions League and the statistics relating to his teams at Juventus, AC Milan, Chelsea and Real Madrid. But his transfer record counted against him because the check system devised by Edwards and Liverpool's analysts placed less emphasis on a manager's recruitment in his first year. Their theory was that a manager might not have the ultimate say when it came to transfer business during his first season but, in years two, three, four and five, that manager's influence would be greater and signings would not happen without his input. A lot of Ancelotti's recruits were deemed to be on the older side and that jarred with Liverpool's thinking. Edwards and the hierarchy wanted players aged 26 or under who were approaching their peak years and would still have a re-sale value three or four years later.

Howe's reputation at Bournemouth was for developing younger players and playing attractive football and, though his stock might have fallen recently, this was a time when he was considered for lots of elite jobs and being acclaimed as a future

England manager. He had also been a player at Portsmouth when Edwards was working there at the start of the century but their friendship never came into it because, if there is one thing to know about the current Liverpool regime, it is that they do not let sentimentality influence their decision-making.

Howe did not have the experience of competing in the Champions League, whereas Klopp ticked every box in terms of achievement, transfer business and playing style. Edwards made his recommendation to Liverpool's owners, Fenway Sports Group (FSG), and left them to get on with the business of making it happen.

Since then, perhaps the best indicator of Edwards' influence is to consider Klopp's line-up for his first Liverpool game, a goalless draw at Tottenham Hotspur on October 17, 2015, and compare it to the team that can expect a guard of honour on Thursday from Manchester City, the now-deposed champions.

Simon Mignolet was in goal behind a back four of Nathaniel Clyne, Martin Skrtel, Mamadou Sakho and Alberto Moreno. Lucas Leiva, Emre Can and James Milner formed the midfield and the front three had Adam Lallana and Philippe Coutinho either side of Divock Origi. Liverpool's substitutes were Adam Bogdan, Kolo Toure, Jerome Sinclair, Joao Carlos Teixeira, Connor Randall, Jordon Ibe and Joe Allen, who never did fulfil Rodgers' description as "the Welsh Xavi".

Edwards had to help Klopp build virtually an entirely new XI but, first of all, he had to get the confidence of the manager and create a relationship where they fully understood one another.

"It is a very good relationship," Klopp says. "He is a very thoughtful person. We don't always have to have the same opinion from the first second of a conversation, but we finish pretty much all our talks with the same opinion. Or similar opinions."

It was Edwards, for example, who pressed Liverpool to sign Salah and convinced Klopp to disregard the fact the Egyptian had

LIVERPOOL'S FIRST GAME UNDER KLOPP
TOTTENHAM 0 LIVERPOOL 0
OCTOBER 17, 2015

SIMON MIGNOLET

NATHANIEL CLYNE
MARTIN SKRTEL
MAMADOU SAKHO
ALBERTO MORENO

LUCAS LEIVA
EMRE CAN
JAMES MILNER

ADAM LALLANA
DIVOCK ORIGI
PHILIPPE COUTINHO

SUBS: ADAM BOGDAN, KOLO TOURE, JEROME SINCLAIR, JOAO CARLOS TEIXEIRA, CONNOR RANDALL, JORDON IBE, JOE ALLEN

LIVERPOOL'S WIN WHICH CLINCHED THE TITLE
LIVERPOOL 4 CRYSTAL PALACE 0
JUNE 24, 2020

ALISSON

TRENT ALEXANDER-ARNOLD
JOE GOMEZ
VIRGIL VAN DIJK
ANDY ROBERTSON

JORDAN HENDERSON
FABINHO
GEORGINIO WIJNALDUM

MOHAMED SALAH
ROBERTO FIRMINO
SADIO MANE

SUBS: ADRIAN, DEJAN LOVREN, NECO WILLIAMS, CURTIS JONES, ALEX OXLADE-CHAMBERLAIN, HARVEY ELLIOTT, NABY KEITA, DIVOCK ORIGI, TAKUMI MINAMINO

THE ATHLETIC

struggled previously with Chelsea. Klopp's initial preference was said to be Bayer Leverkusen's Julian Brandt, a future Germany international he knew well from his time managing Borussia Dortmund. Edwards persisted. Klopp listened, took it in and placed his trust in his colleague.

Edwards' success cannot just be measured, however, by the players Liverpool have signed because some of their more spectacular business has revolved around the ones they have moved out.

Coutinho's £142 million transfer to Barcelona was the biggest deal, but Liverpool also raised significant sums by offloading fringe players. Ibe and Brad Smith went to Bournemouth for a combined £21 million. Kevin Stewart moved to Hull for

£8 million. Leicester City paid £12.5 million for Danny Ward. Sakho went to Crystal Palace for £26 million and when the two sides met at Anfield last week he was the player many suspected Klopp's team targeted as their "pressing victim", the opponent who might be vulnerable to being chased down in possession. Liverpool won 4-0 and it was noted in Anfield's corridors of power that Sakho had looked "terrified".

All this is masterminded, to a large degree, from Edwards' first-floor office up the stairs at the Melwood training ground then along the corridor on the right. His door is always open. It is directly opposite Klopp's office and on the wall is a poster-sized picture of the 'Class of Melwood'. Every year the entire staff – from the security and kitchen workers to the first-team players and manager – pose for an all-in-it-together photograph.

In his trade, Edwards is respected by his peers and one rival sporting director says he has become one of the most "prominent and eloquent" voices at the Premier League technical director meetings which take place every six weeks: "He is good at his job. He always has a clear position and he sets out why. He always cuts very strong financial deals for Liverpool and there have been times we couldn't find a middle ground. They drive a hard bargain and the proof is in the pudding of his success."

Edwards and Klopp, the older man by 12 years, are described by one colleague as "kindred spirits", freely wandering in and out of each other's offices. During the transfer window, Edwards' television will be on and showing the rolling news coverage. The two men swap opinions, they debate and sometimes they disagree. They also spend many lunchtimes playing paddle tennis, after getting hooked on the sport during a winter training camp in Tenerife. They even arranged for a court to be built at Melwood and it will be the same when the club move to their new £50 million training ground in Kirkby.

Edwards ran the London marathon last year with three colleagues to raise more than £57,000 for Prostate Cancer UK. All four wore specially designed Liverpool shirts bearing the No 19 (to signify the calendar year, not the fact Liverpool were aiming for their 19th title). Mike Gordon, FSG's president, donated $5,500 ("as the son of a cancer victim, thank you"). Werner gave $5,000. Jorge Mendes, the 'superagent', €1,200. Ramy Abbas, agent to Salah, added £1,000. Jordan Henderson (£5,000), Andy Robertson (£1,000), Trent Alexander-Arnold (£500) and Daniel Sturridge (£1,000) all contributed. Gordon Taylor, the Professional Footballers' Association chief executive, put in £250. Edwards himself donated £3,000.

All of which demonstrates a level of togetherness that was not so evident, perhaps, before Klopp was in the building.

Brendan Rodgers, the previous manager, saw Edwards as a threat to his authority at a time when the workings of Liverpool's 'transfer committee' had created all sorts of political divisions behind the scenes. It was a permanent source of regret inside Anfield that the club's American owner, John W Henry, had ever coined the name.

In reality, it was the kind of operation that could have been found at just about every major club, where there was an understanding that the manager was too busy to go on overseas scouting missions and become embroiled in negotiations that could take months. Edwards was part of a group that included then chief executive, Ian Ayre, along with the analytics team, senior coaching and scouting staff and sometimes representatives of the club's commercial department. "It is a group that makes sure a deal works for everyone," one of the relevant people explains, "rather than an individual making a big call because their mate, who is an agent, has recommended some player."

Rodgers still had the power to veto transfers and, early on, was probably entitled to question Edwards' knowledge. Liverpool had made a flurry of signings – Iago Aspas, Luis Alberto and Tiago Ilori, to name but three – who passed through Anfield without making a favourable impact. Lazar Markovic was the most expensive failure, costing £20 million, and not everyone appreciated Edwards' occasionally blunt, matter-of-fact manner.

Edwards was trying to push a new way of thinking at a club where they had traditionally relied on old-fashioned methods and, inevitably, there was some resistance.

A number of scouts were moved out, some unhappily. Mel Johnson, the talent-spotter who had recommended Henderson, claimed in one interview that Liverpool missed out on Dele Alli because of the club relying on their "computer and stats-led" approach. The game, Johnson complained, was "not played on a computer", pointing out that experienced football people were being edged out. "Some of these IT guys have come straight out of university and landed jobs at top clubs, despite having no football background whatsoever."

Associates of Edwards say he was prepared for, and unmoved by, the opposition. "You cannot have a closed mind under Michael," one says. "But to be clear: it is not a war between old and new. Liverpool's biggest strength is they move with the times in terms of analytics but they also pay attention to old-fashioned scouting, too. They encourage people to go to games. It is a middle ground."

Rodgers never put it quite that bluntly but he, too, found it difficult to trust Edwards and did not try particularly hard to conceal the fact. The politics eventually contributed to Rodgers losing his job and, five years on, he might have to accept that he underestimated his former colleague, particularly when it comes to the £29 million signing of Roberto Firmino from Hoffenheim. Rodgers had not been keen on Firmino, whereas Edwards and the scouting team were certain the Brazilian would be an ideal fit. Chief scout Barry Hunter had tracked him in

Germany and the numbers showed how, by being involved in 45 league goals in the two seasons up to 2015, Firmino was the second-highest performing Brazilian in Europe – second only to Neymar. Rodgers remained unconvinced and, to begin with, Firmino was used on the right wing.

Everything came to a head with the signing of Mario Balotelli and it remains a source of astonishment inside Anfield that Rodgers gambled his position on a player Jose Mourinho once described as "unmanageable". Luis Suarez had been sold to Barcelona and, with a week to go before the new season, a training-ground match had made it painfully clear that Rickie Lambert was short of the level Liverpool wanted. Balotelli was available. Samuel Eto'o, too. Loic Remy had failed a medical. Rodgers cranked up the pressure.

"He (Rodgers) was wielding his veto power a little bit," one person with knowledge of the deal recalls. "So Liverpool said to him, 'OK, fine'. That (Balotelli) was not a deal Liverpool wanted to do but he insisted on it. Basically, it got to the point where there were a few transfers in which Brendan said, 'It is my way or the highway. I need this player and you need to back me as manager. We have lost Suarez, so this is what we need to do'.

"They (Liverpool) said, 'OK, that's fine, but under our model if we all fuck up together on a few transfers, it's everyone's responsibility and we share that. If you tell us you want to take the decisions, then you will have to take the responsibility for that'. He went, 'Yep, fine, I will do that'. The next season was not great and he ended up getting sacked.

"Some extremely senior sources were pretty adamant they would not have sacked him for the results that season if they had shared the responsibility more for transfers."

——————— **A** ———————

When Barry Fry is asked if he has any particular memories of Michael Edwards, the former Peterborough manager has to apologise.

"I'm embarrassed to say no," Fry, now the League One side's director of football, tells *The Athletic*. "This is my 25th year at the club and I don't remember the boy at all, I'm sorry."

Edwards had been part of a junior football academy in Southampton before being recommended to Peterborough for their youth system, going on to sign a two-year apprenticeship at London Road.

"Probably not the most talented, but he worked hard," is the verdict of one former team-mate. "A proper squad player, who made the best of what he'd got. He was never going to be a star but he was always quite dependable. And very clever. He was probably old for his time, the way he thought about everything and the way he spoke. You could tell he had a good head on his shoulders."

Edwards was a right-back who would occasionally be moved into a holding midfield role and, though he was not regarded as loud or a shouter, there was one occasion when he turned on two team-mates and accused them of thinking they were "big-time".

"There were two colleges in the area," another former Peterborough player says. "Some of us – the ones who never got the better qualifications – went to Huntingdon College. Michael went to Cambridge to do leisure and tourism with the more intelligent lads, one day a week. Academically, he was very able. And on the pitch, you could see he understood the game."

Ultimately, though, Edwards left Peterborough without making a first-team appearance and had to make a new career for himself. He went back to college and enrolled for university, obtaining a degree in business management and informatics.

He returned to Peterborough to start his first teaching job but colleagues say he missed being around football and was not enthused by his new profession.

His breakthrough came in 2003 when Portsmouth agreed to take on Prozone, the football data company. Other clubs had already signed up and Simon Wilson, one of Edwards' former Peterborough team-mates, was in the relevant department up the road at Southampton.

"I said to Simon we had won a contract with Portsmouth and needed an analyst," Barry McNeill, then Prozone's business development manager, says. "He rolled off a few names and said, 'There's one guy I know who's probably not happy where he is, why don't you have a chat with him?'"

Edwards was in his early 20s. "We found him working as an IT teacher," McNeill says. "He clearly had pretty low motivation for that vocation. I interviewed him at a service station between Peterborough and the M1. I explained Prozone, showed him the technology and within a month he was on-site at Portsmouth's training ground."

Though Edwards might not have enjoyed teaching, McNeill thinks the experience hardened him for the football business. "The first few years (of teaching) are the toughest because you are totally out of your depth. You need a spine. That was probably great preparation."

This was a time when data was still relatively new to football and, all these years later, it is strange to hear one of Edwards' fellow analysts say "it was only *The Sun* on a Monday that had passing and possession stats".

Redknapp had been persuaded by his assistant, Jim Smith, that Prozone was worth a go. Smith had been the first-ever manager to take it on at Derby County. Steve McClaren, one of Smith's assistants, then took it to Manchester United. Sam Allardyce, then at Bolton Wanderers, was another advocate. And, as soon as word got out that Sir Alex Ferguson was using it at Old Trafford, other clubs started to follow.

"I would be in Sam's (Allardyce) office after games," McNeill says. "If they had beaten Portsmouth, Sam would say to Harry, 'What the fuck are you doing? Why have you not got this? It is as expensive as your cheapest squad player.' He would almost embarrass people to jump on the bandwagon."

Even so, it took a while for Redknapp to get to grips with it. "There is a famous story where Eddie is trying to get through to Harry," one of Edwards' former associates says. "This is folklore in analyst circles. Harry said, 'Does your computer say we are going to win today?' Eddie said, 'Yes,' quite flippantly. They lost and Harry quipped, 'Maybe your computer can play next time'. Nobody even knows if it is true, but we all repeat it."

In Edwards' early days, Redknapp called to ask why he could not get anything out of a CD-ROM filled with player data. It turned out Redknapp had put it into the CD player of his car.

Edwards had his own office and was of an age when he could mix with the players without it seeming unusual. "On the team bus, for example, he would be with the lads and we would play Mario Kart," Gary O'Neil, their former midfielder, says. "You might have an eight-person league and Ed would be in it. He didn't overstep the line, though. He wouldn't be on lads' nights out because he was, technically, staff. We were good friends and he came to my wedding."

O'Neil remembers Redknapp never previously being stats-orientated – "we basically never used them at all" – but something must have gone right because Edwards followed the manager to Spurs in 2009.

"Michael came to Portsmouth as a very young analyst," Redknapp says. "I remember a massive game, the year we stayed up (2005-06), at Fulham. We were second-bottom and he put this video together to play on the coach. He was scared to show it because it took the mickey out of me. I thought it was a great laugh. He was a smashing lad and when I went to Tottenham I took him with me."

Edwards stayed at White Hart Lane for almost two years before Damien Comolli, then Liverpool's director of football, headhunted him as part of FSG's instructions to implement a new data-led approach, in keeping with their management of baseball's Boston Red Sox. Comolli had previously been at Spurs, whose chairman, Daniel Levy, was then further dismayed to discover Liverpool had taken away another of their key men.

Spurs had an exclusive agreement at the time with a data company called Decision Technology and Liverpool wanted to see if they could muscle in. Edwards, however, persuaded his new bosses to leave Decision Technology alone and instead target Dr Ian Graham, the data scientist who helped to run their operation.

The two men were on the same eight-hour flight to an analytics conference in Boston, Massachusetts. Thirty-seven thousand feet in the air, Edwards convinced Graham to join him as Liverpool's head of research. The task was aided by the fact that Graham is a boyhood Liverpool supporter. Graham, who holds a Cambridge doctorate in theoretical physics, informed Spurs when he returned to England. He now heads up Liverpool's research and analytics department, based at the club's training ground, and informs their decisions across recruitment, sport science, medical and finance departments. Graham works alongside Will Spearman, a former Harvard graduate student who was previously with the European Organisation for Nuclear Research.

———————————— **A** ————————————

On the night Liverpool's first title since 1990 was confirmed, Edwards was having a socially-distanced gathering with colleagues from their scouting and analytics staff. Julian Ward, who manages Liverpool's loan deals, hosted the event to show Chelsea vs Manchester City on a large screen in his garden. They celebrated together: the team behind the team.

Much like Liverpool supporters across the country, they soon switched to LFC TV and watched the three-minute montage the club had prepared for this moment. Klopp could be heard explaining the meaning of Liverpool's anthem, *You'll Never Walk Alone*. His colleagues listened, taking it all in.

Presumably, if Edwards could ever be persuaded to do an interview, he would pay tribute to Graham and a department that also includes chief scout Hunter, head of recruitment Dave Fallows and head of football projects David Woodfine.

Fallows is another Prozone graduate who cut his teeth under Allardyce, while Woodfine is a long-serving associate and worked alongside Edwards at Portsmouth. Hunter, Fallows and Ward were previously colleagues at Manchester City and were recruited by Edwards after he was tasked by the Liverpool ownership to construct the club's recruitment department in 2012. Edwards became Liverpool's first sporting director in 2016, a year into Klopp's reign, after impressing FSG president Mike Gordon in previous roles as the head of analytics and technical director.

It has been a remarkable success, underpinned by this extraordinary statistic: Liverpool's net transfer spend of £92.4 million from the last five years is less than Watford's, not even half that of Brighton & Hove Albion or Aston Villa and a fair bit behind Mike Ashley's Newcastle United. Only Crystal Palace, Sheffield United, Southampton and Norwich City have a lower net spend in that time. Manchester City's total is £505.6 million, Manchester United's £378.9 million.

"Their (Liverpool's) recent record is ridiculous, really," one person with inside knowledge of analytics says. "They have barely had a failed signing. I don't think that can continue, I don't think anyone is that good. If you get 15 out of 15 transfers right, it can't always be that way. He (Edwards) is over-performing and it will regress to a mean at some point."

It is certainly a far cry from the time, in 2017, when an online petition was set up by a Liverpool fan campaigning for Edwards to be sacked. The petition rustled up 36 votes and the first comment – "he's useless, just useless" – has not aged well.

It was Edwards who insisted when Barcelona bought Coutinho that a one-off clause was written into the deal to stipulate that the Catalan club would have to pay a £100 million premium to sign any other Liverpool player over the following two years.

Colleagues talk about the period in 2018 when Edwards had it in mind that Real Madrid, their opponents in that season's Champions League final, might increasingly be attracted to the idea of signing Salah, Firmino or Sadio Mane. Liverpool's response was to tie all three to new contracts, none with release clauses.

Edwards was unflinching when Emre Can, coming to the end of his contract, told the club he would sign a new one but wanted a release clause in it. There was a stand-off. Edwards refused to budge and Can was allowed to leave on a free transfer rather than the club setting a precedent.

What will never change is Edwards' reticence over letting us hear what his voice sounds like. "I didn't even realise how well he had done," one former Peterborough team-mate says. "Then I saw something about him on television and, 'Oh my God, that's him! That's him at Liverpool!'"

"You'd never imagine the guy sat in the tiny Prozone portakabin at Portsmouth would go on to be the guy who plays such a big role at the biggest club in the world," O'Neil adds.

Good luck, too, trying to find a photo of Edwards with the Champions League trophy. Klopp invited all his staff onto the podium in Madrid to join in the celebrations, but Edwards preferred to keep to the edges and take photographs of the jubilant Liverpool supporters. He consoled some of his former colleagues from Tottenham, including Levy, and helped to make sure Liverpool's kitman got a picture with the trophy.

Then the quiet man of Anfield disappeared into the background, just the way he likes it.

UNDERSTANDING JURGEN KLOPP – "IT'S NEVER ABOUT HIM"

RAPHAEL HONIGSTEIN

JUN 30, 2020

Jurgen Klopp completed his very own 30-year cycle last week. Exactly three decades after signing his first professional contract at perennial second division strugglers Mainz, he's won the Premier League with Liverpool as a manager – a career-high that's even more pronounced than lifting the Champions League the previous year, such was Liverpool's all-consuming fixation on the domestic championship.

This season's achievement has put Klopp into a managerial category all of his own, at least until the Champions League resumes in August: he's the one manager working at a top-level club who has achieved all the goals for which he was hired.

That's a huge chunk of contentment to digest for one man over the coming weeks. But Liverpool supporters needn't worry that the German's metaphorical full belly will sate his appetite for continuing his work with the same fervour and commitment going forward.

"That's not who he is," Martin Quast, a German football reporter and one of Klopp's oldest friends, tells *The Athletic*.

"Kloppo doesn't know the meaning of the word 'satisfaction'. He will be deeply happy, of course, but there's no sense of 'this is it' nor of 'I've finally done it'. 'It's never about him and it's never about proving a point. He doesn't draw motivation from negativity, whether that's other people's attitudes or a personal fear of failure. Kloppo does what he does because he loves football, he loves life, and especially what winning feels like. More importantly, he loves sharing these wonderful moments with those who feel the same."

Quast met Klopp while reporting on Mainz for the local paper in 1990. A year or so later, the fast but technically-limited striker started an internship at the regional sports desk of TV channel Sat 1, where Quast was freelancing. Klopp was always worried his lowly-paid contract at Mainz could come to an end if they were relegated and wanted to learn a different trade, just in case. He produced features about regional sporting luminaries such as the Roschinger sisters, two snowboarding champions, but as the youngest member of the editorial team his main duty consisted of procuring a regular supply of cola-bottle sweets from the nearby wholesale store. "We sat there and threw cola bottles into each others' mouths from three or four metres away," Quast says incredulously, as if recalling a strange dream. "Everything was a competition for him."

Klopp loves winning so much because he and those close to him have lost very often, Quast believes. As a player, his career was one endless battle for survival in Bundesliga 2, save for an unlikely flight of fancy that saw Mainz lose the key promotion game 5-4 against Wolfsburg in 1997. Klopp scored a goal but also committed a grave mistake in the tumultuous match.

Two more attempts to go up with the self-styled 'carnival club' as a young manager in 2002 and 2003 ended in traumatic fashion. Klopp had taken the unstoried minnows to the brink of a first-ever season in the Bundesliga, only to be thwarted each time in the final match of the season. They lost 3-1 at Union Berlin when a draw would have sufficed and then missed out on goal difference the next year as their rivals Eintracht Frankfurt scored twice in stoppage time. Many thought the club would never recover from those disappointments but, led by Klopp's indefatigable positivity, promotion was at last achieved in 2004 with relatively little fuss. The whole town partied for a week.

Last year, Quast brought Klopp and some of his former players together to make a film about the 15th anniversary of the feat. "They were laughing about all the stories and enjoying each other's company. It's that spirit of togetherness that Klopp enjoys most, the sense of collective happiness. It might sound funny for someone who's won two championships with Borussia Dortmund and the Champions League with Liverpool, but he said – from the bottom of his heart – that the 2004 promotion with Mainz was the greatest sporting moment he ever experienced, a real-life fairytale and happy ending that had gone against all the odds."

Liverpool's championship procession has been a little less incongruous by comparison, but Klopp will be just as pleased that he's been able to put the biggest possible smile on their supporters' faces, the lack of public celebrations with them notwithstanding.

"He's not one to fret about things he has no control over," Quast says about the postponement of the trophy parade. "In fact, his ability to take setbacks big and small in his stride is one of his most remarkable features. He always finds a way to turn a negative into a positive. It's a little bit weird right now but he knows that people won't value the trophy any less. And they will party eventually, I'm sure."

He adds that the prospect of a global pandemic derailing Liverpool's season was perhaps strangely typical of a coaching career that has come with a fair share of tough disappointments: two lost finals in 2016, goalkeeper Loris Karius making two mistakes in the 2018 Champions League final in Kyiv or Liverpool missing out on the 2018-19 title despite one league defeat all season.

"Dealing with the COVID-19 break and all of the uncertainty was not easy for him, professionally," Quast says. "But he's used the slower pace of life to recharge. He's in top form, very relaxed."

Christian Heidel agrees with that assessment. "He's been focused but also very at peace with himself and a little more chilled over the last few months, as Liverpool's title win has increasingly looked certain," the 57-year-old says. Heidel was Mainz's general manager in the Klopp years, and they have remained close: in February, Klopp watched Neil Critchley lead a young Liverpool side in their FA Cup fourth-round replay against Shrewsbury at Heidel's place in Mallorca. The two giggled as a series of commentators wrongly speculated about the manager's winter-break whereabouts. "Klopp is delighted that Liverpool have won the league but I wouldn't say it's a matter of pride for him. He's not like that. He's proud that he's made the fans proud," Heidel says.

With Klopp, the communal dimension of the game always looms large, as Virgil van Dijk confirmed 12 months ago. "I've never experienced such togetherness," the defender said after last season's Champions League final win. "It comes from the manager. He always says to us, 'You don't play only for yourselves, you play for those who are always there, for your team-mates next to you, the supporters, the people at Melwood and in the stadium who do everything every day in order for you to do your best'. It really touches us. We do everything for them."

Amid all the songs and the dancing at Madrid's Wanda Metropolitano stadium, and later at their Eurostars hotel, it had been noticeable how pleased everybody felt for each other – the manager for his players, the players for him, and everybody for the fans. Klopp's emphasis on the social aspect of their work had truly taken hold.

In the hour of victory, Liverpool resembled less a collection of immensely well-paid athletes and more of a mutual society, toiling for the benefit of everyone involved. A team built in the image of their manager, who wanted to become a doctor "in order to help people" in his youth and whose religious belief has instructed him to see one's time on Earth as a chance – and a duty – to make a difference.

"I'd say our mission is to make our tiny piece of land more beautiful," he said to the newspaper *Westfälische Nachrichten* in 2007. A year later, he told *Stern* magazine that life was "about leaving better places behind. About not taking yourself too seriously. About giving your all. About loving and being loved".

The noise might sadly be missing right now at Anfield but the love has only grown. "The thing he will enjoy most is looking at the happy faces of Liverpool fans, whenever that's possible," Heidel says.

Quast adds: "Their joy is his. He doesn't want to be at the centre of it all, and he would never agree to have a statue of himself put up. When someone suggested that idea at Mainz, Kloppo said statues were only good for collecting bird droppings at the top and for dogs peeing on them at the bottom."

Quast suggests that his friend's conviction that true happiness is a social emotion is best summed up by the image of his current autograph card, which curiously doesn't show his face at all.

Instead, we see Klopp from behind, lifting the European Cup in a Liverpool tracksuit, with the viewer's gaze getting drawn past him, towards thousands upon thousands revelling in red ecstasy. They are what this is all about.

JUNE RESULTS

Premier League, June 21 2020
Everton 0 Liverpool 0

Premier League, June 24 2020
Liverpool 4 Crystal Palace 0
Liverpool scorers: Alexander-Arnold 23, Salah 44, Fabinho 55, Mane 69

JULY

LIVERPOOL HAVE DOUBLED THEIR INCOME IN SIX YEARS. NOW THEY'RE CHASING MAN UTD

MATT SLATER

JUL 2, 2020

Billy Hogan joined Fenway Sports Group in 2004, the year the Boston Red Sox, the company's first big purchase and prize asset, snapped an 86-year curse by winning the World Series.

A born salesman, Hogan rose through the ranks and was the obvious choice to take charge of Liverpool's commercial operation in 2012, two years after Fenway had added the Reds to the Red Sox. After all, if he had spent eight years working with one of the most famous franchises in American sport, what could be so special about a team that had just finished eighth in the Premier League?

Hogan, who was only 37 when appointed chief commercial officer, soon found out that the Boston Red Sox open doors from California to Connecticut, but Liverpool get you out of windowless rooms on the other side of the world.

"I was travelling on club business some years ago to Jakarta and when you get there, you pay £25 or something for a visa that they put in your passport," Hogan tells *The Athletic* a week after the team have broken their own 30-year title hoodoo.

"But when I tried to do it, there were no more pages left and this caused a bit of an issue. I was taken off to some office deep in the airport and this guy was waving my passport around while smoking a cigarette and talking to somebody on the phone. He wasn't very pleased and I was thinking, 'Well, I'm not going to make my meeting'.

"But then he asked me what I was doing in Jakarta and I said I was there on business, and he asked who I worked for, so I said Liverpool Football Club. He immediately put the phone down and said 'Big Reds' and gave me a big hug. That's our supporters' club in Indonesia.

"He peeled off a little stamp that was on the visa and stuck that in my passport. He then led me through the airport, gave me another hug and waved me on my way.

"It's always nice to see the red 'B' on caps all over the world and certainly, in the US, you would say the Boston Red Sox and New York Yankees are the two biggest brands in baseball. But Liverpool are different because football is the most popular sport in the world, the Premier League is the most popular league in that sport and Liverpool are one of the most popular teams in that league. It's just a different scale."

In purely financial terms, the two teams are pretty even. The Red Sox, who have won the World Series three more times since 2004, have an annual turnover of more than £400 million, while Liverpool cleared the £500 million barrier in 2019, the season they won their sixth Champions League crown. But in its 2019 sports team valuation list, the business magazine *Forbes* had the Red Sox £800 million higher than their soccer stablemates. That is a reflection of the huge broadcast contracts and tight wage control which help most US sports franchises make steady profits, year in, year out, with no fear of relegation. But Liverpool look pretty safe in the Premier League and when you factor in their potential to grow as a business, it is not hard to see what gets Hogan out of bed at 7am to answer questions about the club's digital strategy.

The Red Sox have 2.1 million Twitter followers, Liverpool have 14.8 million. On Instagram, it is 1.8 million versus 26.6 million, and on Facebook, it is 5.2 million against 36 million. And the weight of those numbers is starting to tell.

According to Deloitte's Football Money League, the £553 million Liverpool earned last season is the seventh-highest income in global football, only marginally behind Manchester City in sixth place. Barcelona led the way with earnings of £741 million, £74 million more than Spanish rivals Real Madrid. Manchester United were third on £627 million, with Bayern Munich and Paris Saint-Germain completing the top five.

Deloitte Football Money League 2019-20

RANK	TEAM	2018-19 REVENUE (€M)
1	Barcelona	840.8
2	Real Madrid	757.3
3	Manchester United	711.5
4	Bayern Munich	660.1
5	Paris Saint-Germain	635.9
6	Manchester City	610.6
7	Liverpool	604.7
8	Tottenham Hotspur	521.1
9	Chelsea	513.1
10	Juventus	459.7

But Liverpool, now the English, European and world champions, look like a club with the wind in their sails. Their income has doubled in the last six years and, as Deloitte noted, they "have the clubs above them in their sights rather than those behind. The long-term ambitions of a top-five Money League position in future editions are not unrealistic".

Tim Crow is a sports marketing expert, who advises leading brands, teams and sports. "The historic context is important," he explains. "Liverpool were dominant in the years before 1990 and this gave them a very big fanbase in this market and elsewhere, which is something they have in common with Manchester United.

"These two are by far the biggest brands in British football and while Liverpool can talk about Shankly and their European titles, Manchester United have the Busby Babes, Best, Law and Charlton. And these allegiances have been handed down from one generation to another, which is why you have all these 30-year-olds celebrating their first Liverpool title."

So does that mean anyone could have made a financial success out of Liverpool? Is it not so much that they are back but that they never went away?

"If I had to use a word to describe Liverpool before Fenway took over, it would be 'chaotic'," says Crow. "To give you an example, I worked on a campaign with Betfair when it was launched. We wanted the biggest possible audience and we also wanted to create a sense of competition, because that is how the betting exchange works, with fans betting against each other. So we decided to go out and sign deals with Barca and Real, and Liverpool and United. We signed with Barca and United pretty quickly, but we couldn't get Real because they already had a betting partner, which happens.

"But with Liverpool, the talks were such a shambles, we decided to walk away. I had to advise Betfair that these guys just

LIVERPOOL'S INCOME GROWTH

Year	Income
2019	£533M
2018	£455M
2017	£364.2M
2016	£301.8M
2015	£297.9M
2014	£255.6M
2013	£206.1M
2012	£169M
2011	£183.6M
2010	£184.5M

wouldn't be good partners. There are very few times in my career when I've walked away from a deal like that.

"But from the moment Fenway came in, things have changed. They're just very smart."

Hogan is too modest to say if he agrees with that but he does not pull any punches about the situation Fenway inherited when they bought Liverpool from American businessmen George Gillett and Tom Hicks for £300 million in 2010.

"The position of the club was pretty stark. It was on the brink of bankruptcy, not in a good place at all," he says. "The statement we heard a lot was that Liverpool was a sleeping giant and that seemed quite accurate. We knew Liverpool had a massive supporter base and wherever you travelled in the world, you could find Liverpool fans. But everything is based on the success of the team. It's why Fenway does this – whether that's with Liverpool, the Red Sox or any of our other entities.

"The goal is to win in a sustainable way and the more you win the more commercial success we can have, which in turn, can help the football side of the club. It's a virtuous cycle."

For Hogan, that cycle started in 2012 when Adidas walked away from a renewal negotiation for Liverpool's kit deal, saying the club's on-field performance was "not in the right balance" with Fenway's valuation of the shirt. Many would have panicked. Hogan and his team went out and doubled the club's money with a £25 million deal with Warrior Sports, a Boston-based brand keen to break out of their ice hockey and lacrosse niche, into the world's favourite game. Three years later, Warrior's parent company New Balance took over the contract, a changing of the guard that coincided with Jurgen Klopp's arrival on Merseyside.

"Look at how they played the long game when Adidas walked away in 2012," says Crow. "They went with Warrior, who nobody had heard of and it brought them a load of stick, but that became the New Balance deal, which has been a proper partnership, benefiting both parties. And now they've signed a deal with Nike that should take them to the next level.

"On the sponsorship side, they've got Standard Chartered on the shirt front, Western Union on the sleeve and Axa on the training kit as their pillars, with a Manchester United-style multi-partner model that sits underneath that. It's all very calculated and strategic.

"They rode out the bad press. New Balance wanted to keep the relationship and they did a very good job with it. It was a world-class problem for Liverpool to have."

The problem Crow refers to is that New Balance loved working with a resurgent Liverpool so much it was willing to take the club to court last year when Fenway received a more exciting offer from Nike, the world's largest sportswear company. Liverpool won that argument and, from next year, will be wearing the company's Swoosh on their chests and seeing their shirts in shop windows from Boston to Beijing.

"The general sense in the market about Liverpool under Fenway is they are smart operators, who have installed good people in the sponsorship and sales teams – they've really invested in talent and that has made a good impression," says Daniel Haddad, the head of commercial strategy at the sports marketing firm Octagon.

"What they've been able to do much more successfully over the last two or three years is communicate what is unique about Liverpool as a club. They've learned how to speak to brands

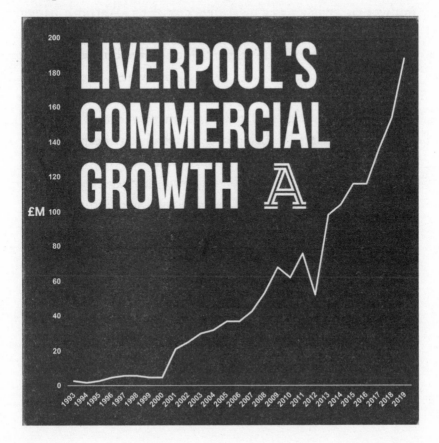

about the club's appeal and not just fall back on how big they are or how many followers on social media they have. All of that is important, and some sponsors still only really care about the eyeballs, but the brand side of things is vital these days and Liverpool have been very good at behaving like a brand.

"People take the piss out of the 'This Means More' stuff but it has been very effective because they've committed to it. It's more than just a sales pitch."

Ah, yes, the slogan that one executive from a rival club recently told *The Athletic* "just winds me up. What does it even mean? It's just typical of them!"

So, Billy, what does 'This Means More' mean?

"It's a marketing phrase to some degree but it's based on some work we commissioned a marketing company to do for us. They surveyed our fans, and people who aren't fans, and asked what Liverpool meant to them," explains Hogan (the company, by the way, was Octagon).

"To our supporters, Liverpool FC is a family. We wanted to know how it felt when you pull on your shirt to watch the game. For our fans, Anfield isn't just a stadium, it's home. There is something magical about our club.

"OK, you can say it's marketing lingo, but the idea is based on data from our fans and it does resonate. Of course, to work, it has to be authentic."

And it does appear to work. Liverpool's commercial income has tripled in a decade from £62 million to £188 million. Scroll down to the bottom of the Liverpool website and you will find a squad of official partners every bit as strong as Klopp's team.

"'This Means More' sounds more like a campaign to me than a motto but their sponsors love it," says Richard Adelsberg, managing director at the sport and music agency Ear to the Ground.

"It's broad enough to apply to almost any brand and it's easy to understand and translate. Having slogans like these does help you get your ducks in a row when you're talking to potential sponsors."

But what really impresses Adelsberg, whose agency uses data from over 6,000 'tastemakers' to inform clients about what's hot, and what's not, is how Liverpool learned to let go.

"Liverpool were quite traditional in their approach," he explains. "A bit like United, they could almost be a bit arrogant about how they dealt with brands because they knew, barring a catastrophe, they would still be a big club.

"But a couple of years ago, they noticed that younger fans were moving towards Manchester City and Chelsea. These younger fans aren't interested in what a club did 30 years ago. They're interested in what is happening now. What they really like is where sport, fashion and music intersect.

"Liverpool spotted this just in time, to be honest, and they changed their approach just as the team picked up. One of the first things they did was reach out to Liverpool fans in the esports world, which gave them access to a huge, younger audience."

It's unclear whether this was a result of, or the reason for, Fenway hiring Peter Moore from gaming giant Electronic Arts to be Liverpool's chief executive in 2017, but the results are obvious. Last year, the club's FIFA Ultimate Team star Donovan 'Tekkz' Hunt lifted a championship trophy before club captain Jordan Henderson, although in this case, it was the ePremier League.

"They have also been clever with how they have supported independent outlets like Redmen TV and (fans' website) Empire of the Kop without trying to control them," says Adelsberg.

"Another good example would be the relationship they have with (musician) Jamie Webster and his BOSS Night events. They could have ignored this and decided it was too edgy or risky. Lots of other clubs would have backed away, but Liverpool didn't and it's developed into something that really resonates with young fans."

——————————————— **A** ———————————————

So they have a massive potential customer base, a good product to sell, a catchy slogan, some tunes and they are down with the kids. But there is more.

"Liverpool never really went away but they have also certainly grown," says Rory Stewart-Richardson, founder and chief executive of Connexi, an online marketplace that puts sponsors together with rights-holders and vice-versa.

"Manchester United are still smashing it on the sponsorship front because of their heritage and the success they enjoyed under Fergie – that is still hugely appealing to brands, even if they haven't been as successful on the pitch since Fergie left.

"Liverpool were a bit like that, but even before they started winning again they were closing the gap commercially and the secret has been their digital strategy.

"They have massively increased the level and amount of content they put out for their fans. They've done heart-warming and funny videos, interviews and vlogs, they've embraced new technology like AR (augmented reality) and VR (virtual reality), and they have invested in cloud-based communications technology.

"Liverpool have the fastest-growing social media presence in football. Everybody is doing it but nobody is doing as well as them. Yes, success on the pitch helps but Liverpool have nailed the digital side. Everyone wants a viral video, but Liverpool's output is so varied and of consistently high quality. It's genuinely fan-first content and that's why it gets more clicks, more likes and more shares."

Football's fight for clicks, likes and shares is almost as competitive as the matches. No club can get away with a photo of a manager watching a new signing pretend to scribble their name on a piece of paper these days.

This week's viral sensation comes courtesy of the Football Association of Iceland – a two-minute video to launch their new logo that references *Game of Thrones*, the Cod Wars, Gylfi Sigurdsson's dead-ball prowess and the Viking Clap – but Liverpool's digital team have been slaying dragons, too.

Recent highlights include a Nivea for Men-branded video of Henderson surprising a life-long Liverpool fan with a Zoom call. The fan had recently lost his mum and dad and needed a good day. His parting comment that the call had "made my life" suggests it works.

But Anfield churns out comedies, too, with February's advert for coconut milk firm Chaokoh making unlikely light entertainment stars of Roberto Firmino, Joel Matip and Andy Robertson.

"We have focused on digital because it's quite simply the only way to reach and engage with a fanbase like ours, which is global," says Hogan. "We don't believe there is any one-size-fits-all solution, so while we work hard on our platforms – our app, our website, our social channels – we are present everywhere we need to be. So we're on (communications app) Line in Japan, (video-sharing network) Douyin in China, TikTok and so on, and each platform brings a different demographic."

Of course, there will be some fans rolling their eyes at this point – assuming they got past the bit about 'This Means More' – or shouting: "What have silly videos and computer games got to do with winning football matches?"

But it really is simple. The club's wage bill has almost doubled from £166 million to £310 million in five years, and Liverpool's amortisation costs – the best indicator of how much they are spending in the transfer market – have gone from £59 million to £112 million over the same period. Every deal Hogan and his team can get over the line provides more money for sporting director Michael Edwards and Klopp to spend on players.

"Liverpool's Champions League win in 2005 was vital to keeping them at the top table, just as buying top talent like Fernando Torres and Luis Suarez was important, too," says Octagon's Haddad. "But what we're seeing now is them holding on to their best players: they are not a stepping stone to somewhere else."

So what is next?

"Our plan is to continue to leverage the club's size and scale, as well as target growth in key markets like China, India and the United States, which in football terms, are developing markets," says Hogan.

"The prospect of where we might get to is amazingly exciting. We have said it's important to enjoy this moment but we know this is a very competitive world on and off the pitch. Our philosophy is not to focus on others but to concentrate on what we're doing. And my role is to keep helping this club grow."

Celebrate, concentrate, collaborate – it sounds like a good plan. Watch out Real, Barca, United: Liverpool are coming for you.

POWERING THE CHAMPIONS: APPLE JUICE LACED WITH CAFFEINE, SEA SALT AND CHERRIES

JAMES PEARCE

JUL 12, 2020

The last time Liverpool were crowned champions of England, legendary coach Ronnie Moran was still taking the players' food orders.

"There were four choices back in 1990," former midfielder Jan Molby tells *The Athletic*. "It was chicken and chips, fish and chips, pie and chips or sausage and chips. Ronnie would write it all down and then, after every away game, we'd always stop off at a shop to collect our order for the journey home.

"That was the refuelling back then. All washed down with a few bottles of beer. We'd always have a few beers on the bus."

How times have changed. Thirty years on, Liverpool have finally landed the big prize once again, with Jurgen Klopp saluting the contribution of the club's head of nutrition Mona Nemmer. It's telling how often she's been name-checked by the manager during interviews since the title was wrapped up.

"What Mona did food-wise and with nutrition is amazing," he beamed. Klopp joked that his players would have starved during the COVID-19 lockdown but for the tireless efforts of

Nemmer, who sent out recipes and coordinated the delivery of food packages to ensure every member of the squad had the required ingredients to make dishes tailored towards bolstering their immune system.

"World class" is Klopp's assessment of someone he regards as one of the most important signings of his five-year Anfield reign.

Nemmer was recruited from Bayern Munich in the summer of 2016 along with head of fitness and conditioning Andreas Kornmayer. Together they have helped to take sports science at Melwood to the next level. They are key figures in Klopp's marginal gains strategy, which has turned Liverpool from contenders into champions.

"Food is like kerosene," remarked former Arsenal boss Arsene Wenger, who revolutionised eating habits in English football in the 1990s. "If you put the wrong one in your car, it's not as quick as it should be."

The fuel Liverpool have been running on has enabled them to blow their rivals away in establishing what is on course to be a record-breaking margin of victory in the Premier League.

Nemmer, who oversees the club's team of chefs, sources the finest organic – and preferably local – produce, from corn-fed chicken to Atlantic cod loins and roast venison. She redesigned the canteen at Melwood to introduce fruit, granola and yoghurt, juice and salad stations. She offers one-to-one consultations and cooking lessons to both players and their families.

Whiteboards provide educational messages for players about the importance of hydration and stocking up on carbohydrates and protein. That's especially important to aid recovery when there's a quick turnaround, like Saturday's visit of Burnley following the midweek trip to Brighton.

After games at Anfield, there are pasta and rice stations close to the home dressing room. Chicken, lamb, fish, steamed broccoli and mashed sweet potatoes with pumpkin are among the items on offer. All the sauces and dressings are made from scratch, with players having the option to take doggy bags home. Sea salt is used, rather than table salt.

Intra-squad games at Melwood have resulted in the losers having to cook cakes for the victors, with Nemmer overseeing proceedings. Molasses are used instead of sugar.

Every player has his own individual diet plan for four meals a day based on a range of factors including his position in the team, height, body weight and ethnicity. Those who cover more distance during games, like full-backs Trent Alexander-Arnold and Andy Robertson, expend more energy, so need to take on board more calories.

Heart rate and body-fat percentages are regularly checked, with blood tests revealing whether someone is deficient in certain nutrients, such as iron or vitamin D and in need of supplements. Nemmer receives daily updates from the coaching and the medical departments, so she can tweak a player's plan accordingly.

Liverpool work closely with a number of UK universities to ensure they remain at the cutting edge of nutritional developments. Research findings are put into practice, like the increased use of blueberries and morello cherries, which contain antioxidants and help protect the body from the risk of illness.

Data collected by Liverpool John Moores University in 2017 showed that Klopp's players expended an average of 3,566 calories a day and consumed an average of 3,789 calories on match days and 2,956 on training days. However, they weren't taking on board enough carbs on match days. To optimise glycogen resynthesis (replenishing energy reserves in the liver and muscles), they required seven grams of carbohydrate per kilogram of their body weight but those tested only consumed 6.4 grams per kilogram. More screening was done to up carb intake on some days and reduce it on others.

When Graeme Souness initially tried to change eating habits at Liverpool in the early 1990s, he ran into trouble. Experienced players were resistant to change as bacon and eggs on toast was taken off the Melwood breakfast menu.

"I'd always have a cheese and ham omelette three hours before kick-off and then a cup of tea with four sugars at half-time," Molby says. "Ian Rush's pre-match was a medium fillet steak with baked beans. But when Graeme came in he said, 'You can't have that any more'.

"Suddenly, it was all boiled fish, boiled chicken, pasta and vegetables. Graeme had spent time in Italy at Sampdoria and had gained an understanding on how it was done elsewhere.

"He was right to do what he did but to this day, I just believe he went about it in the wrong way. He could have sat us down and explained why he was doing it and most would have nodded and understood. But we were force-fed it and players struggled to buy into it."

Nemmer has had no issues on that front. Players have bought into her ideas because they enjoy the quality and the choice of food on offer and can feel the benefits. They have embraced drinking fresh apple juice laced with caffeine at half-time rather than sugary snacks.

Key to her strategy is that no one is forced to eat or banned from eating anything. The idea is that the more healthy food there is on offer, the less likely that players will miss unhealthy options. She teamed up with Liverpool executive head chef Chris Marshall to create the club's own recipe for sourdough bread, which is on the breakfast menu.

Before the appointment of Nemmer, Liverpool had only employed nutritionists on a consultancy basis. "The opportunity to create something at Liverpool Football Club was just amazing," she told club media earlier this season. "Working so close with so many lovely people, you can feel the passion, you can feel the dedication. I think we all know that if you put love and passion into something you, in our context, can smell it or taste it.

"In our menus and how we provide the meals, players always have to make decisions. Over the four years, we've installed a system where the players are always able to find something and learn for themselves what's needed, what the body is craving for, how to organise best recovery. They are so well-trained that they know what to do."

A frustrating 1-1 draw with Burnley ended Liverpool's proud run of 24 successive home league wins stretching back 18 months. When the final whistle sounded on Saturday, Nemmer and the rest of the club's sports science staff were already focused on Wednesday's trip to Arsenal and the task of refilling muscles with glycogen to repair and rebuild damaged tissue.

Endurance and durability have been at the heart of Liverpool's title triumph. Virgil van Dijk, Roberto Firmino and Alexander-Arnold have played a part in every single league fixture. Georginio Wijnaldum, Robertson, Sadio Mane and Mohamed Salah have hardly missed a game, either.

That is testament to the team behind the team.

LIVERPOOL'S TITLE WINNERS – BY THE COACHES WHO DISCOVERED THEM

SIMON HUGHES, JAMES PEARCE, CHARLOTTE HARPUR,
OLIVER KAY, RAPHAEL HONIGSTEIN and JACK LANG

JUL 21, 2020

Liverpool are champions for the first time in 30 years. When that achievement last happened, the make-up of the squad had an exotic twist. Bruce Grobbelaar came from Zimbabwe, Ronny Rosenthal from Israel, Jan Molby from Denmark and Glenn Hysen from Sweden. Yet the majority of players were English, Scottish, Irish and Welsh and their back-stories were similar. Academy football did not exist and apprenticeships, if a player was lucky, were served from the age of 16 at the earliest.

The landscape of the game has changed dramatically. Liverpool's team now includes three world-class Brazilians. The wingers are the best in Africa. There are two mainstays of the Dutch national side. The early careers of some players were shaped by the consequences of civil war in eastern Europe. Unlike stars at other clubs, not all of Liverpool's players were predicted to become legends. The majority have followed uncertain routes, their paths to the top less trodden.

The Athletic has spent the last six months attempting to track down each player's first coach. Where health has intervened, we

344

have interviewed the next coach along in the process. This pursuit has taken us to villages in rural Egypt – where Mohamed Salah was spotted by a scout before he'd even played a competitive game of football. It has also taken us to the housing estates of the Netherlands and the suburbs of Switzerland.

The subsequent testimonies are determined in order of number of league appearances before Liverpool's players got their hands on the Premier League trophy following their game at Anfield against Chelsea. For the players who have made a handful of appearances nearer the end of the season, we look forward to telling your stories in the coming years.

We hope you enjoy the piece.

A

"The hairs on the back of my neck stood up when
I saw him for the first time."
Trent Alexander-Arnold (36 appearances)
By Ian Barrigan, his coach at Country Park, Liverpool

Trent's career could have turned out differently. I have no doubt he'd have become a top-class footballer because of his talent and focus. Without the story of Ian Dawes, though, maybe his path doesn't involve Liverpool.

My father-in-law Jimmy Aspinall was a famous scout who identified a lot of junior players for Liverpool. In the mid-1990s he was desperate to sign Ian, a lad from the Litherland-Aintree area. He was a centre midfielder who'd been at Everton but he decided to leave because they played him at left-back.

I knew Ian's dad, Alan. I'd worked with him for years. I went to see him on behalf of Jimmy and managed to persuade him to sign for Liverpool. It was a big catch because everyone else at Liverpool had failed, as had scouts of other clubs. Steve Heighway asked Jimmy how he'd managed to bring Ian in and

Jimmy told him about my involvement. That led to a meeting with Steve, who asked me to do some more scouting for him.

The arrangement was ideal because I'd just started running a team in the Walton & Kirkdale League called Country Park. It was the most competitive junior league in Liverpool and it meant I was seeing a lot of talented players every weekend. The standard was so high in the league that Crewe Alexandra entered a team in one of the age groups – and they didn't finish top.

As Country Park grew as a club, with other ages playing under our umbrella, my role at Liverpool evolved. By 2005, I was in charge of Liverpool's development centre in Norris Green. This was a place for players to come and train if they weren't already signed on. It was an opportunity for lots of kids.

Jimmy had always told me that whenever you see a player with incredible talent, the hairs on the back of your neck stick up. That was what happened when I saw Trent for the first time. He showed up as a six-year-old at the development centre one night and I just thought, "Jesus…"

I was surprised that he wasn't already training with Liverpool full-time. I walked straight over to his mum Diane and asked, "Is he definitely supposed to be here?" I wondered if he was meant to be at a session at the academy in Kirkby, five miles away, instead. She got a bit defensive about it, thinking that I was questioning whether she'd taken a wrong turning. Trent lived on Queens Drive near Muirhead Avenue and Diane explained that she knew her way around. I was, like, "Listen, he's really good… he's better than the development centre already."

I got straight on the phone that night and made sure the coaches at the academy had a look at Trent as soon as possible. He was six but they decided he should be playing with seven-year-olds. Meanwhile, Diane told me that Trent was looking to play for a Sunday league team as well. He'd trained a couple of times for a few sides but hadn't signed for anyone. I was managing Country Park's under-sevens, so we brought him in.

It quickly became clear he was far too good for his own age group. He'd score 10 goals a game. So he often played in higher age groups with Country Park. Diane would tell me that he didn't enjoy under-sevens so much, because he found it too easy. I thought it was important that he still played there because the way he dominated games gave him confidence. Sometimes, if you promote players too quickly, they forget what joy feels like.

These were small-sided games and he'd always play in the middle of midfield because he was the best player. Once he was in possession, you couldn't get it off him. He was so driven. Sometimes in training, I'd spice things up by giving a few penalties against Trent's team. He hated that. He'd go home and tell Diane he never wanted to play again because of the injustice. But he was always there the next week.

Diane has been such a positive influence on Trent's career and life. Even now, she doesn't place him on any pedestal – always reminding him of how far he has to go. Back then, she was at every game and she'd collect the subs off the parents. She was my debt collector.

On one occasion, both Trent and I missed the opening game of the season for Country Park. I had to attend a scouting meeting at Liverpool while Trent was in London with his mum and his brothers visiting his father, who worked down there.

I asked a guy called Frank Kelly to take charge of the under-sevens, and we lost 2-0. I wound Frank up, telling him that we'd win again the following week 10-0 – that the defeat must have been down to him being the manager. I knew Trent was playing, of course. Frank was doubtful. He knew the team was OK, "but there are no superstars", he told me.

Frank went back to his role in charge of the under-11s. The next weekend, they'd kicked off a bit earlier than us on the same pitches and Frank came running over after about 20 minutes, asking how we were getting on. We were already 6-0 up, but I'd lost count. I had to ask someone for the score. The next thing, Trent gets the ball, charges down the wing and blasts a shot into the top corner. Frank goes, "Where the hell's he come from?"

"Haven't you met Trent?"

----------------------------- **A** -----------------------------

"I called him Alberto but he never corrected me."
Roberto Firmino (36 appearances)
By Hemerson Maria, his coach at Figueirense, Brazil

I first met Roberto in 2008, when he came for a trial at Figueirense. I was under-17s coach. Those usually last two or three weeks, which is enough time to know whether a player has the ability or not. Roberto's trial lasted 30 minutes. He smashed it. He scored two overhead kicks, just like that. He showed real technical quality; there was a big difference between him and the other boys. He was a class above. I knew that if he maintained that level of performance and dedication, he could become a top player – at our club and even abroad.

For some time, I called him Alberto. It was, "Over here, Alberto! Make that run, Alberto!" He just kept responding to the name, because he was an obedient kid. He didn't even correct me. He never came up to me and told me his name was actually Roberto. One day, the fitness coach gave me a nudge. "Hey, Hemerson. That kid's name is Roberto, not Alberto." I called him over. "Alberto, get over here!" In front of the fitness coach, I asked him what his name was. When he said it was Roberto, I asked why he had been responding to Alberto that whole time. He said, "Ah, professor, I was just following your lead." That showed the simplicity and humility of the kid.

What caught the eye was his vision of the game, his capacity to see things before they happened. He saw things that others didn't see, which is a mark of the great players. He was also a very good finisher and had real discipline: he would track back and give his absolute maximum in every training session. He wasn't just one of the most talented players I trained, but also one of the hardest workers. Honestly, he was an example to the other boys of his age.

He was a really shy kid. Roberto was never a leader in the sense of talking a lot, putting himself out there in public. In the dining room, the dormitories or the team bus, he was very quiet and watchful. But he was always smiling: he was a happy kid, who had charisma. His leadership was to do with technique. He expressed himself out on the pitch: that was where he felt at home. He was respected by the other members of the group. Sometimes the best player gets jealous looks or thinks he's above the rest, but Roberto was never like that. Everyone loved him.

He came from a very poor part of the country, from a very modest family. As a result, he did not eat well for a significant part of his childhood and adolescence. We picked up on that and knew he would have to put on some more muscle mass. Especially because of the kind of player he was: he was aggressive and liked to go at his opponents. Sometimes he would be at a disadvantage when it came to physical contact, shoulder to shoulder. We worked on that a lot with him.

We also wanted him to be more objective. He was technically gifted, perhaps the most complete player I have ever worked with, but he sometimes lacked clarity when it came to finishing moves. He liked to 'decorate', to do the aesthetic thing when he needed to keep things simple. We talked about that with him; he understood and improved.

That move where he looks one way and plays the ball the other? He already did that when I knew him. He would do it quite often, to the point of exaggeration. It used to really annoy his opponents, who thought he was mocking them. He got a lot of kicks because of that. We told him he didn't need to do it all the time. Time has shown that it's one of his trademarks, but he picks his moments now.

I remember one moment that really showed his desire to succeed. We had a few days off at the end of a regional championship, which we were going to use to prepare for the Copa Sao Paulo youth tournament. Roberto quite simply didn't want to go home. He said he needed to keep training, to work on a few things. And that if he went home, it would just be one more mouth to feed. He said he'd only go home when he became a big player – when he had done something with his life. That was soon after he arrived. If I'm not mistaken, he went seven months without going back home. He had an objective, and things happened very quickly for him: he was one of the standout players at the Copa Sao Paulo, catching the eye of various teams around the world. After the tournament, he was moved up into Figueirense's senior squad.

I lost contact with him. I became a coach in senior football and life just got in the way. But I have great admiration for the boy: not just the player, but the person. He's one of the good guys; I don't think he has changed despite becoming a big global star. He has the same personality, and he has not forgotten his roots. If I saw him now, I would congratulate him and tell him that he is reaping what he sowed all those years ago. All that hard work, commitment, sacrifice... the things he is achieving today all came from that. I wish him all the best and hope he keeps being the same marvellous person that I knew.

A

*"It looked like he was taking it easy
but a fire burned inside of him."*
Virgil van Dijk (36 appearances)
By Rik Kleijn, his coach at WDS'19 in Breda, Holland

To explain Virgil's story with WDS'19, you have to begin with Jordy Brugel, the goalkeeper for our team. I have a photograph of that team. It was taken in 2001 – the year we conceded just one goal all season. In the photograph, Virgil is kneeling in the front row rather than standing on the back row and that reminds you he wasn't the tallest player. He was an average-sized boy, but he was a central defender, and nobody seemed to be able to pass him even then. This meant that Jordy became very bored. Most games, he had nothing to do and we became champions. It proved to be Jordy's father who recommended Virgil to (Tilburg-based club) Willem II and the rest, as they say, is history.

His background in Breda had involved outdoor soccer courts, promoted by Johan Cruyff's foundation. There is at least one court in every city and the one near Virgil's home, in the Kesteren area of Haagse Beemden, was very popular. The court is surrounded by more than 10,000 social houses built in the early 1980s and I suppose it has a bad image, but lots of good working-class people come from there.

The Cruyff court on the Kesterenlaan was a meeting place for people of all ages. It enabled young players to test their skills against older players. This would accelerate their understanding of the game; when to release the ball and how to ride tackles. I am told that teams would stay on the court until they lost. Virgil wasn't always the most obvious competitor because he played the game at his own pace and sometimes this translated as him taking it easy. But a fire burned inside him, and I am told he'd regularly spend hour after hour on the courts of Breda, because his team would keep winning.

Our football club was two miles or so from Virgil's home. The club has teams from six years old up to the veterans of 60-plus, who participate in walking football. It is a very community-minded place. There is a canteen that serves food and beer and, even in the winter, we host barbecues. We played in blue and white stripes and photographs of many of the successful teams that have represented the club decorate the walls of the clubhouse.

Aged nine, Virgil played seven-a-side every Saturday morning. We had a squad of eight with one sub. I would be lying if I said I thought then that he would become a Premier League and Champions League winner, as well as the captain of Holland. To me, he was simply an outstanding player who had a chance of becoming a footballer.

Frank Brugel was Jordy's dad and he had been a professional footballer, a goalkeeper with RBC Roosendaal and Willem II, where he still did a bit of informal scouting. Because Frank was a goalkeeper, I think he felt as though he knew a thing or two about defensive positions. I remember him telling me that what stood out most about Virgil in those early days was his athletic ability, as well as the way he struck the ball. It helped that Virgil was able to stride forward like Ronald Koeman and contribute goals. He could take free-kicks. All of this led to Frank inviting him to Willem II when he was 10. When he left, it is fair to say our team was not as good as it was before.

— **A** —

"He never panicked, he was always calm."
Georginio Wijnaldum (35 appearances)
By Claudio Braga, his coach at Sparta Rotterdam, Holland

Georginio joined the Sparta academy at the age of six. He was a perfect boy, always smiling. He performed so well. It's rare for someone so young to have such a high technical level.

What made Georginio stand out from the rest was his ability to make the right decisions in games when he was in difficult situations. He never panicked. He was always calm.

He was a young boy with a winning mentality and he made a lot of goals. As coaches, what made us believe that he would reach the top was that he had more than just talent, he had the right attitude too.

He was 100 per cent in love with football. Before training sessions he would be playing on the streets or in the grounds of the academy. After the sessions it was always the same. He would stay around with a ball at his feet working on his movement or his shooting. It was beautiful to watch.

He had the ability to play as a striker, a winger, a No 10 and a defensive midfielder, but it was clear that offensive midfielder was his best role. He had lovely skill. He was always in control of the ball.

I remember in games he would find himself in complex situations when the opposition tried to press him. But he always used his body well and found a way out of those situations. He had a great eye for a pass and created a lot of goals, which was very important for someone in his position. He had great vision. He was so good at bringing the ball forward and turning defence into attack. He would switch the play from one wing to the other intelligently.

When he was part of my under-13s team, he was the reason why we had a lot of coaches and a lot of scouts coming to watch our games. They all knew we had a good one here. It wasn't difficult to see. By then, he was in the Dutch international youth teams.

He didn't like going to school too much, he just wanted to play football. I remember his grandmother and his uncle would bring him to training and to matches. He always took on board advice from coaches about how to improve himself. In the locker room he was always friendly and helpful to his team-mates. He certainly wasn't an introvert.

It was clear at that stage he was going to the top. At the age of 14, he made the decision to take the step to Feyenoord. Believe me, every club in Holland wanted to sign Georginio at that stage. They all knew he was a special kid.

I am delighted with what Georginio has gone on to achieve in his career and watching him win big trophies with Liverpool. But for me there's greater pride in seeing what kind of man he's become. He's someone who always looks to help others. He's still a role model.

—————————— **A** ——————————

"A boy who didn't give up and made the best of what he had."
Andy Robertson (34 appearances)
By Bernie Airlie, his coach at Giffnock
Soccer Centre in Glasgow, Scotland

We used to play three or four small-sided games against different teams at one hub on the same day and there would always be a bit of waiting around between matches.

Kids being kids, most of them would be messing about, playing tag, chasing each other around. Not Andy. I remember he used that time to kick a ball off the wall – left foot, right foot, over and over again. Andy was so dedicated. A bit of a throwback in many ways.

My son Mark and Andy became good friends. They went to St Joseph's Primary School and St Ninian's High School together nearby and keep in contact to this day. Andy captained the high school team and his dad Brian, who was a good footballer himself, was a coach at the club.

He must have been about eight when I first coached him. He was a wee bit small for his age but he was always full of energy.

He was predominantly left-footed, but pretty comfortable on his right too.

Andy was always great at getting up and down the pitch. He was a naturally fit boy with huge enthusiasm for the game and composed on the ball. I always envisaged him being a left-sided player – his athleticism meant he was perfect for full-back or wing-back.

You could see from an early age that he was a good player but, as my son and I always say, Andy wasn't an absolute standout. He was surrounded by good players. You wouldn't have said he was head and shoulders above the rest. You wouldn't have guessed you were looking at a future Champions League and Premier League winner.

At these match hubs, you'd have 200 to 300 kids all playing, so it was a good place for scouts to take a look. At the age of 10, Andy was picked up by Celtic. That meant he couldn't play for us anymore.

A lot of kids get hoovered up by professional clubs and then released further down the road. It's a conveyor belt. That's what happened to Andy. Celtic thought he was too small but that rejection only made him more determined to succeed.

The history of football is full of examples of really gifted young players not making it to the top. You've got to be exceptional. You need an inner belief and you need to be willing to make sacrifices to fulfil your dreams. That's Andy. He was never going to be Messi or Ronaldo, but he maximised his ability and he learned and developed to become one of the best left-backs in the world.

Andy is an inspiration to the kids at Giffnock. Some of the younger boys didn't realise he'd played for the club until we talked to them about him. It's a great example of what can be achieved if you are completely dedicated and if you respond positively to setbacks along the way.

A boy who didn't give up and made the best of what he had – there's a life lesson there, as well as a football lesson.

---------------------- **A** ----------------------

"Working in the fields made him tough."
Sadio Mane (33 appearances)
By Abdou Diatta, scout at Generation Foot in Dakar, Senegal

Our groundsman first spotted Sadio in Mbour, which is 200 miles away from his hometown of Bambali. The first time I saw him play, I was astonished. I asked myself how the club had not seen him up until now. He was formidable. He gifted us that day with his talent. He scored many, many goals.

But on his first day of training, he was very, very shy. He was alone and kept himself to himself. The team would carry the equipment all together but when he came to the pitch he would stay to one side and carry his boots. When I saw that, I went up to him and said, "In football, you can't be shy like that. You have to approach your team-mates – you have to try."

I spoke to him as if he were my son. "You have come all the way from Casamance for football. You have left your family. Here in Dakar, it is very tough. In order to succeed, you have to work hard and commit."

He said to me, "Dad," – because he called me Dad, he didn't call me by my name – "don't worry, I am going to succeed at football."

That's my most treasured memory of him, and he has succeeded. Gradually, he became more confident, talking to the team, drinking tea and eating together. Sadio was always very physical, that's why his physicality doesn't surprise me when I watch him play today because he already had it from a young age. He never got tired.

I'm from the same region as him in Casamance and in our

region we work every day in the fields. Parents would say, "Get up, you have to go to work." He already had the mental toughness as a child because if you don't, you can't work in the fields. That's what life is like over here.

We speak, but not often. Sometimes he calls me to say hello. And some years I don't hear from him at all. He's a very busy man, a global sportsman. If he's preparing for a match, he can't be on the phone to me.

A

"We should watch this boy closely when he puts his kit on."
Mohamed Salah (32 appearances)
By Reda El-Mallah, a scout in Nagrig, Egypt

The pitch in Nagrig had no grass. In the summer, there was only dust. When it rained, it turned into mud. And there was only one pitch. The fields surrounding the town were filled with jasmine and garlic. You could not play football on them.

There are thousands of villages like Nagrig across Egypt, places built out of the countryside and often without safety permits. Most of the properties in Nagrig look the same. Bricks and cement. Very little planning.

The sports field in Nagrig was surrounded by such buildings. Each night, hundreds of children would play there. Games were not organised. There was no official league. But scouts recognised there was talent to be found in villages like Nagrig, where players had nothing and their determination to do well took them further than kids from Cairo, who had more.

I heard about a game that took place every week involving dozens of children so I went along to have a look, hoping I might find a player. The boy everyone in Nagrig was talking about was called Sherif. I had high hopes for him. He was a good footballer but not on the same level as Mohamed. Because he was so young, he was only asked to play because we did not have enough players to make up two teams.

After the trial I went to Mohamed and asked him whether he'd be interested in training with Tanta Club. Tanta is a city an hour's drive from Nagrig. All of the roads are bumpy. Mohamed told me that he'd only ever been as far as Basyoun, a much closer village. He had to ask his father for permission.

I thought he trained well at the trial but the youth coaches decided to monitor from afar rather than invite him back. I was very surprised because I thought they would have more sense – his talent was obvious.

The following week, I arranged another trial at Tanta Club's city rivals, Othmason. It was difficult for any player to stand out that day because so many games were going on at the same time. Mohamed was waiting for his chance on the side of the pitch and he was still wearing his jeans when a ball was cleared and he managed to control it using his chest. There was a coach called Farag El Saidy, who said, "We should watch this boy very closely when he puts his kit on."

El Saidy was smart and invited him to join the team straight away. Mohamed played for Othmason for nearly a year before scouts from Cairo started watching him. He joined Al Mokawloon because of Refaat Ragab. He was a legend of Egyptian football and was running a youth training scheme in association with Pepsi. When he saw Mohamed's speed, he told the people he knew at Al Mokawloon and his life changed from there.

——————————— **A** ———————————

"He missed a penalty in a shootout and his lip went."
Jordan Henderson (30 appearances)
By Shaun Turnbull, his manager at Fulwell Juniors, Sunderland

We played every Saturday morning at Monkton Stadium in

Jarrow. Fulwell Juniors were the best youth team in Sunderland and every side in the region was desperate to beat us. We played in black and blue stripes with black shorts and socks.

Jordan was a talented player but there were no duds at Fulwell. Each boy brought something different to the table. Jordan as a bairn was the footballer you see today. His commitment was off the scale. And he could run for England.

After matches, he'd leave the pitch lathered in sweat. Even if we were winning by a big margin, he'd keep going. He was always desperate for more and he'd demand the same of his team-mates. Even though he was more of a right midfielder, he set the tone for the team. He wouldn't allow commitment or standards to slip.

When he felt like he'd let others down, he'd sometimes get in a bit of a state. I remember him missing a penalty in a shootout and his lip went. His dad was on the side of the pitch, reminding him there was still a chance we could go through. Fortunately enough, we did and in the final he scored twice. When I look back now, I think this was an important lesson for Jordan because it made him really realise how much of a team game football is. On other occasions, he was there to bail others out.

Jordan and his best mate Michael McKeown came from Herrington to play for us. That's about four or five miles away from Fulwell, the other side of the River Wear. Him and Michael were as thick as thieves when they were kids and both of them would join Sunderland and play for the successful youth teams there. We also had Kallum Griffiths, who went to Sunderland as well.

In 1999, Jordan was nine. That was the year we went the whole season unbeaten, 60 games or more. We scored 150-odd goals and Jordan, I think, must have had 25 or 30. Jordan and Michael were jointly awarded the league's player of the year trophy. You couldn't have separated them at that point. They did everything together. They were also different players. Michael was all left foot and he made the game look easy. He could win you matches in an instant. Jordan was different, of course, but his energy helped us win on many occasions as well. When opponents were tiring at the end of matches, Jordan tended to go up a few gears. They were mentally and physically tired, but he always seemed to have a bit more petrol in the engine.

A

"My line manager said, 'I see you've got your pension there'."
Alex Oxlade-Chamberlain (28 appearances)
By Mark Chamberlain, his father and coach at Southampton

I was a footballer and played eight times for England. My career took me from Stoke to Sheffield and then to the south coast with Portsmouth, where the family settled. We didn't live in the type of house where there was memorabilia all over the place and football photographs on the wall. Football was a central part of my life but I wanted my sons to follow their own interests. Alex is my first son of two. But he's Alexander at home.

When he was really young, I was still playing. He was two when I signed for Exeter. For the next few years, I was away while he lived at home with his mum.

After retiring, I ran a soccer school in Portsmouth and that's when Alexander started playing a bit more. He went to a private school called St John's and the focus there was rugby union. There was also cricket and hockey. Alexander liked sport. He also played a lot of cricket and golf. But he never played Sunday league football. His experience at that point amounted to one or two games for his school team but mainly him having a kick about with me on a park field. I let him beat me all the time...

I became the under-11s coach at Southampton. I looked at the under-nines and remember thinking to myself, "Alexander is as good as these…" It was the early days of academy football and the standard wasn't particularly high in the youngest age groups. So I arranged for him to come in on a trial. The environment suited him well. Expectations were different at Southampton during this period. Team results didn't really matter. I worked there for nine years and the atmosphere between the coaches was really special. We just wanted the boys to enjoy themselves. Whatever they were good at, we encouraged them to do. We were never negative around them.

We ended up with some good players in Alexander's team in the early days, but they kept losing and sometimes it was quite heavy. The boys were asked to make their own targets from game to game. Some would want to complete three nutmegs, others would want five shots. They were allowed to make mistakes and try new things – results really didn't matter. Over time, they came to appreciate that the game of football is not just about the spectacular things you do. Getting the simple things right wins games.

We used to travel to training together, even though sessions started at different times. The under-11s tended to start before the under-nines. Alexander would hang around on the side of the pitch and I'd ask him to join in. The best player in my team was the centre-forward, so I'd ask Alexander to play at the back. He wasn't particularly tall or strong but he was a competitor. I remember this centre-forward saying, "Can you take him off now?" He couldn't get any change out of him. Alexander was so sharp and so bright that it didn't matter that the lad was 18 months older than him. It was at that point where I started to think he was doing OK. Steve Wigley, my line manager, wandered over to me one day and pointed at Alexander: "I see you've got your pension there…"

I used to try to guide Alexander as much as I could but I wanted him to form his own impressions. As he got older and became a professional, I stepped back and let him know that I was always there if he needed me but he's his own man now and he rarely asks! I don't mind, though.

———————————— **A** ————————————

"Sometimes he would watch the birds at the side of the pitch."
Fabinho (27 appearances)
By Elio Sizenando, his coach at
Paulinia FC in Sao Paulo, Brazil

There are two clubs in Campinas – Ponte Preta and Guarani – but no one was training the younger kids. This is the Sao Paulo region, where everyone is obsessed with football. Yet there was no structure behind that obsession.

We brought together a few coaches for a new project in Paulinia, thinking that we could improve the level of youth coaching in the area. We started watching youth tournaments in Campinas – futsal, seven-a-side – and selected 60 kids aged 12 and 13. That was when I saw Fabinho. He was born in 1993, but we brought him in with the 1992 intake.

I wasn't Fabinho's coach at first, but I watched him play every week. He was very good technically and carried out his role well. I started training him directly in 2006, when he was in the under-13s. I was with him at under-14 level, and again when he was 17.

At 16, he hardly played at all because he was a late developer. We were runners-up in the Campeonato Paulista, but he didn't appear in a single game. He had always been a starter until that point. Always. I didn't understand it, but that was the coach's decision. I don't think he was very happy about it. But he knew that he was a year younger than the other boys and that he'd get his chance the following year.

When he turned 17, he had his growth spurt and started to really stand out. That was when the scouts started to pay attention to him. It was a drastic change from one year to the next. He was one of my key players for the under-17s side in the first part of that season. I was under-20s coach that season as well, and it wasn't long before I moved him up. He was playing in that team at 17 – three years early.

He was always a right-back in the lower age groups but I started using him in different positions: as a defensive midfielder, as a centre-back, as a left-back. It was born of necessity, but he was a very intelligent kid and really understood the game. He absorbed everything that we taught him. He played mostly in midfield at under-20s level, either just in front of the back four or a bit further forward. But it was as a right-back that he caught the eye at the Copa Sao Paulo in 2011. He was mature and confident and he pushed the team forward. He could put his foot on the ball and pick out a diagonal pass and he could shoot from range. I even let him take the free-kicks because he struck the ball so well. Everyone fell in love with him at that tournament. That was when he introduced himself to the world.

He was always intelligent, but at 13 or 14 he didn't have the same focus that he has today. Fabinho didn't arrive at the project thinking he was going to be a football star. He was there to have a kick-around and to enjoy himself. He was a real joker, a cheeky kid who liked to mess around. On the pitch, he could be quite distracted. I always told my assistant, "Keep an eye on Fabinho". He would fall asleep and we'd concede a goal from an attack down his flank. Sometimes he would watch the birds at the side of the pitch. We would laugh and say, "Stop staring at the birds, Fabinho!" You had to keep grabbing his attention. But at 16 or 17, he started to mature. That's when he started to get that level of concentration.

He was a quiet kid, softly-spoken around adults. Fabinho wasn't the kind of boy who would demand everyone's attention; he was more modest. But he was a good talker, a good communicator among his peers, and very popular.

I always compared him to Maicon, who was doing really well for the Brazil national team at the time. He was a good decision-maker, good in the air and struck the ball well. He was starting to get really strong. He could switch the play bloody well, and he was a good crosser. I would demand a lot from him: "You need to improve this, improve that." I really bugged him, challenging him to get better. That's why we have such a strong friendship, and why he speaks so fondly of me today. I really saw his potential at 17 and wanted to stretch him.

I spoke to him the other day. I asked him about his injury and when he'd be back playing. We mostly talk when he's back in Brazil; he invites me to his house for dinner and we have a good chat.

I've been a coach for nearly 15 years. You always hope one of your kids can make it, but you know that it's tough. He's not someone who loves the spotlight. He doesn't have tattoos and he doesn't wear jewellery. He has a plain car. He just wants to play football. That's what he likes.

In Brazil, we lose a lot of talent because kids don't know how to deal with the fame and the money. Fabinho came from a modest background. His dad was a pastor, and he came from Dique, a neighbourhood on the outskirts of town. We had a lot of kids who got lifts to training from their parents, but Fabinho always arrived by bus. The respect he has for his mum and dad is obvious. It's lovely to see.

—————————— **A** ——————————

"He was cold-blooded and had a serenity about him."
Alisson (27 appearances)
By Daniel Pavan, his goalkeeping coach
at Internacional in Porto Alegre, Brazil

I first met Alisson when he was very small. This was before he joined Internacional's youth set-up. He would come to training to accompany his older brother, Muriel. That was when he first started to really pay attention to football and the position of goalkeeper. His brother was his great inspiration.

Even from a young age, his technique was above average. But what really caught the eye was how quick a learner he was: he was able to assimilate everything he was taught. He was a good kid, with a marvellous family structure around him.

He was always a calm, cold-blooded goalkeeper. Even in tough moments, he had this serenity that allowed him to resolve situations in the quickest and best way possible. He had a very strong personality, even as a boy. He was able to marry technical qualities with coolness under pressure. The ability with the ball at his feet is the thing that has improved most during his time playing in Europe.

I remember that he almost stopped playing at 13. He had built up all the skills and foundations you need, but biology hadn't kept up: for his age, he had not matured physically. That often meant that other goalkeepers – who were technically inferior, but bigger – were picked ahead of him. Size can make a difference at that age. He was quite disillusioned, and his parents thought about taking him away from football. But I spoke with them and was able to convince them that he should keep training and that he could yet have a bright future as a goalkeeper.

I speak with him whenever possible. We exchange messages on WhatsApp, and there is also a group with him, Muriel, Dida, and the goalkeepers who are currently at Inter. We're always in contact. Alisson will always be an example to youngsters at this club, as a goalkeeper but also as a person. He really deserves it all, and he is capable of winning a lot more yet. He is aware that everything he achieves brings us great happiness.

————————— **A** —————————

"He was flat-footed, so we helped him change the way he ran."
Joe Gomez (26 appearances)
By Peter Lodge, his coach at Lewisham Youth FC, London

I'd worked with Kasey Palmer (a future Chelsea academy star and England Under-21 international) from the age of around five and Joe was one of his best friends. One day, Joe came along with him to Charlton Athletic's development centre in Lewisham. He had just turned eight. I looked after the under-sevens and under-eights for Charlton and ran Lewisham Youth as secretary and coach.

Kasey, who is now at Bristol City, was an exceptional talent. He stood out more because he was so good technically. Joe had potential but he was a slow-burner, a late developer. He always wanted the ball. He was full of passion and desire. He didn't like people getting past him.

We used to train in an indoor sports hall. Joe used to run on his heels and you could always hear him flapping around! It sounds harsh, but he was flat-footed. The coaches who came in to assist me could see the problem too as they stood and listened.

We decided not to sign Joe to Charlton at under-nines. We decided it would be better for him to spend the following season playing for Lewisham Youth instead. It was a very talented (Charlton) squad and we feared that if we put Joe in at that stage, he would have got lost in the system. He wouldn't have got much game time. The decision was taken to develop him away from the glare of academy football.

He was always a strong kid but athletically he couldn't get around the pitch quickly enough. We worked hard with Joe on his speed and agility and making changes to how he ran.

Joe was such a great kid. He embraced it 100 per cent. He trusted me. He was like a sponge, taking advice and information on board. He knew he had a big challenge in front of him but he was fully committed to it. He always wanted to get more out of himself.

We never had an ounce of trouble from Joe. He was so dedicated. He was never distracted by anything outside of football. His dad, Gus, was a massive influence and a great role model with tremendous family values.

Some kids are better receiving the ball with their back to goal. But Joe always preferred having the game in front of him. That's why, right from a very young age, he looked likely to be a defender.

After a season playing for Lewisham Youth, we felt he was ready to take the next step and he joined Charlton Under-10s. Talented midfielders and forwards tend to stand out more. As a young defender, it's more difficult to grab the limelight. But Joe got better and better and by the time he was 17 he was playing for Charlton's first team.

I'm still involved at Lewisham Youth in the background and I'm back working at Charlton's academy. I always mention Joe's rise to the kids.

I'm still in touch with him. The year before last, we brought a group up to do the stadium tour at Anfield. I got my picture taken in front of Joe's shirt in the dressing room.

I sent him the photo and joked that I was going to nick the shirt. He sent me one back saying, "Don't do that, I'll send you one!" I left it where it was!

— **A** —

"I played against him in training because it was too easy against the other kids."
Divock Origi (26 appearances)
By Michel Ribeiro, technical director at Genk, Belgium

I first worked with Divock when he was nine years old. He had started out at a junior club called Zwaluw Diepenbeek and then moved on to Park Houthalen, close to Genk, which is where we scouted him.

The first thing that struck me was how tall he was for his age but he was also very comfortable with the ball at his feet. He had great technical ability. It was clear that he had a really good base for us to work with and develop.

Divock was always a hard-working, friendly and humble kid. As a coach you couldn't ask for any more from him. He never caused a problem for anyone.

It helped that he had his dad Mike, who played for Genk, to guide him away from the training ground. There were never any occasions when Divock stepped out of line. He was always so committed to making it as a professional.

At Genk, we always play young players in a number of different positions rather than pinning them down to just one. It was clear early on that Divock would be an attacker so we never played him at the back. He had such good feet. He led the line as a No 9, he played out on the wing and he played centrally a bit deeper sometimes.

I think that stood him in good stead because at Liverpool and for Belgium he has been used out on the left at times.

As the technical coach, I used to give Divock a lot of homework. I wanted him to work on his mobility. When kids are tall like that you need to ensure that they don't just rely on how big they are. You have to work on their technique and their movement.

When he started having it too easy in the one-v-one at the age of 12 or 13, I made things a bit harder for him. I put myself as the defender and used my body to make things more difficult. It was about working with him to try to ensure he had the full package and not just relying on the physical side. We would work a lot on his quick turns and the need to have fast feet.

By the age of 12 we were playing him a year above his age group. That wasn't just because of his size, he deserved it. He was too good to stay in his own group. We needed to challenge him more. At the age of 14 he was playing two years above in the under-16s. He wouldn't always play the whole game, we would carefully manage his minutes. We didn't move too fast with him.

We played in a youth tournament against Schalke and a number of English teams, including Liverpool, and Divock played so well. We tried to do everything we could to keep him. But by the age of 15 he had attracted interest from a lot of clubs in England, Spain and France. In the end he and his family made the decision to move to Lille.

When a young player is in such demand like that they can start acting like a superstar. But Divock was never like that. He didn't change. We lost him in one sense but the relationship remained strong. We parted on good terms. There were no bad words exchanged.

We still keep in contact and when I talk with him on the phone it's clear that Divock still hasn't changed.

A

"Other teams complained he shouldn't be allowed to play."
James Milner (20 appearances)
By Jim Ryan, his coach at Westbrook Juniors, Leeds

I was a school teacher but I was also coaching a team called Westbrook Juniors in Horsforth, Leeds. We had an under-12s team and I remember this little lad being brought along by his mum. He was two years younger than all the other lads and he looked far too frail and fragile to be playing with the bigger boys. I was concerned he would get hurt.

But we let him join in and he really could handle himself. He could hold his own. He was very gifted, very fast, great coordination and, although he was small, he was quite strong physically. He could evade tackles and, even if he went down, got straight back up again. He always wanted to be involved in every aspect of the game and – this won't surprise you –

he would be up and down, up and down, covering the whole pitch.

Even playing among boys who were two years older, he stood out. It ended up with some of the other teams' managers complaining to the league secretary that James was too young and shouldn't be allowed to play. I think what really bothered them was that he was such a good player. The league didn't enforce that, fortunately. We won the league that year and he was the difference. I remember saying, "Mark my words. That lad will play for England." It was slightly tongue-in-cheek at the time, but I think we all knew he was very, very gifted.

But that was the only year he played for us because the following season his dad informed us that he was going to be joining Leeds United's academy. I remember his dad telling me there was only one other player in his age group who was as good as James – and that was a lad called Rooney at Everton. And by the age of 16, James was playing in the Premier League for Leeds.

I think James is the perfect example for young players. He's not into flash things or drinking or nightlife. You hear of players who play a few games and they think they've made it. James has always kept focused. I know he has this reputation for being boring or whatever, but I think that's something he has cultivated. He has got a great sense of humour.

It's been great to watch him progress, playing for England, playing for Liverpool, but I can't take any credit for it at all. I added nothing to his game. I was just privileged to see him develop.

A

"I used to say to him, 'If you want to be like Deco, you have to be braver'."

Naby Keita (16 appearances)

By Alya Soumah, his coach at FC Alya de Dixinn, Guinea

Every morning I would cycle to Naby's house just before seven and ask his mum's permission to take him to training. He would sit on the back of my bike and off we went to the stadium, three or four kilometres away. He was eight years old.

There wasn't a president of the club. We didn't have much equipment, so I had to buy everything, balls, cones, the lot. I sometimes asked the children to see if their parents could lend the team some money.

Naby's family couldn't afford much. His mum used to sell a dish called akyeke, made from grated cassava, usually served with fried fish and ground pepper, to feed the family. He sometimes ate at mine but his mum didn't want him to live with us.

I took Naby under my wing. I bought his kit. He was like a son to me. The other players used to say that I loved him more than everyone else but they didn't know all that I was doing for Naby.

He scored some incredible goals. With his small stature, he could go round one, two, three players, even past the goalkeeper. We nicknamed him Deco, after the Barcelona player.

If someone hurt him though, he would start crying straight away. He didn't like contact that much. I used to say to him, "If you want to be like Deco, you have to be braver. Football is difficult." I told him that it would be a real shame if he didn't use his talent. He said he wasn't going to give up, professional football was his dream. He would do anything for football.

I still speak to him often, once or twice a month. He has bought me a television and a motorbike and a car. I'm always there for him, like a father. I give him some advice. I tell him he can be like Lionel Messi.

—————————— **A** ——————————

"He had a low centre of gravity and great balance."
Adam Lallana (15 appearances)
By Terry Wateridge, his coach at Bournemouth

We used to run community football sessions on Monday evenings and I remember Adam coming along at a very, very young age – no more than five or six years old. He was desperate to play with the older lads even then. He was a really bubbly young lad, really full of it. He just wanted to play football all the time. That was difficult at first because he was so young and he was very small at that age but he joined in and his enthusiasm was limitless.

He had a real natural talent and was always going to be a good player. Even though he was so young, you could just tell. And because he was so small, he had a very low centre of gravity and great balance. He was two-footed and he would move very, very quickly with the ball.

We had some very good players at the time, but Adam was the one who really stood out, which is how eventually Southampton ended up taking him from us. He was a player we really didn't want to lose. It was a shame, but Bournemouth managed to get a very good sell-on clause which eventually they did very well out of when he moved on to Liverpool.

He has had his share of injuries over the last few years, but he has done very well for himself, getting into the England squad when he was at Southampton, getting the move to Liverpool and doing well there. It's nice, as a coach, to see someone do well like that and think that you've played a small part in helping to get there.

A

*"He was a right winger until he made
the sacrifice to become a keeper."*
Adrian (11 appearances)
By Javier Lozano, his sports teacher
at Colegio Altair in Seville, Spain

Adrian is a goalkeeper now but he used to play as a right winger. He was fast and would time his runs into the opposition box well, so he would score in nearly every game. He also provided good cover to his full-back. He was a great team-mate to the others, very supportive.

He changed position aged 11 or 12. We had three goalkeepers at the start of the season, so he was still flying down the wing and scoring goals. But one of our goalkeepers had an operation on both legs, the second moved to Seville with his parents, and the third picked up an injury. So I gathered all of the players and asked for some volunteers to go in goal. Adrian raised his hand immediately. He said, "Mister, I'll sacrifice myself for the group."

He was a kind, happy kid. He had a mischievous streak, like quite a few of the boys. But he was also a good student and responsible at home. Aged seven, he studied at another school but lots of his friends were at Altair and they played in a football team together. At a barbecue, he was convinced by his friends to enrol at Altair, a college in the south-east of Seville close to the ring road.

He was a very determined boy with perseverance, so I was always sure he would go far and have a long football career. Have I continued to follow his progress? I have seen almost every game he has played since he moved to Real Betis as a youngster, including matches for West Ham and now for Liverpool.

We have remained very close. There is a WhatsApp group with most of his team-mates from that time, and they added me to it.

We still meet several times a year – the parents and their children – for a big meal. And Adrian brings me a new football jersey every time we meet up.

A

*"His dad sat in the car in the dark with
the headlights on so Dejan could train."*
Dejan Lovren (10 appearances)
By Sanjin Lucijanic, his coach at NK Karlovac, Croatia

I was in my mid-twenties, fresh from the coaching academy, when I first came in contact with a 10-year-old Dejan Lovren. His family had moved to Karlovac from Germany.

I don't want to come across as falsely modest. But I can't really claim any of the credit for developing Dejan into the player he is now. I think he would have made it just as well with any other youth coach because of his extraordinary talent and, even more so, his attitude.

Of course, I did my best to nurture his skills in NK Karlovac's *mladi pioniri* (under-12s) youth category, but to go any further than that in my claims would be distasteful. I've never seen a kid so eager, so determined to succeed. His work ethic was remarkable and he was absolutely dedicated to becoming a top professional footballer. And by that, I don't mean he thought he'd make it to Dinamo Zagreb – even then he looked beyond that and had his mind set at playing for one of the biggest clubs in Europe one day.

His skills easily topped those possessed by kids who were two years his senior. We continued to work together at *stariji pioniri* (under-14s), so I had the privilege of coaching him for three or four years. If you look hard enough, you can still find my quotes from back then, when I said Lovren was going to make it to the very top. We were all sure of it – sure of him, above all.

Some say Lovren was a shy and withdrawn boy who spoke better German than he did Croatian. If you also consider the fact that he came from a Bosnian refugee family, you might think he would have struggled to fit in. But I never got that impression. He was a normal kid and I don't remember him having any real social problems. His family had been through war horrors and hardships, but I believe they were well accepted in Karlovac. Dejan was completely focused on football and the only problem he had was other kids and their parents sometimes complaining because of him jumping age groups. But they stopped when they saw how good he was.

Lovren's father Sasa had coached Dejan while they were still in Munich. His dad's support was invaluable. I had Dejan do some additional individual training; the two of us worked on some technical aspects of his game and he didn't want to stop even after it got dark outside. So his dad would come, park his car by the side of the pitch and turn the headlights on so that Dejan could continue.

At the time, our approach at the club was to rotate kids in various positions so that they learned the requirements and specifics of different roles. Dejan played all over the pitch as well, although he had already been cast as a defender when he came to us. I often used him as defensive midfielder though, because he had such a good understanding of the game and would dominate in that role.

He played defensive midfielder in one game against Dinamo Zagreb when he was two years younger than most other players. We won that game 3-0 and he was the best player on the pitch by some distance. After that, we knew we couldn't keep him for much longer. I got calls from Dinamo that very day. They wanted his family to move to Zagreb so that he could play for them.

(*Additional reporting: Aleksandar Holiga*)

A

"He scored effortlessly from kick-off."
Joel Matip (9 appearances)
By Thomas Vossing, his coach at
SC Weitmar in Bochum, Germany

SC Weitmar were a well-established club in south-west Bochum but our youth football set-up was a little basic in the mid-90s, to put it nicely. The kids were playing on a red clay pitch and there were no qualified coaches, it was all done by volunteers without any qualifications or particular plan. When they were looking for a coach for the kids, they asked the players from SC's under-19 team whether anyone felt like teaching the youngsters how to play. I had said yes.

Joel joined Weitmar's under-sixes aged four in 1995. His family lived nearby and still do today. One of his nephews plays for Weitmar now.

At that age, many kids are easily distracted. They look at butterflies during the game or forget what it is they're supposed to be doing. Joel – or Jimmy, as his nickname went – was totally different. He was physically more developed than the other kids but most importantly, he simply played football. You gave him the ball and he'd pass it back, straight and crisp. He had an intrinsic understanding of what needed to be done.

I had never seen a kid who was so good at his age. He basically scored with every shot he took. But for someone so much better than anyone else on the pitch, he was the opposite of selfish: always tracking back, always looking out for a better-positioned team-mate. The classic Joel move was to win the ball in his own half, zip past three opponents and then put it on a plate for a team-mate. To say he made the difference for our team would be a crass understatement. With him on the pitch, we won 5-0 or

6-0. Without him, we lost 4-0.

I remember the kids coming up with their own ploy for a while, they decided that he should score straight from the kick-off. He did, almost effortlessly. His shot was miles more powerful than anything you saw at this level.

Joel was an extraordinary talent but no-one realised how far he would go when he left to go to Bochum's biggest side, VfL, three years later. Weitmar has produced a few players who went on to become professionals. But he's the first one to win the Champions League and the Premier League. We're all incredibly proud of him.

————————————— **A** —————————————

> *"He would only pass to those who had*
> *his understanding of the game."*
> **Xherdan Shaqiri (7 appearances)**
> By Michael Meier, his coach at junior
> club SV Augst, Switzerland

The first thing that people from other countries often get wrong about Xherdan is the pronunciation of his surname. It is Schatschiri. All of the Kosovan Albanians in Switzerland say it that way, but it hasn't travelled very well.

He came from a big family. His father Isen arrived in Switzerland at the start of the 1980s while the rest of the family stayed at home in Kosovo. It was only later that Isen's wife Fatmire joined them with the children, including Xherdan's two brothers, Arianit and Erdin. They lived in a small apartment but when his sister, Medina, was born they moved into a farmhouse just outside Augst which had wood heating.

When Xherdan was eight years old, he made football look easy. He was so far ahead of other players in terms of his speed and strength and he wasn't afraid of trying new tricks. He wanted to try to be spectacular. Other boys would place their shots but Xherdan went for power and was able to reach the high corners of the goal. He was a match-winner.

He understood the levels of his team-mates. He would only pass the ball to those who he shared an understanding with because he always wanted it back as quickly as possible. He was addicted to the possession of the football. He was so enthusiastic, it was impossible to stay angry with him for long if you ever thought he'd done something wrong.

We won leagues and cups and Xherdan was the central player. It was no surprise when the club found out that Basel wanted to take him there. It was the nearest club and only a 20-minute drive away from Augst but Xherdan was reluctant to go at first because he liked being around his friends. There had already been much upheaval in his life and I don't think he wanted to go through that process again. After a few training sessions at Basel, though, he met new friends.

He has returned to the club a few times since becoming a professional footballer. He has always tried to help. He has a reputation that associates him with confidence but I always think of him as humble and considerate of other people's feelings.

LIVERPOOL'S SEASON: KLOPP'S *FRIENDS* QUOTE, WEIGHT LIFTED, WHO'S COMING THROUGH?

JAMES PEARCE

JUL 27, 2020

James Pearce relives Liverpool's remarkable 2019-20 season that saw them lift the UEFA Super Cup, the Club World Cup and the Premier League trophy.

A painful 30-year wait for domestic glory was ended in record-breaking fashion as Jurgen Klopp's side blew their rivals away.

Best goal they scored
So many special ones to pick from. Curtis Jones' stunning winner against Everton in the FA Cup, Trent Alexander-Arnold's unstoppable free-kicks, Alex Oxlade-Chamberlain with the outside of his right boot away to Genk and Mohamed Salah from a seemingly impossible angle in Salzburg.

But the finest for me was a beautifully worked team goal that ripped Manchester City to shreds at Anfield back in November. It showcased the pace, the precision and the finishing quality in this team. Alexander-Arnold intelligently switched play to send Andy Robertson scampering away down the left flank. The

Scottish full-back had a touch to control and then delivered a pin-point cross into the penalty box. Salah didn't even need to break stride as he emphatically nodded past Claudio Bravo.

Worst goal they conceded

Anfield was rocking in March. Roberto Firmino had just ended his goal drought on home turf early in extra-time to put Liverpool on the brink of a place in the quarter-finals of the Champions League at the expense of Atletico Madrid. Then disaster struck. There was no sign of danger as Alexander-Arnold played the ball back to stand-in keeper Adrian. Inexplicably, the Spaniard decided to clear it first-time and scuffed the ball straight to Joao Felix. He teed up Marcos Llorente, whose low strike evaded Adrian and nestled in the bottom corner. Anfield was silenced and Liverpool wilted after that blunder. Hopes of retaining their European crown were dashed.

Funniest moment

It would have to be Pep Guardiola's touchline tantrum at Anfield last November. "Twice!" he raged at fourth official Mike Dean, holding up two fingers after City had a second penalty appeal turned down. One of the memes of the season was born. Liverpool fans lapped it up. Guardiola had lost his rag and his team had lost their grip on the Premier League crown.

Most interesting person I spoke to

I was fortunate enough to have 45 minutes with Jurgen Klopp in his Melwood office back in November. Time like that is a real privilege. No cameras, just a voice recorder on the table in front of us as he sat down on the sofa with a large bowl of fruit and yogurt for his breakfast. I decided to focus the interview on the psychology of management, the environment he has created and how he gets the best out of both players and staff. The insight he provided about that side of the job was fascinating. He's an inspirational figure. I loved writing it up.

Moment you won't forget

This is an easy one. The torrent of emotion unleashed inside Anfield when Salah ran half the length of the field to beat David de Gea and wrap up victory over Manchester United in January. Until that point, nobody wanted to tempt fate. Once bitten, twice shy and all that. But as Salah whipped his shirt off and Alisson won the footrace with his team-mates to mob the goal scorer, the jubilant Kop delivered a booming rendition of *Now you're gonna believe us, we're gonna win the league*. It was spine-tingling. Liverpool were 16 points clear.

Strangest quote

"Maybe I'm a bit smarter than the Joey role, but my talk with girls was never as good as his. 'How are you doin?' It wasn't so easy in my life." Klopp revealing that he initially learned to speak English by watching the TV show *Friends*.

Biggest controversy

The main issues came off the field rather than on it. Liverpool tried and failed with a bid to trademark the city's name, prompting an angry backlash. There was also fierce criticism in April when they took the decision to furlough around 200 staff during the COVID-19 lockdown. The reaction led to a swift U-turn. Liverpool had to condemn scenes at the Pier Head and outside Anfield as thousands of fans ignored pleas not to congregate as they celebrated the title triumph.

Player who should get more credit than he does

Georginio Wijnaldum. The Dutch midfielder has been absolutely key to what Liverpool have achieved this season. He's a selfless team man. He links play intelligently, he shuts down space relentlessly and so much of his best work goes under the radar. His versatility is a huge asset. There aren't many players who can say they have played centre-back away to Brighton and centre-forward away to Barcelona. He's a class act.

Biggest question answered this season
There's been a lot of discussion over the years about whether Liverpool's great history can be a burden at times. Ending the title drought became not so much a target but an obsession. There's no doubt that nerves and anxiety played a part in the minor wobble that saw the seven-point lead Klopp's men enjoyed going into the new year last season disappear. Ludicrously, considering they ended up with 97 points, some labelled them bottlers. Such talk has been silenced emphatically. The drought is over. History isn't a burden when you write your own glorious chapters. Liverpool are no longer the nearly men.

Biggest question to answer next season
Can Klopp ensure Liverpool maintain these blistering high standards without a show of force in the transfer market this summer? The impact of COVID-19 on revenues means it's likely to be a relatively quiet window. Klopp has talked about promoting from within and handing more opportunities to youngsters like Curtis Jones, Harvey Elliott and Neco Williams. Their rivals will gamble and splash the cash to a much greater degree to try to bridge the gap. Those who criticised Liverpool's inactivity in the market a year ago were made to look foolish as they ran away with the title. The big question will be whether their stance is vindicated once again.

Who can break through next season?
I'm really looking forward to seeing more of Elliott. The teenage

winger is such an exciting talent and he will certainly have a bigger role to play. There are also some gems coming through from the academy. Keep an eye out for Layton Stewart and Billy Koumetio. This might sound strange considering it will be his third season at Liverpool but I'm excited about the potential of Naby Keita. So far we've only seen flashes of his brilliance. His Anfield career has been so stop-start. If Keita stays fit, I expect him to light up the Premier League in 2020-21.

Who needs to leave the club?
Some loyal servants are moving on, with Dejan Lovren set to follow free agents Adam Lallana and Nathaniel Clyne out of the exit door. There are likely to be a couple of other squad players off-loaded. Loris Karius needs to leave. His loan at Besiktas didn't materialise into a permanent move but there's no way back for him at Anfield. Xherdan Shaqiri is also expected to pursue a new challenge if a suitable offer is tabled. The Swiss attacker only made three starts in all competitions during an injury-plagued campaign.

What's most exciting about next season?
I'm looking forward to a season starting without the annual chat about whether this will finally be Liverpool's year. No talk of droughts and barren runs. They no longer have that weight of history on their shoulders. They are winners rather than challengers. What's most exciting for me is that this team hasn't peaked yet. That hunger still burns bright. There's so much more to come. Still room for development with the best manager in the world at the helm.

Liverpool have continually evolved tactically under Klopp, adding new strings to their bow and I want to see where he takes them from here. I can't wait for the day when supporters are finally allowed back into Anfield and you can feel that buzz around the place as the Premier League champions go about their business. As the banner on the Kop reads: "Football without fans is nothing."

JULY RESULTS

Premier League, July 2 2020
Man City 4 Liverpool 0

Premier League, July 5 2020
Liverpool 2 Aston Villa 0
Liverpool scorers: Mane 71, Jones 89

Premier League, July 8 2020
Brighton 1 Liverpool 3
Liverpool scorers: Salah 6, 76, Henderson 8

Premier League, July 11 2020
Liverpool 1 Burnley 1
Liverpool scorer: Robertson 34

Premier League, July 15 2020
Arsenal 2 Liverpool 1
Liverpool scorer: Mane 20

Premier League, July 22 2020
Liverpool 5 Chelsea 3
Liverpool scorers: Keita 23, Alexander-Arnold 38, Wijnaldum 43, Firmino 54, Oxlade-Chamberlain 84

Premier League, July 26 2020
Newcastle 1 Liverpool 3
Liverpool scorers: Van Dijk 38, Origi 59, Mane 89